TRACY SHIELDS

girl rebuilt

advice on how to ditch Mr. Unavailable
and become the girl of your dreams

ISBN: 978-1-09831-384-5

DEDICATION

This book is first and foremost dedicated to my mother, Rose, who, despite me refusing to listen until it was almost too late, taught me almost every lesson I know. I would also like to dedicate this book to my wonderful husband Douglas, for simply existing, and loving me the way I need to be loved, and to my sons, Daniel & Julien, without whom I would only be half the person I am today.

CONTENTS

Forward.. 1

Part I: Are You (Gasp) Addicted to Love?............................ 7

   1.   How Can a Love Addict Help Me Find Healthy Love? 9

   2.   You're probably NOT a love addict, but....................... 21

   3.   40 Questions 25

   4.   Obsession.. 31

   5.   Self Avoidance 39

Part II: Should I Stay or Should I Go?.............................. 45

   6.   You Deserve Better Than Scraps 47

   7.   Assessing Your Current Relationship(s)........................ 53

   8.   Do You Need to Let Go? 61

       i.   **Ambivalence**... 66

   9.   Don't Call Him! (No Contact) 73

       i.   **Who Can Take Away My Pain?** 80

  10. Prepare for the Detox Jitters (Withdrawal) 83

       i.   **Got Withdrawals?** 86

       ii. **Still Want to Go Back?** 87

  11. Who Are You Without Your Relationship?........................ 91

  12. Ten Lies We Tell Ourselves to Keep Hanging On 99

Part III: Rebuild Yourself, Girl.. 105

13. Values... 109

    i.   Putting Your Values to Work.. 115

14. Self-Esteem 119

15. Boundaries and Self-Control... 123

16. Growing Up (responsibility).. 131

17. Facing Your Fears... 137

    i.   The "Void" We Think We Need To Fill 140

18. Choosing Dignity... 145

19. Positive Self-Talk (removing negative talk) 149

    i.   Dialectic and Cognitive Behavioral Therapy...................... 153

20. Taking Action and Aligning Your Actions with Words 155

21. Aligning Logical Brain and Emotional Brain................................ 161

22. Say Goodbye to Fantasy... 167

    i.   Fixing Something that Isn't Broken 170

    ii. Inventory Time! 171

    iii. Needs and Expectations... 172

23. Lose Your Bad Behaviors (drama, manipulation and venting, oh my!) 175

    i.   Venting.. 178

24. Managing Stress Now That You Can't Hide Behind Your Defense Mechanism.. 183

    i.   Responding to Conflict 190

    ii. Falling Without a Net.. 191

25. Gratitude & Mindfulness 193

PART IV: Dating, the New You.. 197

  26. Are You Ready for a Healthy Relationship?................... 201

    i. **Are You Available?**.. 206

  27. The Importance of Being Single.................................... 209

    i. **The Purpose of You** 213

  28. Find a Better Model of a Loving Relationship............... 217

  29. A Successful Healthy Relationship Looks Like… 223

    i. **Signs of a Healthy Partner** 232

    ii. **Look for a Partner Who Does This, Not That** 235

  30. Are YOU a Healthy Partner?.. 239

  31. How Healthy Might Feel Awkward................................ 243

  32. How to Avoid the Avoidant 247

    iii. **How (Not!) to Attract an Avoidant** 257

  33. A Little Bit More About Red Flags.................................. 261

    i. **20 Reasons He/She Is Not Your Soulmate** 267

    i. **Tips for Healthy Dating** 274

  34. How to Have a Healthy Break Up 283

    i. **Dealing with Rejection**.. 288

    ii. **Not Seeing the Results You Want** 290

PART V: Relapses, Resources and Rules, Oh My! 295

  35. Fell Back Into Your Old Ways? Here's a Quick Fix 297

  36. Essential Laws of Love 305

  37. Hotlines, Recovery Facilities & Treatment Centers,...... 311

Acknowledgments.. 314

"*The truth is at the bottom of a well. You look in a well, and you see the sun or the moon, but if you jump in, there's no longer the sun or the moon; there's the truth.*"

–Leonardo Sciascia

FORWARD

When I was forty years old I was at my wits-end when it came to love and romance. I had a history of bad relationships, each one lasting, tops, six months; I had a failed marriage, and post-divorce, was heading back into bad relationship territory by making the same stupid mistakes I made when I was 20. Only this time I was angry with myself. Why hadn't I figured this out? Why was I doing the same stupid things? I was smart. I was cute. I wasn't at one end of the crazy spectrum or the other. I simply couldn't figure out, for the life of me, why I had such bad luck when it came to love. I spent some time wailing incessantly and imploring the universe for an answer to what seemed like the most important question: *Why do I only attract unavailable guys?!* And I eventually got an answer that made sense. But that answer entailed looking at my life through the perspective of a psychological and behavioral condition that I would have never have thought applied to me—addiction. Accepting that I was an addict—a love addict, no less, was very hard to do. And yet, once I did, I discovered that my questions finally had answers. And my problems had solutions. And from this, came a roadmap to my future self that led me to a life of peace, purpose and love. While I don't think that everyone's relationship issues can be solved by applying the same ideas of addiction recovery, I do think everyone can benefit from the clues addiction and even obsession offer us about love. I mean, let's be perfectly real here. We know love and addiction go together like spaghetti and meatballs, or rather, like dopamine and norepinephrine. These hormones are released during both normal healthy attraction, and unhealthy addiction—as if there's no difference (and often, there's not). They are the hormones responsible for feeding the brain's reward circuit, basically anything we do that makes us feel good. And, according to Xiaochu Zhang, Zhiling Zou, and Andreas J. Fallgatter in *Beyond Reward: Insights from Love and Addiction*, "Individuals in romantic love show many symptoms of drug and behavioral addictions, including tolerance, craving, emotional and physical dependence, relapse, and withdrawal."[1]

In other words, when healthy people fall in love there exists a very real, very intense chemical response to love that is essentially the same chemical that creates the uglier side of love—addiction, obsession, compulsion.

So, don't be afraid of the word addiction. It's just a teaching tool. And, don't think everyone who has relationship trouble is automatically a love addict. They're not. Heck, you don't have to use the term *addict* at all. It's kinda scary, I know. But I can say for certain the lessons offered by the world of addiction recovery are brilliant and fitting when applied to love, especially for those of us who have suffered from an obsessive or anxious history of loving an unavailable partner.

The GirlRebuilt.com blog was another driving force for this book and for my recovery. Ten years ago I thought it would be cool to blog about my issues. *Whaagh, I was dumped, let me tell you about my suffering.* I had been reading other love addict blogs and figured, what the heck; why not jump into the discussion? What bothered me, though, was that all the love addict blogs I read, while alluring, fashionable, and entertaining, didn't exactly offer any kind of help.

I didn't just want to be entertained, I wanted to get better. I wanted the pain to stop. I wanted the pattern to stop repeating. And so, in time, my blog morphed into one based on solutions, not just my own personal venting. That blog grew from nine followers to thousands. I quickly realized this wasn't just some cultural craze, but a serious issue many women and men were struggling with, and not just in America, but everywhere.

---

1   https://www.ncbi.nlm.nih.gov/pmc/articles/PMC5108782/

And so, GirlRebuilt.com not only became a testament to my own struggle, but the struggle of others. I knew then I had a mission. I had to continue to share what I learned with as many people as possible, in the off-chance I could help someone else. And while the website is still a thriving community for women and men to gather and talk about their relationship woes and ways to improve them, this book is something more. It's a compilation of the best advice I've gathered in hopes that it helps you as much as it's helped me. I'm sharing what I've learned in my journey, and ways to help you understand things in a tangible, hands-on way.

So How Does this Book Work? And who is it for? When I was younger, I was a rebel. I tried to break all the rules and I definitely believed there was no right or wrong way of doing things. Social conventions? Laughable. If I wanted to sleep with someone before knowing his name, I was going to do it. But somehow, all the hilarity, wackiness, and gratification I got out of being a rule-breaker didn't quite lead me to the place I wanted to go, which was to find deeper, more intimate love. I eventually realized I would have to follow a few rules if I wanted that. And so, this book is for anyone who has tried to do it their way, but after months or years of feeling like a failure, might be looking for a new way. It's for anyone who feels as though they just can't seem to get relationships right and keep repeating faulty dating patterns. It's for anyone who wants to retain their rebel soul, their uniqueness and individuality, but just needs to be pointed in the right direction. And it's for anyone who…Here, let me make it easier for you.

This book is for anyone who…

- Feels like they obsess over partners or relationships
- Constantly ends up with Mr. Unavailable
- Feels addicted to their partner or relationship
- Realizes their relationship is more pain than pleasure

- Stays in an unfulfilling, toxic, frustrating or abusive relationship and can't seem to break up

- Wants a better quality relationship with their current or future partner

- Asks themselves time and again, *Will I ever be able to have a healthy relationship?*

I'm a hands-on kind of person, so what I've created is a workbook self-help book hybrid with loads of exercises for you to develop a better sense of who you are and where you'd like to go. I've really tried hard to get you used to focusing on and answering the tough questions we often avoid when it comes to self-exploration. Also, look out for important need-to-know details that include:

- Statistics and facts that might surprise you on love, relationships and dating

- Exercises you can do to help guide you in a bit of soul searching

- Tips for healthy dating

- Red Flags to watch out for

- Resources you can turn to for further learning

This book is intended to be an invaluable, in-hand guide, something to keep on your nightstand to help strengthen your quest for a truer understanding of yourself and a healthy love relationship with someone else. I mean, even if you only glean one *ah-ha* moment or one new personal truth from this book, I've done my job. It just took me about 80,000 words to do it (*sheesh*).

Oh and a word on advice.

I have a friend who, every day, asks me for advice. I give it. I give it in cosmic, elephantine doses. Long-winded, desperate harangues. *What do I do?* she says. Well, you do this. And then you do that. And if that doesn't work, you do this other thing. She never takes any of my advice. And we continue with our friendship, same as always, laughing and carry on, with an occasional "I told you so," thrown in if she does the very thing I told her to avoid doing and it turned out bad. It reminds me of the quote from John Steinbeck, in his novel *The Winter of Our Discontent*, when he writes, "No one wants advice, only corroboration." The truth is, I cannot fix anyone's problems. No one can fix anyone else's problems. Advice is really only random (or focused) suggestions from someone who got up and did something and it worked. And, advice is gobbly gook until you're ready to make changes and do something new and different all on your own. Because let's face it, all the advice in the world and you're still going to do whatever you want.

But if corroboration is what you want, well, I can do that too. I can absolutely back you up with the idea that we're both going to rebuild ourselves, we're going to learn how to love in healthier ways and we're going to be stronger, smarter, happier individuals. If that works, *onward!*

PART I:
ARE YOU (GASP)
ADDICTED TO LOVE?

CHAPTER 1

How Can a Love Addict Help Me Find Healthy Love?

"Your task is not to seek for love, but merely to seek and find all the barriers within yourself that you have built against it."

–Rumi

You know the theory that you become a world-class expert after devoting at least 10,000 hours of "deliberate practice" to something? It's what made the Beatles the best in the music industry, Bill Gates a computer tech billionaire, and Michael Jordan the greatest basketball player in history.

When I came upon this theory a few years ago in Malcolm Gladwell's book *Outliers*, it hit me like a hard punch to my stomach. What, if anything, had I devoted 10,000 hours to? Sadly, the only thing I could come up with was…men. And worse than *just* men—as if that's not bad enough—unavailable, avoidant men. I had practically devoted my entire life to becoming a master at bad relationships. At least, it felt that way.

Years before this realization, I had another one, a big one. I was a love addict. There's no real "disorder" for love addiction. It's certainly not listed in the Diagnostic and Statistical Manual of Mental Disorders. So maybe I was; maybe I wasn't. But I was so desperate for answers, I didn't care about labels. What mattered to me was getting healthy. And, I remember the exact moment the truth to all my problems made itself known. I was chipping away at my 10,000 hours, obsessing over trying to figure out what was wrong with my current avoidant, unavailable, drug- addicted boyfriend, *(nothing was wrong with me, of course)* when I came across this little chart online that defined the "love addict/avoidant pattern." There, for the first time in my life, right before my very eyes was an actual definition of my relationship. In fact, it defined almost every relationship I had ever had. I am including it here for you.

"Love Addict"/Avoidant Pattern*

Person	Desires	Attracted to	Behaviors	Process of person's relationships
Love addict	Security, safety acceptance, "oneness" (merger) *Fears:* • Greatest fear is abandonment • Underlying fear is healthy intimacy (in enmeshment the core of the person is actually sealed off)	Self-contained individuals who appear strong, stable (often avoidant or obsessive compulsive, like their families of origin)	Line up next relationship before leaving current one--forming love triangles Instant closeness, looking for "magic" feeling Idealizing partner Obsessing about partner Talking obsessively to others about him or her Acting out anger and revenge for being abandoned	Enters relationship in haze of fantasy--found this stable, strong, accepting individual Gets high from fantasy Denies how walled in avoidant really is Avoidant gradually becomes distant and shuts down, abandons relationship in some way Love addict acts out anger & revenge, turns to affairs and addictive sex Partner capitulates and renews relationship, or love addict moves on to new relationship Sense of self and self esteem does not develop--love addict remains in dependent position. Ability to tolerate fear and discomfort must develop for growth to occur
Avoidant	Wants to be connected, but not closely *Fears:* • Greatest fear is intimacy/engulfment • Can have a hard time rejecting others or saying no	Individuals who provide much of the enthusiasm and intimacy for both of them	Ambivalence all the way through may be in relationship because can't say no	May show initial traditional romantic pursuing, but ultimately enters relationship because love addict provides most of the "intimate energy"; may fear would never make into a relationship otherwise As love addict wants more and more attention avoidant attempts to please by giving it to them--at least initially Eventually avoidant becomes overwhelmed by enmeshment and/or neediness of love addict, becomes critical, and eventually backs off from relationship or abandons it Feels relationship has failed, sometimes gets involved with addictive behavior or affairs to distance, distract, or numb out May return to relationship out of guilt or fear of being totally alone, or moves on to connect with another partner Cycle of abandoning and returning can go on and on, especially if love addict starts to move on

*Much of this pattern of relating has been described by **Pia Mellody** in her 1992 book "Facing Love Addiction."

I stared at it for a very long time. How could I be an addict when I'd grown up with an alcoholic father? There's only room for one addict per family, right? All the rest of us got to be victims, or co-dependents. That was the pattern that was drilled into me, and the pattern I believed. And yet, here I was, unable to deny this description of myself. An addict. I was feeling an enormous sense of shock and disbelief, because for so many years, I'd lived with the same, nagging, unanswered questions:

Why do I keep attracting the same type of unavailable, avoidant, men?

Why do I always feel so needy in my relationships?

Why am I such a failure when it comes to finding love?

But I also felt relief. For the first time, I felt like I was pointing in the right direction. Or at the very least, I was at a starting point that had the potential to lead me down the right path.

Little did I know I was in the very first few minutes of 10,000 new hours of learning how to have healthy relationships.

Here's a story for you. When I was a kid, I was well-loved. I received my fair share of hugs and kisses from both parents, ate well, laughed a lot, had an enormous loving family and for the most part, got along well with my brothers. My mother was a relatively quiet, loving, beautiful, tolerant woman who not only adored my father, but believed in him. She was the quintessential doting housewife, and loving, stay-at-home mother whose whole life revolved around the care of her family. My father was hugely charismatic, funny, clever and talented. He taught himself how to play guitar, banjo, drums, harmonica, and even the violin all before the age of 18. He told amazing stories, wrote his own music, was an excellent businessman and created many amazing companies out of nothing but ideas. He loved my mother more than anything—well, almost anything. I say "almost" for one simple reason. He was an addict. And that's kind of where the magical childhood memories derail. His addictions often got in the way of what might have been an average, but amazing life that from a distance and even at times close up, many people envied.

Lurking behind the façade of a "perfect childhood," were many deep-rooted problems. Despite all the love and affection among us, we moved 14 times, from Hollywood, California where I was born, to New Jersey to New Hampshire and back to NJ again. Most of the houses we lived in were big and ostentatious—an odd phenomenon considering that my father almost never held down a traditional job. None of the houses were "ours." My father always "lease-purchased" or rented our homes in an attempt to dodge creditors or loan sharks, some of whom would find us anyway and show up at our front door, telling my mother, "Make sure your husband knows that we know where he lives."

I went to seven different schools in six different school districts, had virtually no friends until the sixth grade and was a very poor student. On top of my father's addiction to alcohol, he was bipolar, most likely ADHD, and equally addicted to gambling, pornography, prescription drugs and money. These addictions and disorders were the price he paid for his brilliant creativity; but, they were also attributes of his personality that caused massive dilemmas too numerous to count. And yet, no matter what kind of chaos ensued, no matter what dangers lurked in our lives, we were connected by love. And so, love is all you need, right?

Wrong.

The story of my parents may be the perfect backdrop for a Hollywood blockbuster: bad boy falls in love with beautiful girl, they marry, have kids and despite a constant stream of familial wackiness, their love for each other is unbounded—the glue that holds them together. True love conquers all. Love saves the day. All you need is love.

Blah, blah, blah.

In actuality, the story didn't exactly start or end in a way that should leave an audience feeling all warm and fuzzy inside. My mother not only had very low self-esteem when she met my father (at age 18 and 19, respectively) but she was never permitted to go out or do anything, and so, when she met my dad, she saw him as the perfect opportunity to get out of her house and live. For many years things were great. But, by the time I was six, my father's drinking and gambling worsened to the point where hit men waited outside our home, threatened my mother, and brutally attacked my father, making one attempt after another to get their money back. My father was arrested many times, some for petty crimes, other times for instances so humiliating to our family that we just wanted to pack our bags and move. One time in particular, when I was about 16, my father was arrested for "terroristic threats" he had made to a business partner. We only found out after a neighborhood friend showed us the article in the local newspaper. *So*, that's why he missed my high school spring choral concert, I realized. Aside from feeling overwhelming shame, I also remember overwhelming anger. Another time he created a publicity stunt to jump over the Grand Canyon. After he'd raised money from investors, he dropped the plan. When the investors tried to get their money back, we packed up and left town. This went on for years. We were often so broke that I remember our phone and electricity being turned off because we couldn't pay the bills. My father would disappear, then reappear after several days, leaving us wondering where he'd been. Eventually, after nearly twenty years of marriage, my mother stopped "believing" in my father when she realized her children's lives were in danger. She left him when I was about seventeen.

Without him, the tranquility in our house bewildered me. The lack of the chaos and drama my father brought to our lives felt like a noticeable hole. And so, we kids decided to take over where he left off and cause trouble ourselves.

But my behavior "problems" started way before that. When I was in grade school I would do outrageous things to get attention. In third grade, I lifted my shirt to a group of boys on the playground who wanted to see what boobs looked like (not much at age eight, that's for sure). And, by high school, I became obsessed with love and sex and would cry almost every night because I didn't have a boyfriend. Not unlike many teens, I thought I was unworthy of love, and so, I settled for sex. But unlike most people, who grow out of that phase, I remained there, unable to recognize my worth, unable to grasp my own personal values, and completely unable to know the difference between healthy and unhealthy love.

I spent most of my adult life struggling in and out of painful relationships, making loads of self-negating choices, and suffering miserably. I had zero boundaries, a high tolerance for insults and abuse, and no real sense of who I was, what I wanted to become, and how I would get there. Unbeknownst to me, my childhood had been the breeding ground for confusion. I'd learned that the definition of love wasn't exactly addiction or gambling or stealing, but, rather, the *acceptance* of these things. My mother, after all, chose to stay with my father no matter how he behaved. Why? Because she loved him. Because when you got married in the 60's, that's what you did. Because her parents, who also had a toxic marriage despite being "in love" (they screamed and yelled and threw things at each other to the point that my mother would sit, at age seven or eight, crouched on the landing, crying in fear and praying they'd stop) had taught her that there was no leaving. That you need to respect your husband and accept him, good or bad. And so, she approached her married life with great love and hope as well as fear and powerlessness. Moreover, no matter how bad things got, she didn't believe she could survive without my father. And so, the lesson she never meant to teach me was that love means acceptance of behaviors that are not only undesirable but dangerous. And that no matter how much suffering and pain you incur, you must stay. Couple that with the fear of living alone I picked up from her, and you have a recipe for disaster.

Sadly, my mother was far from the only woman of her generation who believed in these often-times hazardous concepts of fidelity. Some women got lucky and found loving, respectful husbands. My mother wasn't so lucky.

And neither was I. And one consequence was that I was never taught the difference between self-love and self-hate, and healthy and unhealthy love.

Instead, avoidance was the life-tool of choice. And boy, did I know how to use it well. Not only did I watch my father avoid his family responsibilities by drinking and gambling, he was also avoiding me, personally (and everyone else, for that matter). He rarely, if ever, came to see any of us perform in school functions or play sports. He never spent any quality time with us. We shared no interests to bond over. And he never really sought ways to have a personal relationship with me or any of my siblings. If I wanted quality time with my father, I'd have to be the instigator and show interest in whatever it was he was into—which typically meant accompanying him to a bar or a casino. Otherwise, he was just not present in my life. My father took me down to Atlantic City for a little father-daughter time when I was fourteen. I think I had whined to my mother one too many times that "Dad doesn't love me," and so, with her prompting (*Tim, for god's sake, spend some time with your daughter*), my father took me down to AC, propped me up in one of the lounges, bought me a glass of red wine and told me to enjoy the show, he'd be back shortly. He returned hours later, completely broke. I can't remember if I drank the wine. What I *can* remember is falling in love with the young, hot singer on stage who belted out a cover of John Cougar Mellencamp's Jack and Diane.

My mother, for her part, paid us loads of attention. I want to make that perfectly clear. She loved her children dearly and spent every waking hour with us. On a personal level, one-on-one, she cared for my brothers and

I physically, emotionally, mentally. But oh, that avoidance she modeled. She did her best to ignore my father's behavior. Until she didn't.

She finally realized that their toxic relationship would never improve and it had to be ended. It just took her a while. She reminds me to this day that we are a family of late bloomers. And, as Sharon Olds writes, "anyone who blooms at all, ever, is very lucky."

Bottom line, both my parents taught me avoidance. So, here's the kicker. A child in this situation inherits two consequences from parental avoidance: she feels an overwhelming sense of abandonment from her parents' avoidance (of her, yes, she takes it personally), and simultaneously, she learns to use avoidance as a coping mechanism, as they did. And that's where love addiction comes in. Love addiction, and its concurrent way of processing romantic relationships, is, as we will see, a direct result of the avoidance of the self, intertwined with nasty abandonment issues.

Whoa. OK. Too much too fast? I get it. Learning is a slow process. But...keep reading. We will get to why all your problems are not actually wrapped up in your love life, or lack thereof, but rather in avoidance. A few other points first...

So, early on, I learned from my mother (and chances are, you learned something like this from yours), that:

1. Addiction is bad, but as long as you love your spouse, it's still acceptable to stay married to an addict, even if their behavior is harmful.

2. An avoidant narcissist is the ideal mate.

3. A heterosexual relationship is typically not built on a partnership; rather it's built on a patriarchal framework that gives the wife little power

4. Personal and joint suffering goes with the territory of marriage

5. A wife's personal interests, needs and safety are not important

6. Love is the only glue needed to hold partners or a family together.

I learned from my father (and chances are yours taught you something similar), that…

1. Men cannot be expected to participate in family because they have other more important things to do (like work, play golf, drink, socialize, network, etc.)

2. Men can be irresponsible and avoidant

3. Men need to be the center of your world in order to give and receive love from them, even if they don't give you much attention

4. Men lie, and can and should have secrets, and that's OK

5. Love is a word, not an action

6. Communication is not necessary

7. Fathers prefer their sons to their daughters

A few bad lessons about love, indeed. All of which can wreak havoc in mature adult relationships. My point here is that learning to deal with the world and all the problems within it by avoiding is not healthy. And the first place it tends to play out is in your relationships.

If you were lucky like me, your parents grew to learn healthier ways of doing things. I reaped the reward of their newfound knowledge after they divorced and went their separate ways. They both grew up a little more and avoided a lot less. My mother spent years learning how to love herself, stand on her own, and face unpleasant realities. She met and married a wonderful man (we'll get to that later!), and spent over 30 years of her life as a press photographer and photo editor. My father, although plagued with addiction the rest of his life, went on to create a successful vitamin supplement company specifically designed for people who suffer from heart disease (ironic, or what?). He died of leukemia a mere three year after he started the company, but to this day, I praise his devotion to and hard work in creating a product designed to help others.

However your family drama played out, there's a gargantuan amount of wonderful resources to help you unlearn whatever faulty lessons you learned in childhood. Your first exercise is designed to bring these lessons out of the darkness, and into the light...

Exercise: Think back to your childhood. What was the dynamic between your parents? Between you and your siblings? Were there open displays of love? Coldness? Sexual abuse? Avoidance? Physical abuse? Ambiguity? Instability? Happiness? Joy? You're trying to get a clear idea of what "love" looked like when you were growing up. Many experts agree love addiction stems from childhood issues of abandonment, trauma, abuse and addiction.

While all families have differing levels of dysfunction, love addiction, according to Pia Mellody in her best-selling book *Facing Love Addiction*, tends to be the result of "unhealed pain from childhood abandonment,"[2] as well as growing up in a toxic household in which the child's "needs went unmet." And while, love addiction is not always the result of a lack of hugs and kisses, it can be the result of growing up in a setting of inconsistent messages about love paired with more serious traumas like addiction, avoidance, denial and even abuse. Mellody calls this "the pain of the precious child,"[3] which stems from the child being "denied the opportunity to grow properly."[4] Look back. Try to form a clear and logical (not emotional) picture of your childhood. How did you learn to love? Write it down. Write down the positives of your childhood and the negatives.

Your answer is your beginning. It is how you learned to love.

2   Facing Love Addiction, Pia Mellody, 2003
3   Ibid.
4   Ibid.

CHAPTER 2

You're probably NOT a love addict, but...

"A bird sings in the morning, an owl hoots at night...it's still a bloody bird."

– Oliver Reed

Whether you consider yourself a love addict or not, is not really the point of this book. It is not designed nor intended to convince you that you're a love addict. It's created to help you learn to have healthy relationships and stop wasting your time on unavailable partners. And if you can learn some of the lessons I myself have learned through my recovery process as a love addict, then all the better. But if you truly want to know if perhaps you could be a love addict, a great start is author of *Addiction to Love,* and *The Art of Changing,* Susan Peabody's 40 Questions, which will come at the end of this section.

But first, a story on "love addict" resistance.

So, I go into this cafe recently and sit down to have a latte and a blue-berry scone (biggest weakness ever). And I end up talking to this amazing woman sitting at a table next to me, who somehow ends up telling me the story of her life -- how she's in her second marriage, and he treats her like garbage, so she started having an affair with someone else, and then she fell in love instantly, but now she can't seem to let go of the hubby...and....

And then she started crying and said, "I'm at my wit's end. I don't know what to do."

I came right out and said, "You sound like a love addict." And I proceeded to write down the web address to GirlRebuilt.com, thinking I was doing this poor girl the biggest favor ever. But she looked at me like I had five heads, and quickly replied, "Umm. I am NOT a love addict."

There I go. Making assumptions. Labeling people without their approval. Thinking I know best, when in reality, I don't have a clue. And yet, I kinda do.

I quickly apologized and said that I didn't mean to upset her. And then I added that she should just check into the site anyway, because there's some really great relationship advice on it. She was OK with that. We actually hugged goodbye and went our separate ways. Months later, she reached out to me in an email and admitted she was a love addict. "I never knew," she wrote. "I wasn't a stalker, and that's what I thought a love addict was."

Oh gosh, no.

And while there are love addicts who will stalk, commit suicide and even murder the object of their addiction, those are extreme cases and not the defining characteristics of love addiction.

For starters, let's define, as best we can, what a love addict is and what she or he isn't. Urban Dictionary aside, there are several good definitions. Brenda Schaeffer, author of *Is It Love Or Is It Addiction*, writes:

Love addiction is a psychological and behavior disorder in which a person looks to another person to satisfy a hunger for security, sensation, power, identity, belonging and meaning. (Schaeffer)

Pia Mellody writes:

Love Addicts assign a disproportionate amount of time, attention, and "value above themselves" to the person whom they are addicted, and this focus often has an obsessive quality. Love Addicts have unrealistic expectations for unconditional positive regard from the other person in the relationship. Love Addicts neglect to care for or value themselves while they're in a relationship. (Mellody)

And Susan Peabody explains the process of love addiction like this:

It all begins with what seems like an innocent attraction to someone, which quickly turns into infatuation (idealizing someone you don't know very well). The potential love addict, who is insecure and hungry for love, takes this infatuation much too seriously and easily becomes blinded by the exhilarating effects of "love at first sight."

Once Cupid has hit his mark, the soon-to-be love addict quickly becomes excessively preoccupied with the loved one. Every other aspect of his or her life becomes less important than this new lover, and endless hours are spent fantasizing about how the relationship is going to develop." (Peabody)

The two key elements in defining a love addict therefore are obsessive behavior towards someone *plus* a neglect of ones' self. We will talk about both of these behaviors in the next chapters.

And while many individuals follow the above process of falling in love with one person, others can be more addicted or obsessed with relationships than people. Some are addicted to friends or family members. Some individuals never have actual relationships but are obsessed with the fantasy of someone or the fantasy of a relationship. Others still are obsessed with the memory of a past love and cannot let go. They are known as "torchbearers." All of these styles of unhealthy love and obsession can be a manifestation of love addiction. If you feel as though you fall into one of those categories, it really doesn't matter if you agree with the term love addict or not. What matters is that you keep reading! This book is for you.

CHAPTER 3:

40 Questions

Like I've said before, I can't tell you if you're a love addict or not. And, at the end of the day, does it really matter if you are or aren't? The point I really need to get across is, if you have even the slightest similarities in behavior to what I would call a "love addict," then the advice in this book will mean something to you. And so, if you're like me and you're not adverse to labels, unplug your mobile devices, get out a pencil and get ready to check boxes.

Susan Peabody created a list of 40 questions to help you discover if you may be a love addict. Love addiction comes in many different forms. You don't need to answer "yes" to every question, but the more yeses you check, the more likely you are a love addict. These questions have been taken from Susan's website http://www.brightertomorrow.net, with permission. Keep in mind this is not a professional evaluation. There is no current personality disorder for love addiction. If you would like a professional evaluation, please see the resources in the back of this book.

The Questions

_____You are very needy when it comes to relationships.

_____You fall in love very easily and too quickly.

_____When you fall in love, you can't stop fantasizing—even to do important things. You can't help yourself.

_____Sometimes, when you are lonely and looking for companionship, you lower your standards and settle for less than you want or deserve.

_____When you are in a relationship, you tend to smother your partner.

_____More than once, you have gotten involved with someone who is unable to commit—hoping he or she will change.

_____Once you have bonded with someone, you can't let go.

_____When you are attracted to someone, you will ignore all the warning signs that this person is not good for you.

_____Initial attraction is more important to you than anything else when it comes to falling in love and choosing a partner. Falling in love over time does not appeal to you and is not an option.

_____When you are in love, you trust people who are not trustworthy. The rest of the time you have a hard time trusting people.

_____When a relationship ends, you feel your life is over and more than once you have thought about suicide because of a failed relationship.

_____You take on more than your share of responsibility for the survival of a relationship.

_____Love and relationships are the only things that interest you.

_____In some of your relationships you were the only one in love.

_____You are overwhelmed with loneliness when you are not in love or in a relationship.

_____You cannot stand being alone. You do not enjoy your own company.

_____More than once, you have gotten involved with the wrong person to avoid being lonely.

_____You are terrified of never finding someone to love.

_____You feel inadequate if you are not in a relationship.

_____You cannot say no when you are in love or if your partner threatens to leave you.

_____You try very hard to be who your partner wants you to be. You will do anything to please him or her—even abandon yourself (sacrifice what you want, need and value).

_____When you are in love, you only see what you want to see. You distort reality to quell anxiety and feed your fantasies.

_____You have a high tolerance for suffering in relationships. You are willing to suffer neglect, depression, loneliness, dishonesty—even abuse—to avoid the pain of separation anxiety (what you feel when you are not with someone you have bonded with).

_____More than once, you have carried a torch for someone and it was agonizing.

_____You love romance. You have had more than one romantic interest at a time even when it involved dishonesty.

_____You have stayed with an abusive person.

———Fantasies about someone you love, even if he or she is unavailable, are more important to you than meeting someone who is available.

———You are terrified of being abandoned. Even the slightest rejection feels like abandonment and it makes you feel horrible.

———You chase after people who have rejected you and try desperately to change their minds.

———When you are in love, you are overly possessive and jealous.

———More than once, you have neglected family or friends because of your relationship.

———You have no impulse control when you are in love.

———You feel an overwhelming need to check up on someone you are in love with.

———More than once, you have spied on someone you are in love with.

———You pursue someone you are in love with even if he or she is with another person.

———If you are part of a love triangle (three people), you believe all is fair in love and war. You do not walk away.

———Love is the most important thing in the world to you.

———Even if you are not in a relationship, you still fantasize about love all the time— either someone you once loved or the perfect person who is going to come into your life someday.

———As far back as you can remember, you have been preoccupied with love and romantic fantasies.

_____You feel powerless when you fall in love—as if you are in some kind of trance or under a spell. You lose your ability to make wise choices.

So? How did you do? Did you pull your hair out? (Don't do that). Did you have a moment of personal reckoning? Or did your response tell you nothing you didn't already know? Whatever your reaction, *breathe, and move forward.* This is the point where you either chuck the book in your recycling bin or turn the page with a renewed sense of hope that this may very well be the beginning of the end of a lot of your suffering…

Obsession

"What a liberation to realize that the 'voice in my head' is not who I am. 'Who am I, then?' The one who sees that."

–Eckhart Tolle

Infatuation. It's the best feeling ever. When you think of your love or are near them, the humdrum world melts into non-existence and you slip into Bosch's *The Garden of Earthly Delights* (it's a painting worth Googling). Life is suddenly too good to be true. Except when it isn't. When you're obsessing or fantasizing over one thing, one object, one act, one man, one woman, one whatever, your whole world has shrunken to a pinpoint and your life is no longer under your control. Obsession can be so destructive it can stunt growth. It takes away time from your life you can never get back. That's the bad news.

The good news is you can change.

What is obsession? The textbook definition is "a persistent preoccupation, idea, or feeling," But what is it *really*? Why do we obsess over love? Without getting too much into the science of obsession I can say that studies now show obsession lights up the same brain pathways of reward as passionate love, lust and addiction, which doesn't help explain things very much because all of the above are very different things. And so? What is obsession in the realm of why we do the things we do?

Forget science. Forget chemistry. Just for a moment. From my experience, all my obsessing over G, over Paul, over John or Mark was not because I loved them. I want to be perfectly clear. Obsession is not love. My obsession stemmed from one place: my internal need to avoid myself and all my personal problems. And while the perceived cause of my obsession may have been the fact that these men were unavailable, or didn't love me, or lied to me, or rejected me, and I wanted to get to the bottom of it, the true-north cause was I didn't want to think about anything else because doing that—thinking about my bills, my kids, my work, my loneliness—was far more painful than the pain I felt from obsessing. And what's more, I didn't know how to manage my bills, my kids, my work or my loneliness! But I did know how to manage my obsessing. I was in control. The more I obsessed, the closer I thought I got to a better understanding of my relationship. That, of course, was an illusion.

Obsessing helps us focus on something outside our scope of manageability, even if the thing we are obsessing over is something like our health. It keeps us lazy, immobile, narrowly focused, imprisoned. Ironically, despite the control we think obsessing might give us, we lose control of our lives when we are in its thrall. Also, quite conveniently, we don't have to focus on our lives when we obsess.

But, the truth is, for many of us, obsessing is an uncomfortable if not heart-wrenching, painful tool we use to avoid. We're afraid that if we let go of our obsessive thoughts (or the object of our obsession), we won't understand the world. We'll be derailed. We'll lose control. We will..*gasp!*...have to actually think of more important and more uncomfortable things!

Obsessing, when it relates to our relationships, tends to come in the form of psychoanalysis. We don't believe we are obsessing at all. We are <u>analyzing</u> behavior that doesn't make sense to us or fit our preconceived notions of what our partner's behavior *should* be. We are not losing balance, we are *investigating* the truth, *digging* for clues amidst what seems to be a sea of lies. And we are *deciphering behavior*, words, actions and experiences within the realm of a relationship that at times doesn't add up or make sense. *Why didn't he call me? Maybe he's not feeling well. Maybe he's too scared. Why didn't he ask me out on a third date? Maybe it's because he's too introverted. Maybe the fear of getting attached to a new person so soon after his break-up is blocking him from going after true love...* We give up hours and hours of our waking life to become therapists, private investigators and forensic scientists, all for the sake of figuring *him* out. At least that's what we tell ourselves. The reality is, we are obsessing.

Exercise: Here's a game you can play with your brain. It's a thinking game. Sit in a quiet room where you won't be distracted for about an hour. Unplug! Turn off all mobile devices, computers, music, TV etc. You want to create an atmosphere of compete silence. Now, if you have a stopwatch, set it for one (1) minute. What you basically have to do within that minute is think of anything you want. Anything! Anything, that is <u>except for that which you typically obsess over</u>. That means, NO THINKING OF LOVE OR THE OBJECT OF YOUR LOVE. Got it?

Ready, set, go.

OK, how did you do? In your journal, write down any and all of the stuff you thought about. Anything different?

Now do the same game for five minutes. And repeat. What did you think about? Career? Hobbies? Work? Television? Boyfriend? Girlfriend?

Sadly, when I first did this, I learned a rather disturbing truth: I had nothing else to think about but the guy I was obsessing over. No art, no music, no current events. I knew nothing about the world because I'd wasted so many years obsessing over a man. And that's when it hit me...I am the sum of my thoughts, so, if my thoughts are only about one guy, I am not much else. This was a huge wake-up call. I knew it was time to work as hard as possible to change that. And how did I do it? I got serious about forcing myself to think other thoughts. I picked up the book *East of Eden* by Steinbeck and read it. I looked online for graduate programs. I started to watch the news. When I talked to others, I moved the conversation toward neutral stuff-- NOT relationships--I tried to learn about politics, art, music, and so on. I thought of people I knew who were deeply career-driven and I tried to imitate them. What did *they* think about?

The more relevant stuff I put into my brain, (paying bills, addressing important issues, making critical life decisions, being creative, etc.), the less chance it had to think obsessive thoughts.

The following is a journal entry I wrote while I was in obsessive mode. It clearly shows how willing I was to replace obsessive thoughts for one man with a man I didn't even know (yet). See if you can relate:

I feel it coming on again. It's as if my brain cannot ever be at rest. When one man goes, another one comes. Like spirits that possess the body without the self-knowing. I have shut off mentally to both S and G, with the occasional, lingering sad thought for S. But there's someone else. Not physically, mind you. In fact, we only know of each other in the narrowest sense. He's a long-time friend of a friend. Recently divorced. I saw him for a fraction of a second at a wedding over the summer and his eyes burned a hole in me, he was staring so deeply. At the time I only thought, typical!. But now it all kind of makes sense. He and his wife had just split and I suppose he was single and looking. I have never had any conversation with him, EVER. But he is known as "good" guy. So, time goes by and S and I are over and by a huge error in judgment, I cleared my status with S on Facebook and "Tracy is no longer in a relationship with S..." came across EVERYONE'S newsfeed. I was humiliated, to say the least. However, it gave D (the new guy) a chance to flirt. D is a lawyer. A successful one. He's 38. Plays guitar. Lives on a farm. He likes witty, intelligent, sexy, Italian women who have a tendency to come on strong. This combination in my little fantasy-world is what has kept him in the forefront of my brain these past two weeks. He gives me stuff to think about. I can imagine happiness. Who can't be happy with a lawyer who plays guitar on a farm? The more I think about this, the more perfect he becomes. And so starts the obsessing. I am not obsessed with him yet, but it's like this: If I don't have thoughts of a MAN in my head (not just any man, but one whom I am interested in and who is showing me some sign of attention), I feel completely empty. Detached. Not a part of the world. It's horrible. So, the obsessing keeps me connected. It keeps me grounded. I have said before I am not ready to date. I dread the day I open my inbox only to find "How about a drink sometime after work?" sent from a new guy. I will surely go into a panic. But it is obviously my goal, albeit a subconscious one, to maintain connectivity to a man, any man. That, I believe, is the definition of my love addiction.

How does it feel to read this? Can you relate? Looking back on this particular journal entry I can clearly see I was not nearly as far along in my progress as I hoped to be. A little disappointing. And yet, the "D" I am referring to eventually became my husband. At some point in the future, before I actually met him, I was able to let go of obsessive thoughts and *ahhh*, use my brain power for good.

There are hundreds of books on obsessing. There are movies devoted to characters who are obsessed. We even, at times, glamorize obsessive behavior. Fifty Shades of Grey (2015) comes to mind. Christian Grey has an obsessive fixation on Anastasia and because he's rich, famous and good-looking, we think that's hot. The Twilight (2008) series is another good example. Edward

Cullen is obsessed with Bella (um, he watches her sleep every night!), and we're totally OK with that. Heck, Romeo and Juliet are obsessed with each other to the point where they both kill themselves if they can't be together. Think about it. The mythology of Romeo and Juliet is so engrained in our psyches that it defines our cultural norms on what love is and what love should be. Because of this, a legal defense of "crime of passion" can lead to a lesser sentence. Obsessive love can often be the foundation of what "true love" is. And yet, the reality is, obsession is destructive. It is especially self-destructive. Forget how "hot" Anastasia finds Christian Grey (in the real world, by the way, not many people tolerate being the target of obsessive love); think instead of the emotional suffering Christian Grey most likely endures when all his thoughts are compulsively focused on one woman. There's not much time for joy, that's for sure.

We all tend to obsess at periods in our lives. We obsess over work, relationships, decisions, money and so on. But when obsession becomes our modus operandi it's time to start working towards managing obsessive thoughts. And here's the irony. Obsessing, no matter how good at it we become, will never bring us closer to our obsessive object or person. In fact, we only obsess over that which is not ours.

To someone in the throes of obsession, this may sound impossible, but there are ways to manage obsessive thinking or behavior. Here's a few that have worked well for me:

1. Set Goals: if you are obsessing over the end of a relationship it's time to set new goals. One of the reasons we obsess, remember, is because it's safer than moving forward into the unknown. We know the relationship. We were safe there. The end is scary. It means we don't know what our future will look like. And so obsessing is our way of not moving forward, of holding on to what we know. This is why setting new goals is super important. Start a journal. Envision a new future. What goals can you set for today?

Tomorrow? Next week? Next month? The more you are able to plan and visualize tasks in the coming weeks and months, the more control you will feel over your future.

2. Obsess over something else: we often cannot get over an obsession without a replacement obsession. When I went through my last break-up I obsessed for months over him and then realized I wasn't doing myself any favors. And so I took up running. I ran on the treadmill at the gym and ran my brains out. I didn't win any races. And I only managed to run a few 5Ks. But I was fit as hell and felt great. And that's more than obsessing over men gave me.

3. Stop Avoiding: If we accept the idea that we obsess in order to avoid, it's time to dig deep and figure out what you might be avoiding. Responsibility? Growing up? Being alone? It's different for all of us. We address the idea of self-avoidance in the next section. The important thing here is to get in touch with what you might be avoiding and face it. Confront it. Take some of that obsessive energy and re-direct it to address other issues in your life that seem insurmountable. Yeah, I know. Easier said than done. For now, maybe just keep reading! We will get to conquering insurmountable tasks later.

CHAPTER 4

Self Avoidance

*"The strongest force in the universe is
a human being living consistently with
his identity."*

–Tony Robbins

To better understand our obsessive, addictive behavior we need to look not at addiction or obsession, but at yet another behavior. Avoidance of ourselves.

Humans don't like pain. We drink to avoid it. We pop pills to avoid it. We shop to avoid it. We seek magical love to avoid it. We avoid, avoid, avoid…And sometimes, use our relationships as a cloak to protect us. Love can become a defense mechanism to help us deal with the pain or loneliness we feel in our lives. Worse yet, a bad relationship, even though it's bad, also helps us avoid the pain of who we are. If, for example, you are fretting over the drama and discontent of a painful, unsatisfying, or unrequited relationship, you have no time to focus your attention on yourself and your personal problems. That person you keep obsessing over, keep analyzing, and trying to figure out may not only be in your life because you love him or her, but also as a means to avoid yourself so that you don't have to face your deepest fears. And before you say, *Wait, I'm not avoiding myself! If anything, I'm focusing on myself and trying to work on my relationship!* read on.

Avoidance and obsession are actually the opposite side of the same coin. I learned many years ago that all my love-obsessed behavior was only partially due to the fact that I was boy-crazy. The deeper cause was a subconscious need within me to wriggle out of any and all responsibility. To erase my life. To be someone different. To run away from the pain of who I was and what I couldn't do. While others were avoiding themselves and their lives with drugs, or food, or work, I avoided with love. And so, the more I learned about love addiction, the more I learned it has little or nothing to do with the object of my affection, or love at all. It has to do with the self and the self's inability to find peace and understanding within certain situations. Heck, I shouldn't even have called myself a love addict once I learned this. I should have called myself a "Self-Avoidant." Because that's what I was.

So, how does love work when I am a Self-Avoidant? When I obsess, when I struggle, when I fear, when I feel disgust and I point all those emotions at you, you become the problem, and I am off the hook. When I get involved with a man who ignores me, neglects me, doesn't love me, it forces me to analyze his behavior, not mine. And, when I feel insecure and unloved and keep chasing after someone who doesn't want me in his life, it allows me to have a purpose, a challenge, a passion other than the ones I really have. Or worse, it masks the fact that I haven't developed any interest or passions to begin with!

Self-avoidance also looks a lot like blame. Who among us hasn't thought, "if only he [fill in the blank: stopped lying, loved me, didn't cheat, came over more often, didn't do drugs] all my problems would be solved"?

So often we say, *if only he or she would change.* So often we look to the rest of the world to do the work of making us happy. We are blind to the fact that change, happiness, understanding are experiences that we are responsible for achieving. That there is a struggle going on within us that needs to be resolved and we are the ones responsible for it. Yes, we can ask for help of others. We can lean on family and friends during hard times. But, we alone are responsible for facing the person within us and creating a life worth living. No one else. **By focusing so deeply on someone else to save us, we are avoiding the very real truth that it's our job to save ourselves. Or conversely, that we don't need to be saved at all. We merely need to learn to manage our lives.** My "issue" was not so much that I was addicted to loving someone. My issue was I was always too damn scared to grow up and fix my own problems. And I was scared because I didn't know how.

And therein lies the clincher.

We are afraid of responsibility, of growing up, of making decisions, of being adults because we never learned how to face those things. The more we avoid ourselves the more distance we put between us and the learning process.

In my case, I never learned how to work or how to choose a career. Nothing interested me. I enrolled in college, but quit early on, not believing an education was important. I didn't feel connected to anything. This was partially learned behavior. I never saw my parents work except sporadically. No one in my family until me went to college. And I never had a mentor or a teacher who inspired me or pushed me to go after my dreams. While I did have them, I believed dreams didn't come true. And most detrimental, I didn't believe in myself. Because I lacked all that, I welcomed the opportunity to be saved by a whirlwind relationship because I didn't have the answers, and I couldn't seem to save myself; I welcomed the distraction of falling in love because love validated me when I couldn't validate me. And I welcomed relationship problems in my life because somehow, I could manage *your* problems

(I'm an expert at that, I've been doing it for 10,000 hours, remember), but I couldn't seem to manage my own.

Love, then, became my passion. Love is what I became devoted to. Love is what I depended on. Love saved me. Love rescued me. Love was my life, even unhealthy, toxic love.

This, of course, was escapism at its finest. And, there's nothing healthy about it.

So, there you have it. Obsession and avoidance. Two of the key components that make up love addiction, and coincidentally, two of the most destructive patterns of behavior to drag into a relationship. And while there are other forms of destructive behavior when it comes to love and other unhealthy relationships, I really believe these are the two most responsible for causing trouble. Avoidance of the self, blended with a big dose of obsession gives you the two main components that are the basis for all other combinations of unhealthy. Sounds like a pretty nasty-tasting smoothie, if you ask me.

In my worst hours, journaling my thoughts saved my life. So, I offer you this writing prompt so you can try it yourself. Y'know, saving your own life.

Exercise: Forget your love interest at the moment. Write down a list of things in your life you feel you're avoiding, that you'd rather not deal with. It can be as mundane as "cleaning my house," or as serious as "fixing my marriage." In fact, look for small things you tend to avoid as well as big things you might not even know you're avoiding. For me, one of the biggest things I didn't realize I was avoiding was "growing up." On the one hand, I was hugely responsible. I was a great mom, paid my bills on time, paid my own way through college once I did go back, graduated magna cum laude, and I was, and still am, a very reliable person. On the other hand, I was petrified of working full time, even though I needed to. I couldn't make a commitment to what I did love (I loved to write, but I kept telling myself I was no good). And I was emotionally immature. I believed that I could be "saved" by Prince

Charming, when I wasn't exactly Princess material myself. A note of caution: many people do this exercise and conclude that they try to stay in a relationship because they want to avoid being alone. While fears of being alone and being "abandoned" are very real and may be a driving force behind why you stay in a bad relationship, they may not be. As a love addict, I realized that while I obsessed over being in a relationship, I was mostly alone. In fact, I got really good at it, even though I didn't like it. It turns out I wasn't actually afraid of being alone or being abandoned. I was actually afraid of intimacy.

PART II: SHOULD I STAY OR SHOULD I GO?

"That's it, pack it up, be wise my sister cause
the facts keep stackin up, tell him, to kiss the
you know what make sure the door is shut,
behind you I do believe the brother's out of
luck, and stuck but that's not, your "P-R-O-
B-L-E-M" you gotta let him go and let him
know this is the end..."

–Monie Love, *It's a Shame (My Sister)* 1990

While Part I of this book introduced the idea of love addiction and hopefully helped you decide if the term "love addict" is for you or not, Part II removes labels and just gets to the nitty gritty of your relationship by helping you figure out whether he or she is worth keeping or not.

CHAPTER 5

You Deserve Better
Than Scraps

"'You must never behave as if your life belongs
to a man. Do you hear me?' Aunty Ifeka said.
'Your life belongs to you and you alone.'"

—Chimamanda Ngozi Adichie, Half of a Yellow Sun

Before any talk of our relationships, before I get into why we should hold on or let go, before we talk about the avoidant, unavailable partner or the pain of getting over a breakup, I have to set in stone a mantra we all need to repeat daily, because honestly, I don't think we know it: **you deserve better than scraps.**

Now, when people hear me talk about scraps, they're all like, *Yeah! I don't deserve scraps!* And then they go home to their partner and demand to be treated like a goddess. Meanwhile, they've gone home to the same avoidant, disrespectful, unavailable partner. My point is, many men and women don't know what a scrap is. We need to know. Once we do, we realize we deserve more. Here's a few examples of a "scrap" from my own fully stocked past:

- When I was a teenager, I let a boy who I was completely un-at-tracted to, who had brown broken teeth and bad breath kiss me because I thought I could do no better.

- When I was in my twenties, I went to a community college, not because I couldn't afford better, not because I was saving my money, but because I believed I couldn't academically do better.

- When I went out in the world to get a job, I believed I had no talent, no experience and no education, and so I took menial jobs that didn't require any of those things and paid very little. I wanted to work in publishing, but I never applied to work at a publishing house because I didn't think I was worth it.

- When I was a young woman, I married a man I'd only known for 21 days. I married him on the side of a highway, no white dress, no wedding reception, no gifts, because I didn't believe I was worth a <u>real</u> wedding or that a man would love me after 21 days.

- And when I was divorced with two kids and back in the dating world, I made myself available to someone who never showered or brushed his teeth, who did drugs, wore dirty clothes and never wanted to have sex. I though he was the best I could find at my age (36!). I thought no one would want a divorced woman with two kids.

So those are examples of the scraps I fed myself. But what about scraps our partners feed us?

They often hide in these guises:

- Limited or no availability

- Limited or no intimacy

- Limited or no compliments

- Physical, mental or emotional abuse

- Minimal communication

- Emotionally closed off

The list goes on. But keep in mind that scraps are, generally speaking, relative. A scrap to one person may not be a scrap to someone else. Case in point: Julie K and I had a phone conference. She really needed to speak to me about a man she recently fell in love with while working for two weeks as a yoga instructor at a glamorous resort in Rio de Janeiro. They both promised to stay in touch after she left. But once she was back home, days passed without a lot of interaction from her lover. He sent her a few texts, they talked once a week, but little by little, he became more unavailable. Julie, at first, was OK with his limited communication because, as he had suggested, this was all he could offer—a long-distance relationship. In her mind, as long as he was locked in to some sort of connection to her she wasn't going to complain. She was, after all, busy with her own life in Chicago where she owned a Pilates/yoga studio. But night after night, when she came home, she was completely alone. She eventually became scared to death he would disappear completely or meet someone else; and so, she started to obsess over him. The more she obsessed, the more she would reach out to him and demand some sort of guarantee that they would be together again, or that he would call more often. And the more she did that, the farther he seemed to retreat. At one point in the conversation with me she asked, "Would you accept his behavior? Would you be willing to put up with a long-distance relationship like that?"

I didn't hesitate. "Absolutely not," I said. To me, long-distance relationships are completely unappealing. I know myself well enough to know that seeing or hearing from my romantic partner once every few days, weeks, months, etc. is not something I want. To me, that's a scrap. And I want more. But to someone else, it may not be. In this case, distance wasn't the only scrap Julie was living off of. She was also accepting an emotional distance. He most likely wanted to end the relationship, but didn't want to hurt her. While she may have sensed this, a part of her didn't want to listen or believe it. Only you are the one who knows what a scrap is and what it isn't.

And only you are the one who decides to accept or reject them. That's the hard part. So often we *say* we don't want to be treated badly, we *say* we don't want scraps, but then we stick around and eat them anyway because we (falsely) believe that's all there is.

Well, stop telling yourself untruths. There's more out there. There's better out there. But you first must believe it. And then you must be willing to walk away when you see scraps thrown at you. Oh yeah, and, you must also be firm in your resolve to stop throwing scraps to someone else as well.

When you believe you have value, when you believe you are worth not just a little, but a lot, you do not accept dirty, broken teeth, menial jobs, or people who never want to make love to you, hold you, kiss or be near you (unless, of course, you're really into those things). When you believe you have value you do not put up with neglect, disrespect, abuse, mind games, cruelty, or any other kinds of abusive, disrespectful treatment.

When you believe in yourself, you teach people how to treat you with respect. When you do not believe in yourself, you teach people that they can treat you any way they want and you will accept it.

Part of believing that you deserve better is having a sense of entitlement. I know. We tend to use this word to describe people negatively. Religiously speaking, any of our Judeo-Christian teachings call on us to be humble and grateful for whatever we're given. We're supposed to be content with scraps.

But, when you believe you are entitled to better treatment, you get it. Something in you changes and you no longer accept less. A perfect example of this is <u>food</u>. How many of us would eat from a trash can? Especially if we could afford not to. And unless you were homeless, and might possibly die if you didn't eat what you could scrounge up, how many of us would choose garbage over food we could get at a grocery store, restaurant, or make ourselves? Not many. What about junk food? How many of us would eat fast-food every day, or just potato chips and soda? The truth is, despite occasional junk food binges, most of us have a sense of entitlement when it comes to eating. We want healthy choices in our grocery stores. We want healthy choices for our children. And we want healthy choices for us. We recognize that by eating healthy foods we are doing something good for ourselves. It's that simple.

So, if we can feel entitled about food, why not feel the same about the people we allow into our lives? Why not feel entitled about work, education, income, friends, and so on?

When we lack a sense of entitlement regarding the person we should meet and fall in love with, when we have no clear sense of what we deserve, we accept darn near anything. We end up with scraps.

And let's face it, scraps don't taste good. Eating them is embarrassing. Being seen doing this is even more so. But when it comes to relationships, we oftentimes overlook scraps because we believe we are being fed in other ways—great sex, status, occasional intimacy. We tell ourselves the scraps are worth it.

I'm telling you it's not worth it. I'm telling you it sounds like you've been eating scraps your whole life and by now, you just think this is normal. That scraps taste yummy. And yet, every time you take a bite, you get sick. Relationships are not meant to make you this sick.

Someone once said to me, *How empty of me, to be so full of you.* It confused me at first. Isn't that what true love is all about? To be so full of our one true love? Years later, I realized that this person's words were more brilliant than I'd first imagined. I am "empty" if my only thoughts, feelings, hopes and dreams are about my partner. But what am I bringing to the table? What unique world within me can I offer if I can only mirror back your reflection? So, my advice is to fill yourself with who you are. Fill yourself with an abundance of things you love, other than your partner. Fill yourself with a new sense of entitlement. Focus on your worth. And read the Self Esteem section of this book and check out the Resources section for books on self-esteem.

CHAPTER 6

Assessing Your Current Relationship(s)

"The hardest thing to learn in life is which bridge to cross and which bridge to burn."

—David Russell

Before we decide if our current relationship is worth holding on to or if it's time to let it go, we need to spend some time assessing it. Not emotionally, but logically. Otherwise, we will continue the pattern of going back and forth, hemming and hawing, not knowing what to do, and basically staying or leaving for the wrong reasons. When we don't know what to do, we can become paralyzed, unable to make a decision. We can feel powerless, and being able to assess a current relationship should give back some of that lost power. We are, after all, the deciders of our own fate. And we need to be able to make decisions and be content with our decision-making. Once again, I've found writing to be an incredibly helpful tool for this assessment, so get out pen and paper or flip open the laptop and get writing. There are three main assessment exercises I'd like to share here. They are the classic "Positive vs. Negative List;" the "Emotional vs. Logical List;" and "The Inventory of Past Relationships vs. Current Relationship."

Exercise*: Relationship Assessing*

Positive vs. Negative

Make two side-by-side lists. One list will contain all of your partner's Negative qualities. The second list is all the Positives. Pretty simple. Now, here's a few rules:

1. "He loves me" cannot be on either list. It won't be considered a positive or a negative in this exercise and therefore, holds no weight.

2. Each item on your list has to have a value. Using a numeric range of one to five (five being the most valuable and one the least), grade each quality according to the weight it holds for you. For example, "He's always there for me," gets a five because it's so important to me. Whereas, "he's sexy" might get a three because, while that's important, it's not essential. Likewise do the same for Negative qualities. "She's never available" is hugely painful to you, so that would get a five. Whereas, "She plays on her mobile phone too much," might only get a three.

3. Finally, you have to have the same number of Positives as you do Negatives. I realize this may be an impossibility. Your partner may have 30 Positive qualities and only five Negatives. But, I really want you to try to even it out as much as possible. Now's a good time to be nit-picky, or conversely, generous.

Below are two of my personal relationship assessments. I dug one out of an old journal of a relationship I had with a guy named G. The other, is my current relationship assessment. I wrote down an equal number of positives and negatives and then I rated them by importance to me. Once I did that, I was able to add the numbers in column one, add the numbers in column two, and then subtract. As you can see, poor G got a big fat zero, whereas my husband got a 20 (he's a keeper!). It's not so much the numbers that are important, though, it's the weight that each of these items carry. Honestly, "He's always available for me," in my husband's assessment far outweighs anything in G's assessment. And while G may have been a great communicator, the weight of his negative qualities was so heavy that they trounced his best qualities and made it impossible for me to stay.

Old relationship with G

POSTIVES	NEGATIVES
Fabulous communicator (5)	Smokes too much (5)
We click; we have intense chemistry (5)	Never wants to have sex (5)
He is somewhat reliable (3)	Doesn't take care of himself (poor dresser) (5)
He makes me laugh (3)	Doesn't want to move in with me (4)
I love his hugs (3)	Caught him lying a few times (5)
He's a musician (5)	Embarrasses me in public, sometimes (4)
I'm very attracted to him (5)	Doesn't fit into my family (5)

Score: 33 (Positives) – 33 (Negatives) = 0

Current relationship with my husband

POSITIVES	NEGATIVES
He's always available, always there for me (5)	He can be over-sensitive (2)
He's kind and respectful to me and to others (5)	He's not a disciplinarian w/ his kids (3)
He's very responsible (4)	He's forgetful (1)

He allows me to be me (5)	He's not very good w/ domestic tasks (1)
We communicate very well (5)	He plays on his phone too much (3)
He makes me laugh (4)	He can be too entitled (1)
He's really good with my kids (2)	He's not very good at fixing things (1)

Score: 32 (Positives) – 12 (Negatives) = 20

We do not date half a person. We date a whole person. We take the good with the bad. But don't let that idea mislead you. When the bad far outweighs the good, you need to face up to that. If your partner has 200 great qualities but, for example, physically abuses you, that one negative quality holds an enormous weight. In that case, the Positive/Negative chart exercise won't really work. Some other assessment tool needs to be used.

Emotional beliefs vs. Logical facts List

When we assess our relationships we must give weight to our partner's personal qualities. But where does that "weight" come from? It typically arises from our own personal wants, needs, desires and expectations. More than that, it comes from our logical-thinking and emotional-thinking brain.

We will get into logical thinking versus emotional thinking in Chapter 21. For now, understand this: the ultimate goal when making important decisions is to use both "head and heart," especially when it comes to relationships. But very commonly, because romantic relationships tend to be "matters of the heart," most of us only use our emotions. "But, I need him." "But she said she loves me." "I can't be alone." "I'll never find anyone else." "I will change…" These are emotional responses to a relationship, and while they hold a certain degree of importance when it comes down to the final decision, they shouldn't be the driving force that determines whether we stay or move on. Our logical brain, however, has a stronger, more objective perspective on things, and so, we need to summon that part of ourselves in order to truly assess our relationships. Here's some examples of the questions your logical brain might conjure: Is he kind to me? Does he respect me? Can I be myself in his presence? Is he reasonably available? Do we share the same values? Do his positive qualities outweigh his negative ones? Take out another sheet of paper or open up another writing document and make two lists again. This time we want "Emotional Belief" versus "Logical Facts."

Your list should look something like this:

Emotional Belief	Logical Fact
She loves me	Even though she says she loves me, she's never around, she cheated on me twice and she lies.
I am deeply in love with her	While I am in love with her, I am in a lot of pain from her behavior and I don't trust her
She's perfect for me in so many ways	I am not dating half a person. She is perfect for me in many ways, but she causes a lot of pain.

Along with writing out our emotional beliefs versus logical facts, we can also ask ourselves if our relationship has the top 10 mandatory characteristics of a healthy relationship (see also Chapter 31 on "A Successful Healthy Relationship Looks like...") Now, before you resist the idea that every healthy relationship is the same (they're not), and before you rail against the concept that you and your partner could possibly be average or just like everyone else (you're not), understand most healthy human relationships tend to have the same key ingredients. How does your relationship stack up? How is your relationship different? What is it missing? What's there?

10 mandatory characteristics of a healthy partner

A healthy partner is...

1. Physically, mentally and emotionally available most of the time

2. Willing to communicate (listening and speaking)

3. Respectful to you and others

4. Kind to you and others

5. Responsible in most realms of life (children, finances, work, relationships, health)

6. Honest (doesn't lie or deceive)

7. Trustworthy (doesn't betray trust)

8. Safe (doesn't cause anyone harm, including self)

9. Grown up (may be child-like, but responds to experiences as an adult)

10. Willing to work on issues

Notice the word "Loving" is missing. Love is like a book. It only has value when it's filled with a story, and for relationships, that story is a compilation of these things and more. I need to say it: stop using the word "Love" as part of your assessment.

Exercise: *Past Relationships Inventory vs. Current Relationship.*

Our dating pattern can tell us a lot about who we are in the realm of romantic relationships. It can basically tell us if we always seem to have unhealthy relationships or if our current unhealthy relationship is a blip, a deviation from what's normal for us.

Write a list all your serious relationships. Using a single piece of paper (or a hundred!), describe each relationship using these parameters:

k.) General character (Jake: *fun, avoidant, cold*; Ryan: *warm, inconsistent, playful, irresponsible*; Denzel: *loving, respectful, unavailable;* Brad*: narcissistic, mistrusting, energetic, etc.*),

l.) The overall tone or mood of the relationship (It was *happy, frustrating, passionate, fraught with mistrust, lonely, etc.*)

m.) Your personal feelings for the person and relationship (*I felt lonely, I felt safe, I felt neglected, etc.*).

One of my followers on GirlRebuilt.com described her relationship to her partner like this: "We have a stressful relationship with happy moments, instead of a happy relationship with stressful moments."

See if you detect a pattern, ie, if there are characteristics or traits that keep cropping up in your partners. This exercise can help assess the "type" of relationship you're used to, and as well as what you are and are not willing to tolerate in relationship. For example, if four out of six of your boyfriends were "unavailable," this is a characteristic you not only keep bumping into, it's also one (depending on the lifespan of the relationship) you accept. Ouch! That might hurt to hear, but ask yourself if it's true. If you absolutely hate dating unavailable men why do you continue to do so?

When I answered this question years ago, I told myself *because that's all there is* to make myself feel better:. I believed all men were avoidants. Well, that's not true at all. But the real truth was that I kept dating them. I wanted a kind, respectful, responsible, available partner and yet, I wasn't looking in the right place.

Here's one of my favorite parables.

> There was a young man searching outside his house, in the grass, for his keys. It was a sunny bright day, with lots of mid-afternoon sun streaming down. An old man came by and asked what he was doing. "I'm looking for my keys," he said. "I lost them." So, the old man, wanting to help the fellow out, started looking in the grass alongside of him. After awhile, the old man said, "did you maybe drop them in a different spot, because we've been looking here for a while now and I'm not seeing anything." The young man said, "Oh, I'm sorry, I should have mentioned that I lost my keys inside the house." The old man was dumbstruck. "I'm a little confused," he said. "If you lost them inside the house,

why on earth are you looking for them out here?" "Because there's more sunlight," he said.

CHAPTER 7

Do You Need to Let Go?

*"The self-recognition of breakage is the form
of bravery available to real people."*

–Adam Gopnik

Should I stay or should I go?

That's the question I get asked all the time by many of my readers. And sadly, I am not the one who can answer that. But you can. You just have to know how. If you've read the previous section entitled Assessing Your Relationship, you've already done half the work. You now know that it's imperative to get a clear, logical picture of your relationship, versus an emotional one. Making lists, evaluating your relationship history and learning to think logically versus emotionally should help.

So now what?

Well, a few things. First, you have to understand that by reading this book, your goal is not exactly to save your relationship. It's to save you. And your goal is not necessarily to improve or change or rebuild your partner, it's to change, improve and rebuild yourself. And when that happens—when you change, improve and rebuild yourself —you often outgrow a relationship that started when you were at a totally different place in your life. When your goal is to set higher standards for yourself, expect respect, and embrace the idea you are worthy of an available partner, you have to ask yourself, *Can this partner even give me those things?*

So begins the conundrum of staying or going. By staying, you get to keep your partner, but you relinquish the opportunity to become healthier within yourself. By leaving, you have the opportunity to become a better version of yourself, but lose your relationship. If you're anything like me, you try to improve yourself *and* stay. But that road contains a myriad of problems that we will discuss here.

Susan K asked me: *Can I heal and change and become a healthier person while staying with my current boyfriend?* My short answer was sure, give it a try. My long answer was probably not, because once you get healthy and heal and change you won't want him anymore. It's like Cinderella. When a poor girl in rags who cleans a castle gets swept away by a rich, handsome prince, she doesn't continue wearing rags. She doesn't continue to clean the castle on her hands and knees anymore. Sure, she can go back and visit her old life, revisit the dark and gloomy castle where she was nothing more than a servant to her cruel sisters. But she will never again be the woman she once was. That's what happens when we rebuild ourselves. A handsome prince doesn't swoop down and rescue us. We rescue us. And we change so much we outgrow the old relationship. It doesn't serve us any more. We trade in our rags for riches.

But there's a more significant reason you will probably want to let go on your own, I told Susan. You started the relationship as an unhealthy person, searching for a mate. That means you were not looking for healthy things.

You were looking for intensity, for example, not intimacy. You were looking for someone who probably didn't impose too much of an emotional burden on you, although this was most likely a subconscious choice. You might not have been too picky. You settled for little or no respect. You settled for little or no kindness. And you may have even settled for little or no attention. A healthy person wouldn't put up with any of this, so, why should you? And that's just for starters.

But all that aside, here's a story of letting go…

When I was a kid I had an item many kids have–a security blanket. I also sucked my thumb and had a goofy-looking teddy bear I creatively named "Teddy." And while I was able to get rid of the thumb sucking and the teddy bear, I was unable to let go of the blanket. In fact, it followed me well into my married life. Of course, by then, I didn't exactly call it a security blanket. It was a "throw" that I kept at the bottom of the bed. And yet, it was always near me, tossed somewhere by my side or in between my husband and I. And it still held one of the most important roles any object in the house could have– it comforted me when I was sad or angry or in pain. When I was upset, I would roll it into a ball and press my face into it, touching the soft binding to my skin. And lo and behold, it worked. It calmed me down.

Unfortunately, as I got older I turned to other things, destructive ones, for comfort: cigarettes, food, people, and shopping. Like the blanket, they worked. Yet there was a paradox. The more I clung to these things to comfort me, the more uncomfortable, out of control, and painful my life became.

Relationships are a perfect example. No matter how real and fulfilling a relationship was for a time, if it had come to its end for whatever reason, I inevitably tried to emotionally (or physically) drag it out. The trouble wasn't that I'd made the relationship my security blanket, but the be-all and end-all of my existence. It was the entity that validated, comforted, defined, and saved me. And while every good relationship can and should be considered a comfort, it should **not** be considered something that saves us from ourselves.

That's when we seem to get into trouble. And that's when we hurt the most if the relationship ends.

How so? Well, when we cling to a relationship that is clearly over or is unhealthy, we sabotage ourselves. Sure, the relationship may have been wonderful at one point. But when we do not respect its passing, we do great damage to the self and stunt our growth. It's like wearing your prom gown everywhere, years after you graduated high school. Let that thing go! By hanging onto the past, we deny ourselves a true present. And we fail to take care of our deep human need to be loved—not by others, but by ourselves.

But in order to let go, we need to know why we are hanging on.

We hang on because we don't believe we have anything else. We don't believe we can do better, or find someone who will accept or love us with what we believed was the best love imaginable. And most importantly, we fail to recognize that we—ourselves alone—are so much more than the relationship. The relationship may have ended, but we did not. Also, we hang on because we do not have (and possibly never had) a clear sense of the actual health of the relationship. Wanting the relationship to work more than wanting to face the truth of its flaws puts us in a position of denial. But, if we are to be brutally honest with ourselves, the relationship might have been broken in ways that could not be fixed. This does not mean we have to beat ourselves up over our self-delusion. But we do have to be honest and face a truth we might not want to face. Facing the truth and not holding on to a fantasy helps us heal and move on (again, read Assessing Your Relationship).

The last item is something that happens often with relatively healthy people too: when it comes to relationships, some people give everything away. They sacrifice their identity and become the other, they give up their hobbies to follow the other's hobbies, and they lose themselves almost completely to the relationship. There are clear problems here. When and if the relationship ends, what do they have left of themselves? I can't tell you how many times I've done this. I proudly called myself a chameleon. I would change everything I possibly could about myself simply to fit the experience I was having. If I was dating an artist, I was deep and driven by the nature of art. If was dating a guy who was into sports, I exercised more and learned all the plays of his favorite game. And if I was with someone who was family-oriented, I too, focused more than usual on my family. And for what? Looking back, I find it strange that I was so proud of having no identity of my own and could change so easily to fit into the lifestyle of whoever I was dating.

When I was a teenager, I spent a summer working on a boardwalk at the shore, selling T-shirts for a young but wise Israeli man named Eyal. I had fallen in love with one of my co-workers, and at the end of the summer, when he went back home, I was devastated. I felt like my whole world collapsed and I had nothing. Eyal and I talked about this one night and he said this: "There is an old, Israeli saying that when you fall in love, give everything to the other person, but keep three finger for yourself. Your index finger, your middle finger and your thumb. This way, when you fall, you have a way to get back up again." And he held up those three fingers to show me. This is where your strength lies, he said. The story made perfect logic in the physical sense. Sure, if you fall, you need to be able to pick yourself up. But what did he really mean? What was it that I'd given away that those three fingers represented? That I needed to get back?

And then he explained further. "Your index finger is your work," he said. "Find a passion for something, go to school, find a career. Your middle finger represents your hobbies. Find hobbies you love to do and never stop doing them. And your thumb is your spirituality. Never lose your faith in what you believe," he said, no matter what it is. If you don't believe in a higher power, or you don't consider yourself spiritual, refocus the meaning of this finger into something else—a deeper appreciation for nature and the environment. The point is, these three fingers represent aspects of you separate from your relationship. They can be shared, but they should never be relinquished. They are all yours.

So did you hold on to your three fingers in your past relationships? Or, did you give them away? Perhaps that's why you are holding onto someone and don't want to let go. Do you feel like you'll have nothing if you lose the relationship? Guess what, you have an entire world! You have the time, the space and the aliveness to explore what you love and what you want to do and be. Understand this concept, and it makes letting go of a relationship, if that's what needs to happen, easier.

At the end of the day, this review is much like deciding on travel plans. Do I want to throw myself under a palm tree with a mojito in hand, tool around Europe on a Velib while sipping café au laits, or, climb the world's highest mountain with sherpas? Once you know what you want, you need only figure out which location on the globe can offer those things. My point? If you want to scale mountains, get out of Kansas. If you want a healthy relationship, it might be time to pack your bags and get out of Dodge.

i. **Ambivalence**

> *"And I can't be running back and fourth*
> *forever between grief and high delight."*
>
> – J.D. Salinger, *Franny and Zooey*

Another clear (or, from your vantage point, unclear) reason to possibly let go concerns dealing with a nasty little state called ambivalence.

Come closer…Go away, I need space…not too much…

When you wonder why you're being pulled and pushed, or when you're the one doing the pulling and pushing it's usually ambivalence that's to blame.

I so often felt terribly ambivalent over some of the guys I was in relationship with. And by ambivalent I mean that sometimes I loved the person and wanted to be close to him, while other times, he repulsed me and I wanted nothing to do with him. I learned to accept this behavior as part of my "fear of intimacy." The pushing away then pulling closer behavior was a sure sign that I was simply scared of commitment and closeness with another human being. In fact, at one point in my life, I was engaged to be married to a guy that my family really liked. It was at first a very passionate relationship, but as soon as we moved in together and got engaged I had what everyone assumed was a typical case of "cold feet." Trouble is, it didn't go away, and finally grew so strong that I got physically sick, broke out in hives, and developed a serious stomach ulcer. The more I ignored the truth that something was wrong with the relationship, the sicker I became. My body was screaming at me: *do something!*

My ambivalent path usually went like this: I'd meet someone, see red flags immediately (I'm very good at detecting red flags), push the guy away, and once I pushed, he generally liked me even more, so he would insist we were meant to be together. Aggressive pursuit was always such a turn on for me (I thought it was a sure sign of true love). I would give in. I would fall madly in love with him a week or two into relationship, promise devotion, and we'd have this whirlwind affair.

And then…I'd come to my senses, but keep quiet about it because I was embarrassed.

How could I have made such a mistake? I'd berate myself. But maybe I didn't make a mistake, I'd counter. Maybe I was just scared. Once the initial chemistry of love wore off, the real nitty gritty of the relationship (the unglamorous living day to day stuff), and I thought I couldn't handle it. I thought I had a fear of commitment that I had to somehow overcome. And when I couldn't overcome it, I just figured I was hopeless. I believed I was incapable of true intimacy with someone and everyone I would ever meet would have this same effect on me. That led me to believe my lot in life was to overcome my fear of intimacy and so I tended to force myself to remain with someone longer than I normally would (even going so far as to marry someone I wasn't all that in love with) so I could learn what intimacy was. But there was a much larger (and simpler) issue at play that caused my ambivalence, and it was something I remained in denial about for many years (sadly, when we put ourselves into a box, we deny ourselves other possibilities): **Shockingly, my ambivalence was caused by the simple fact I just didn't like the guy.** Sure, I liked him in certain situations, in others I even loved him, but clearly I had some pretty strong aversions to parts of him that I should not have overlooked, but did. And yet, I kept telling myself I had to take the good with bad. That I would never find anyone without problems. And this is true! You are not dating part of a someone. You're dating a whole person. But you have to love that whole person. I only loved half, or a quarter.

Worse yet, I craved and wanted the relationship, not necessarily the guy. Aside from ambivalence, this craving is relationship addiction at its finest. I believe it comes into play when we force ourselves to love someone whom we inherently, naturally do not love just for the sake of maintaining a committed relationship because the relationship is what we truly crave. Ambivalence, too, can be tricky because love or friendship may exist in part, and we tend to believe if we have this small amount of love for a person, then we truly do love them and should be in a relationship with them. Mentally and emotionally you might even tell yourself, *I'm just scared, that's all;* or, *I'm being too picky.*

But here's the deal. There's good, healthy fear or trepidation about moving forward with someone and then there's red-flag-scared. And if you're not being true to your spirit, your body will start to create warning signals; your body will start screaming at you to listen. Again, back to the guy I was engaged to be married to in my twenties, I moved full speed ahead with wedding plans and everything. And yet, physically, I was breaking out in hives, my stomach was not only in knots, but double constrictor knots, and I was incessantly dizzy. Eventually, I told my fiancé that I needed a break from the relationship. When that happened, it was like a flower bloomed inside me.

I could breathe for the first time in months and my physical body instantly healed. He told me I had a fear of commitment. Years later I realized, I had a fear of commitment *to him*. And I want to make it clear. There was nothing "wrong" with this guy. He was (shockingly) not avoidant or unavailable, he was kind and respectful. But, I just didn't love him. As much as I wanted to, it wasn't there. When something like this happens, the problem of ambivalence can turn into physical and emotional pain, hatred, anger or resentment. Below is a list of the bad kind of ambivalence that generally means there's something wrong and you may be staying in a relationship you shouldn't. The important part to understand is that there is a huge dissociation between what you are saying and what you are feeling, or, conversely, what you think you feel versus what is actually happening to you:

You say you love your partner, but you have trouble looking them in the eyes (not in the beginning, mind you. In the beginning when all those juicy chemicals are coursing through the veins, you can do and feel virtually ANYTHING).

- You say you love your partner, but you're consistently turned off by their breath.

- You say you love your partner, but you have an aversion to their style or the way they dress.

- You say you love your partner, but you become sexually anorexic after a time and don't want to be touched.

- You say you love your partner, but you find their jokes, or topics of conversation consistently uninteresting.

- You say you love your partner, but you want to avoid them more frequently than not.

- You say you love your partner, and you have strong positive feelings for them over the phone, computer or through e-mail, but not in person (or vice versa).

- You say you love your partner, but you dream or fantasize about someone else "better" or "sexier" or more "passionate."

- You say you love your partner, but you feel momentarily happier at the point of break up.

- You say you love your partner, but you constantly prefer to be alone.

- You say you love your partner, but you frequently have feelings of disgust, anger, frustration, hatred, ambivalence, apathy, or coldness within the relationship

- You say you love your partner, but you have little or no respect for them.

- You say you love your partner, but you feel uncomfortable around them.

- You say you love your partner, but you feel physically sick or weak when they are near.

I think because we so desperately want something (a loving relationship), we sell ourselves on a bad deal. We deny our instincts and don't listen to our gut. We think there must be some secret meaning behind our behavior, so we analyze ourselves and the relationship to the point of ignoring the basic truths. But sadly, the truth (as I have found) cannot be denied, and the longer you stay in a relationship that's not right for you, the more your deeper instincts will scream at you to pay attention. Bottom line, this kind of ambivalence comes from wanting the relationship more than the person and that tends to be a clear indication that it's time to go.

So, is there such a thing as healthy ambivalence? Yes! Ambivalence is necessary in the beginning of a relationship when you're trying to decide if a certain person is right for you. Remember, ambivalence means "doubt." And doubt is healthy when you do not know what you're getting into. It's when you are STILL having a lot of doubts after a longer period of time. After six months to a year you should know when someone is right for you. You may not know them completely. But you should have a pretty good sense. Healthy ambivalence looks something like this:

- You love your partner, but you worry if he will accept your family

- You love your partner, but you wonder if his job will relocate him

- You love your partner, but you worry if your living styles are the same when you move in together

- You love your partner, but you wonder if he wants children someday.

These are healthy doubts that should, within time, be worked out via communication if the relationship is a strong one.

When it comes to ambivalence, always remember to be honest with yourself and don't be afraid to question your feelings or thoughts. Feeling uncomfortable or consistently feeling anger or hatred or frustration with a partner is a sign that it's time to go.

So, we've talked a lot about when to leave, but what about when to stay? Staying is often easier to determine because it's built on a very basic concept, ie, reciprocity. We reciprocate, or collaborate in a partnership, which means the desire to become healthy and closer is mutual, not one-sided. Both partners work together, and on themselves, to reach a common goal. But what is that goal? Is it merely to stay together? A healthy goal has to be more substantive than that. Two people who just stay together for the sake of staying together tend to miss the point. How about staying together for the sake of growth—personal and shared? How about staying together because of common interests? How about staying together to build something with your partner, like a family, or a business or a life? When our desire to stay in a relationship is one-sided it often creates demands for the other partner to change his behavior. An example is, "you need to be more available and then we can stay together," or "you need to participate in this relationship if you want to keep me."

Like it or not, people don't change that easily. And they only change if they want to, not if you want them to. One of the hardest lessons I ever learned was that we cannot make people love us. What we can do is accept people as they are and hope that they accept us as we are.

But this is the million-dollar dilemma. Do we simply accept painful, neglectful behavior for the greater good of the relationship? Well, if we want to suffer then, yes, sure. But, if we want to stop suffering, the answer is no. We do not stay and accept pain. We do not stay and accept suffering.

In Chapter 13 we'll talk about values. This will offer a deeper perspective about the concept of accepting people as they are. Until then, let's assume your relationship has come to end. How then, do you move on?

CHAPTER 8

Don't Call Him! (No Contact)

"People have a hard time letting go of their suffering. Out of a fear of the unknown, they prefer suffering that is familiar."

– Thich Nhat Hanh

So, let's say your relationship has ended. Whether you're the one who ended the relationship or it was imposed upon you, it doesn't matter. What does is your commitment to your new life. And that means upholding a little something called No Contact ("NC" for short).

In addiction circles, we talk a lot about NC when it comes to our "person of addiction." And let's be honest here, if you're still craving face-to-face run-ins, and making booty calls or phone calls, or text messages, or late night Snapchats long after the relationship is done, NC should be your new best friend, whether you think you're a love addict or not. In harsher terms, NC simply means quitting your drug of choice, cleansing your system of toxic behaviors and toxic people, and preparing the foundation for a healthier life—in this case, without your relationship.

NC, obviously demands that you physically distance yourself from your ex. Don't see her, don't text her, don't call her, don't stalk her on social media, and don't show up at Starbucks when you know she'll be there getting her morning latte. For most people, physical distance is enough to begin the healing process. For those who are having a harder time letting go, NC also means no *thinking* about your ex. No fantasies, no day dreams, no listening to old songs or watching old movies, no meandering down memory lane, and most important, no obsessive analyzing or wondering what he is up to or who he is with or why he hasn't called, or (this was always my personal favorite), why he psychologically chose to walk away from the most perfect relationship on the planet. Was it his innate fear of commitment? Because he was abused in childhood? Or was it because he's a narcissist and was born without the ability to connect? *Hmm…let me buy a gazillion books on narcissism so I can understand him better.* All these cerebral behaviors are rooted in obsession (and avoiding the healing process) and they will continue to imprison you and keep you from moving forward. Letting go is critical to your happiness.

Unfortunately, this is one of the hardest parts of moving on and rebuilding yourself. Like a true junkie, we tend to keep going back to the source of our addiction for another "hit," because, let's face it, being without him or her is painful. In fact, the pain of going through withdrawal is often so severe that *we* oftentimes *run back to* a painful, destructive relationship just to avoid this new hurt. The agony of the relationship almost seems bearable compared to that of going without.

But trust me, this feeling of withdrawal, be it physical, mental or emotional (or all three!) is only temporary. And staying away from the person you believe, at this point in time, is the source of your suffering, is your most important first step.

Yes, I know, I know. If you just look at her Facebook page for a few minutes to find out if she misses you it will take away the stabbing pain you feel in your heart. If you just send one little text to hopefully get one back it will take away all of this misery. But each time you break NC, the opposite seems to happen. You hurt even more. And the cycle begins again. You heal. Then you get lonely. Then you reach out in some way. The reaching out is never what you had fantasized it should be. You are in pain again. And the healing process starts all over. Just remember, believing that reaching out will take away pain is an illusion. It won't. Like a true mirage, you struggle to get closer to the source, only to find out it doesn't exist.

One of the phrases that has helped many move forward is this:

No contact = no new hurt.

Changing your perception of what NC means to you is also super-important. For many, the thought of not contacting or responding to the person who has been the focal point of your life seems like torture. It might feel like you've "lost" something or someone. Or, your life is empty, lonely, meaningless. It might even feel like when you first go on a diet and deny yourself high-calorie or unhealthy foods. You can't help but feel hungry and cranky as if you've just removed all the fun from your life. A healthy salad seems like a poor substitute for all the comfort food you just gave up.

But, this negative attitude toward NC is detrimental. For starters, all these thoughts and feelings of "loss" are not exactly a correct interpretation of what is really happening. While it may seem like you've lost someone (because clearly they are no longer there), the reality is, you've gained. What have you gained? Your life back, and the chance for a better, stronger healthier relationship with yourself and others. NC is, in fact, a gift you give yourself. It is a way in which you take care of yourself. And it is the first in a long line of many actions you will take toward loving yourself and upholding your worth, self-respect, and dignity. Remember back in Chapter 5, all that talk about scraps? NC is your very first decent, life-thriving meal in a very long while. But you have to recognize it as such.

In order to do that, to clearly understand why you are choosing NC (and it is, after all, a choice), I want you to see the value in this decision. Love addicts often do not see the value in the choices they make. Even the most assertive of us tend to want others to make decisions for us. Not this time. This is the beginning of making choices for yourself and being gratified by them. So, trust your judgment, and ask yourself the following questions:

1. Is my ex a life-giving force? Do I not only feel comfortable, safe and happy when I am with him, but do I feel, respected, healthy, true to myself?

2. I may hear the words "I love you," but do I feel well-loved?

3. Do I feel positive about myself, my life and the relationship at least 80-90 percent of the time? Or is it less than fifty percent?

4. Do I like myself in this relationship? Does my partner like himself/herself?

5. Is my ex available? Am I available? Or do either of us have circumstances or personal inhibitions that do not allow us to commit fully?

6. Am I hurting anyone, including myself, by remaining in this relationship?

Depending on your responses, your ex is either a great catch or he's a cancerous tumor whose removal would save your life. My guess is, if you're reading this book, he might be the latter.

A word of caution. Even the best of us can forget why we are staying away. Especially if you have an ex that keeps reaching out. And so, making a game plan as soon as the relationship has ended is a super-smart choice. I mean, think about good 'ol Chris Columbus. Do you think he just hopped on the Santa Maria to set sail for the new world with only his hat and compass? Heck no. He knew his voyage would last many months so he PREPARED. He had a crew and loads of food and medicines to back him up. Sure, he miscalculated. Sure, he made mistakes (*"What? This isn't the East Indies?"*). But he was as prepared as he knew how to be.

Heading into NC is much the same. You need to plan. The better you are at taking care of yourself during this time, the more you have to fall back on, the less the chance your attempt at NC will fail. Here are a few tips:

1. Exercise! I know, I know. You're in pain and can't get out of bed. But exercise is a proven mood enhancer. You need to force yourself to stay busy, and cardio is by far, at the top of the list for survival tactics.

2. Have a hobby available to keep you busy, or two or three. A lot of people claim that "working with your hands" is the best as it forces you to keep your mind on the task *at hand.*

3. Get ready to eat your favorite stuff. Stock up on "feel good" foods at least until you get through the initial withdrawal phase (if you are concerned about weight, make healthier choices, chew gum, sugarless lollipops etc.!) But right now is not the time to worry about putting on a *few* (and I mean few!) extra pounds. Your NC takes priority. You can lose the weight when you are feeling better.

4. Have friends and family ready to talk and listen. Make sure they know what you're attempting (no contact!) so that you have extra support. If family members aren't supportive, seek out friends or support groups; people who will understand what you might be going through.

5. Make plans, goals and activities that don't require a partner (go to the movies by yourself, attend a concert, visit the bookstore, sit at a cafe and people-watch etc.)

6. If you can, go out and shop. Heck, buy yourself something nice.

7. Go get a massage, a manicure, a pedicure. Go get your eyebrows waxed. My all time favorite: changing the color of my hair. Nothing too drastic. But enough to make me feel revived. A box of hair color at the grocery store is perfect if you're on a budget.

8. Get involved in a series, or a sitcom. Comedy is your best choice. It serves to distract and lighten your mood. Try to stay away from romantic shows for a while. Series like The Affair, or Big Little Lies, or even old reruns of Sex and the City can be triggers.

9. Don't turn NC into a bad thing. You have a choice: you can think positively about what you are doing for yourself, or negatively. Choose positive! This is a happy time, not a sad time. You are not, I repeat, not losing anything worthwhile. You are gaining! You're getting your life back.

10. Remember the Ten-Minute Rule. It's a safety net for those moments of intense craving. For example, whenever you feel the intense urge to call or make contact, say to yourself, "first let me take a brisk walk for 10 minutes." Meditate, breathe, take a shower. Cravings tend to pass within minutes.

11. Visit GirlRebuilt.com and choose an entry to read! My website is filled with support and advice.

12. Practice the art of positive self-talk. You must reaffirm daily your reasons and motivations for wanting to keep NC. If it helps, keep a journal.

13. Some other distractions you can keep in your arsenal if cravings/withdrawal gets bad:

14. Take a shower (you can't use the phone from there),

15. Take a nap,

16. Clean the house,

17. Drive,

18. Ditch your cell phone,

19. Go swimming,

20. Take a bath,

21. Call a FRIEND,

22. Make an appointment somewhere (salon, doc office, dentist, etc.),

23. Do crossword puzzles,

24. Play solitaire,

25. Go to the gym,

26. Ride your bike,

27. Bake a cake,

28. Paint something,

29. Write a novel,

30. Find a new job

31. Research your ancestors

32. Sing

33. Learn an instrument

34. Take a class

35. Get a college degree

36. If you already have a degree, get a second one

37. Invent something

38. Learn how to budget your money

39. Watch all of Suze Orman's videos

40. Volunteer at a zoo or animal shelter

41. Join a political campaign

Bottom line: stay busy and keep your eye on the prize: You. You are doing a good thing for yourself. Getting through withdrawal is hard, but success is a matter of determination and self-conditioning. We've been through much worse pain than this. We can definitely handle a few months of withdrawal. It does get better.

i. **Who Can Take Away My Pain?**

Remember when life coaches were all the rage? *Can't get your act together?* Call a life coach. *Depressed? Stressed? Have no goals?* Call a life coach. They were personal fitness gurus, nurses, therapists, and secretaries all rolled into one, and were the hottest things out there until we all caught on to the fact they were mostly over-paid and under-trained. But, we bought into them because they played on our magical thinking that our lives could be fixed if only we had that one person to tell us what to do, or better yet, do it for us. If only we had one magical pill to make us whole again. If only we had a million dollars to solve all our problems.

I remember being at my rock bottom. I was hunched over in my bedroom, arms clasped around me and crying, begging God to take away the pain and just fix my life. I remember thinking, *This is just too hard for me. I can't do it.* I soothed myself with thoughts of a drug that would make it all go away. I imagined there was a man who existed who would just show up at my door and save me. I was so desperate for help that these fantasies brought me both comfort and frustration. The reality was nothing like that existed. The hard work of figuring it all out was on me. *Crap.* That was a hard pill to swallow.

Knowing that I was the only one who could "fix me" and deal with my pain by myself seemed bitingly cold and lonely. I just couldn't. I didn't think I had what it took.

But I did. And you do too. Somewhere in us there is a fire. At times, it feels like it's dying out, flickering, about to extinguish. But it isn't. It just needs a little air. And, as my mother always used to say, "When you're sick and tired of being sick and tired, you'll do something about it."

This is what your fire needs. This is what you need to know to pick yourself up: you are human. And what it means is that you are perfectly built to handle this--whatever *this* may be-- and while whatever you are dealing with may seem heart-wrenchingly painful right now, it will not last. You actually have all the answers. And they will come to you. You just need to be patient. You are your own life coach. You know what feels right and what feels wrong. You just have to give yourself more credit. You just have to keep practicing.

And here's the best part: while you essentially are the one who must make decisions and figure out your life all by yourself, there are tons of people, resources, friends, family and strangers who will help guide the way, who will hold your hand. And while life coaches and therapists and personal growth strategists won't solve everything for you (they might not even solve anything for you), they might add to what you already know. They might teach you something you haven't yet heard in a way that makes sense to you. That's the hope of this book. That it can guide you, and inspire you to do for yourself.

But you? Yes, you are the one who needs to sit through the pain. Experience it. Be patient. Breathe. And through the static of all the suffering buzzing around you, listen to the voice within you. That is the Master. She knows. She's capable. She's courageous. She will guide you.

CHAPTER 9

Prepare for the Detox Jitters (Withdrawal)

"Smooth seas do not make skillful sailors."

–African proverb

Now that you know about NC and understand the benefits, the truth is that the road ahead is still going to be a difficult one. While your logical brain grasps the importance of letting the ex go, your emotional brain most likely is still trying to hold on for dear life. This temporary but very painful phase after the end of a relationship is known in love addict world as withdrawal, and just like a drug addict or alcoholic detoxing from addictive substance, love addicts will also experience physical, mental and emotional pain associated with the removal of their addictive person. Heck, nearly everyone who breaks up can go through this same trauma. The degree to which you do doesn't mean you loved more. It means it's simply harder for you to let go.

And of course, the more severe the perceived loss of the relationship, the more dangerous this phase can be. Here is an excerpt from Susan Peabody's definition of withdrawal:

"Withdrawal is dangerous and should be taken seriously. It is life or death because there is a high suicide and homicide rate associated with it. The root of the problem is separation anxiety.

"Separation anxiety is listed in the psychological handbook called the DSM IV as a child's disorder. But adults have it too. When they have bonded and become addicted to someone they regress as far back as infancy and feel the anxiety of an infant crying endlessly in his crib for food or attention.

"All children go through a phase when they experience separation anxiety when mother is no longer in sight. They then select an object to take the place of mom and can cling to the object when mom leaves the room without having an anxiety attack. Fast forward into adulthood. The adult/child picks a person to stand in for their primary caretaker to quell anxiety. When you intervene in this with a breakup, then the place in our brain that is still connected to our infant memory is activated. Picture a child clinging to a stuffed toy and someone grabbing it and throwing it in the garbage before the child is ready to let it go. This "snatching away" is as traumatic then as it is traumatic now, especially when the object of affection standing in for mom or dad happens to be your lover." (Peabody, 2005)

But what does withdrawal to a love addict feel like? Look like? Here are actual accounts of withdrawal from members of Love Addicts Anonymous:

I am listless. I am nauseous. I have headaches. My body is exhausted. All I can do is lie still in bed as if I had the flu.

I feel like I'm walking in a fog, nothing is real or very important. I'm crabby and irritable.

I feel empty and lost without him and terrified that I made the wrong decision. Everything seems to remind me of him and contribute to feelings of extreme anxiety and worry that I did the wrong thing.

I feel resentful, suicidal, enraged, used...

I locked myself in my room for four days straight and cried and cried and cried. I could barely take a shower or feed myself. Sometimes, I just laid on the floor and looked up at my ceiling.

At times I felt like I was going to die.

I have all those nervous feelings in my stomach. I am going crazy. I have not even gotten dressed or anything. The worst thing though is my brain. I have constant fantasies and thoughts about him.

I feel depressed. I don't want to deal with people or really talk.

Obsession, obsession all day today. Couldn't even focus on my school work...

I am a mess. The withdrawal is excruciating. I can't focus on anything except my boyfriend.

I have the "highs" and "lows." One day I am strong and hopeful, the next I feel pain and doubt. I ask over and over, "why doesn't my PoA [person of addiction] care that he's hurting me?" Next minute, I remind myself that he's not, that he has no power to hurt me. I am hurting me.

Once in a while I have dark thoughts. Mostly, I have headaches and I feel tired.

This painful part of the rebuilding process is essential. It is the first step in becoming a stronger, healthier person. Keep your eye on the prize, and keep reading. And, if you feel your withdrawal symptoms are unmanageable, please seek help. There are resources at the back of this book.

i.   **Got Withdrawals?**

Withdrawal is that horrible state right after a break up where you feel like you've been ripped to shreds and beaten to a pulp. You can't stop crying, you can't focus, you can't get up and go to work, you can't eat, or maybe you're eating everything in sight! Whatever the case, withdrawal is not pretty.

With anything addictive (food, alcohol, coffee, nicotine, drugs, love, sugar) our bodies reacts in a chemical way. When we repeatedly put a chemical like caffeine into our bodies and then suddenly remove it, ouch! we experience withdrawal (obviously on a much smaller scale) and tend to incur the typical no-caffeine pounding headache. But, coffee aside, the human body takes time to readapt to any new chemical state we put it in, and it especially takes time if the change happened abruptly, as opposed to slowly, over time. Going "cold turkey" ain't for the faint-hearted.

Too often going through withdrawal seems like a never-ending state of misery, and so, what to do? Well, if you're unhealthy, you go right back to the person you're addicted to in order to put out the flame and feel an immediate sense of calm. Of course, that sense of calm, brought on by "going back" to your drug of choice, is an illusion.

Instead, we need to know that withdrawal is temporary and we need to have patience with the "process" our bodies and minds must go through. Love and the high we get from someone is also a chemical reaction, and when it's removed, our physical body and mental state need time to readapt to that as well.

The lesson of withdrawal is patience. This is the time to wait. To sit through the pain and face it. And if you're anything like me, it is incredibly hard to wait because we want immediate gratification. Like a child, we want what we want and we want it now. But healthy adults understand the need to wait. They understand that deferred gratification brings joy. That blowing the paycheck week to week gets us nowhere, but saving money offers security for times of economic uncertainty. It's hard because we don't like pain. I mean, we've lived our whole lives trying desperately to avoid it!

Remember too that withdrawal is the first step in the process of healing. And that after it, comes a much more realistic, well-earned sense of calm *and* an ability to think more clearly.

So, wait. Be patient. Hang on. Do whatever it takes to get through this. More than anything, be patient with yourself. Don't allow the "trick" of withdrawal to lead you to believe you will always feel this miserable. You will NOT. The body heals itself, but needs the time to do so. Withdrawal is tough. But you're tougher.

ii. **Still Want to Go Back?**

So many of us lose sight of the importance of why we broke up in the first place (*Hello?! You were miserable, remember?*), and we go back. So? Go ahead. Go back to your ex. You know you want to. And if you feel as though you should, surely that means it was meant to be, right? Why not! Every emotion you have, even a burp or a fart has huge significance. Right? A sign from the universe. So, follow it and go back to him.

And when you go back....enjoy! And be happy! Be happy he's ignoring you. You don't deserve to be paid attention to anyway. In fact, everyone, including friends and loved ones should ignore you. Because what you have to say is not very important. Other people (who ramble on about nothing and do nothing with their lives) are so much more important than you.

And when you go back....feel that amazing sensation of confusion again. It's fun and exciting to never know what to expect from one day to the next. She's running hot and cold! One day she loves you, the next she doesn't? Perfect. Instability is probably just what your heart desires.

And when you go back...feel the intense love that, let's face it, you are most likely creating on your own because, let's face this too, half the time he's off with another woman. Oh, the lies! Oh, the betrayal! When I was a child. I always dreamed of having a loving relationship filled with lies and betrayal. Isn't that every young girl's dream? I also wanted a guy I had to fight for. Nothing comes easy! Love is meant to be painful and filled with suffering.

And when you go back....celebrate the good times! Because they are few and far between and erratic as heck. And well...they don't exist anymore. Because she's gone. But who cares! She comes around every so often, and isn't that a sign from the gods she's still hanging on and wants to come back? Because people who love you want to spend as little time as possible with you. Ah...the memories! They will keep you warm at night.

And when you go back....rejoice in the rejection and the scraps he's feeding you. Why take anything else? You are not ready for something better. Rejection and scraps are right up your alley! There's no way you could handle a decent, warm meal. Not you! You're too rugged for that. You prefer to eat your meals out of the garbage can.

So, yes. Next time you wonder if your plan to stay away and do better in life is just getting in the way of this great relationship of yours, if leaving him was not worth it, if everything you fought for is just a waste of your time...then, all sarcasm aside, I *do* suggest going back. And maybe then, you'll remember why you left in the first place.

CHAPTER 10

Who Are You Without Your Relationship?

"The most terrifying thing is to accept oneself completely."

–Carl Gustav Jung

Now that you're working NC, and you've hopefully made it past the ugliest parts of withdrawal, it's time to fill all that newly acquired space and time with the mysteries of YOU, which means introspection. Who are you? Let's start there.

When I was younger, most of my relationships were sexual in nature and they were over before they started. There was no real dating, just sleeping with someone when they were available. Strangely, I used to think sex was sacred and if I was having it with someone they must love me or have feelings for me. But, when I tried to talk to them or spend time with them outside of the bedroom, things often fell apart. I cried for hours, days, months, years, trying to figure out why this was so. Eventually I concluded that men were jerks and I was unworthy of real love.

Later in life, I did start to actually "date." I matured a little and recognized sex only begets sex and tends to lead nowhere. Without much of a fight, I gave up the notion I was a sexually liberated woman who had the freedom to hop into bed with whomever she pleased. That, sadly, never panned out for me. So, I tried a different approach and held off on sleeping with a guy right away. A new type of guy appeared in my life and my relationships were definitely a step up from the purely carnal ones. They held passion disguised as love, but were all short-lived. I dated men I met over summer break, who would only be in town for a few months and then leave. I spent about five years in this mode. falling in love with men who were bound to leave me. Men who were unavailable. I blamed it on the men. Why do I always meet men who leave me, who aren't available? Once again, men were jerks.

In later life, after divorcing my first husband, I continued dating men who were emotionally distant, neglectful, and avoidant. Every one of them. And again, I simply couldn't figure it out. Why was I dating guys who avoided me? I wasn't a disgusting, horrible person. So why were men treating me like the plague? Why was my very own husband neglecting and avoiding me? Wasn't I worthy yet of love?

The reason I had such a difficult time figuring out why I kept dating inappropriate, avoidant, distant men was because I never took into consideration my responsibility for dating them. I was, after all, allowing these men in my life. I was, after all, attracted to them and willing to overlook (at least temporarily) their unappealing behavior. At times I was even willing to overlook it to the point of trying to change myself to stop their behavior and neglect of me.

All men weren't jerks. But I was willingly dating the ones who were.

What I didn't realize also, is that they weren't neglecting me, per se, they were just neglectful people. They weren't avoiding me, exactly. They were just avoidant-types. Or they were immature men who only wanted sex, or they were foreigners who lived in other countries, who lived other lives. Their behavior, in fact, and who they inherently were, had very little to do with me. It was me, on the other hand, who had all the control in the world as to who I dated. And it was me who chose to date people who treated me poorly.

Why would I do this if it hurt so much? Why would I consistently date men who were avoidant or didn't treat me well? Here are the conclusions I made that helped me see who I was.

1. **I was** immature. I had a very undeveloped sense of what love was and I didn't put a lot of effort into finding someone who was more compatible for me.

2. **I was** impatient. Immediate gratification was the most important thing in the world to me. Live in the now! I used to say. I knew nothing of the importance of deferred gratification. I acted on my impulses and thought "chemistry" was the only ingredient necessary for a relationship. (It's not.)

3. **I had no model of a loving relationship.** My dad was an alcoholic, my mother was co-dependent. Even my grandparents had weird, distant, avoidant marriages. What did I know of love or compatibility?

4. **I had no values.** I had no standards. Well, my one value (or so I thought) was that I had to be physically attracted to whomever I dated. And I had to have some chemistry with them. But other than that, I figured I could overlook or put up with virtually any behaviors I didn't particularly like. I figured I could "learn to love" anyone. In fact, I used to fantasize being trapped on a deserted

island with someone "hot" so they had no choice but to love me. Looking back, however, I even overlooked the value of being attracted to my partner. In reality, I dated many men I wasn't very attracted to.

5. **I had a very** shallow notion of intimacy. If I liked a guy's looks and he was an artist or musician, what else was there? As one of my friends always said of me, I'd "fill in the blanks" with my own imagination, giving men qualities they didn't actually possess. I also mistook sex for intimacy. If we were having sex, we were intimate. I was so wrong!

6. **I had low self-esteem and little confidence.** Actually, I had a great amount of confidence and self-esteem when I'd walk into a dive bar and flirt with a bunch of intoxicated guys. Shoot low, so you feel better about yourself was my motto. And so that is who I always surrounded myself with. I never in a million years saw myself dating hardworking, kind, successful, healthy men because their expectations of me would be too high. A man in a suit? *Forget it. Not my style.* Truth is, men in suits intimidated me.

7. **I didn't know myself.** When you have no identity, when you only have the vaguest sense of who you are, how in the world can you recognize what you want and need? You can't. You'll take whatever "feels" good at the time, like a child. There's no discriminating, no sense of entitlement, no using your brain to figure out the difference between right and wrong.

8. **I socialized in the wrong circles.** The idea of meeting successful, mindful, hardworking individuals was so far outside my realm of possibility because I simply didn't run in those circles. For years, I only hung out with people who were, for lack of better terms, immature, unambitious, irresponsible. That's not to say everyone in my life was that way. But, those were the people I felt most

comfortable with. Why? Because I was immature, afraid of success and oftentimes irresponsible. Forget the notion that opposites attract. Like attracts like. Water first seeks its own level.

Looking back, I spent a lot of time blaming people and circumstances outside myself for my troubles. Even though people would tell me that I needed to love myself or "fix" myself first, in order to find a better match for me, I didn't get it. I didn't know how. But once I really opened the window onto my own behavior, only then was I able to change things and find a more appropriate partner.

Exercise: Make it your goal to figure out who you are when you're *not* in a relationship. Do this by creating a list of past and present boyfriends, girlfriends, or people you're drawn to. Add friends, family members, co-workers you hang around with. Next to their names jot down words that describe their overall spirit. Are they positive? Are they superficial? Avoidant? Lazy? Calm? Drawn to drama? Shallow? Depressed? Immature? Angry? Game-players? Artists? Drug-addicts? See if you can create a sense of who you are through the people you socialize with. You'll see a pattern in your social ties, and once it's noticed ,you can see if you identify with it. For example, I hung around artists and writers for years because I felt drawn to them. I felt I was one of them. And yet, I hate to say it, many of these artists and writers were a rather unreliable, unstable, chaotic bunch. While I loved the art we were all creating and I genuinely loved the spirit of the group, I didn't share their values. I didn't think it was OK to drink excessively on a week night. I didn't think it was OK to leave your kids home alone five nights a week for the sake of participating in readings and art shows. And I didn't think it was OK to take extended time off from my family to attend writing conferences. I want to be clear when I say, there's nothing wrong with a writer's or artist's lifestyle. But, this lifestyle didn't coincide with who I was and who, I guess, I wanted to be. On the one hand, this lifestyle seemed glamorous to me. I was drawn to it. The reality, however, seemed anything but glamorous. I learned a lot about myself through this experience—primarily, that I am a family girl and a homebody. Hopefully, this exercise will enlighten you as well.

Here's another way to figure out who you are.

- Look at the people in your life, and that is who you are.

- Look at the drama or lack of drama in your life, and this is who you are.

- Look at the anger, fighting, hostility in your life, and this is who you are.

- If most of your relationships (romantic, familial, friendships etc.) are fraught with pain, hostility, anger, frustration, and neglect, this is not a coincidence. This is who you are.

- If most of your relationships (romantic, familial, friendships etc.) end badly, mean-heartedly, and are followed by sadness, pain, cruelty to the other, this is who you are.

- If most of your relationships begin abruptly and end abruptly, this is who you are.

- If most of your relationships are emotionally and intellectually shallow and primarily about sex, this is who you are.

- If most of your relationships lack intimacy, this is who you are.

- If you are hanging around with superficial people who shop for clothes all day and are only interested in looks, this is who you are.

- If most of your relationships are peaceful, loving, passionate, and long-term, this too is who you are.

Take responsibility for creating your own reality. Look at the patterns of your life and the people with whom you associate to determine who you are. Water seeks its own level. People are reflections of the self. Bottom line, you need to know who you are without a relationship, so you have better control over who you are in your next relationship.

Exercise: Take a look at your life and try to define yourself without your partner. Imagine there is no significant other in your life. Who are you? What do you look like? What do you like to do? What are your interests? What are your fears? Are you facing all your responsibilities? Are you avoiding anything? Try to thoroughly question whether you are avoiding something in your life that you'd simply rather not deal with, or that might frighten you.

CHAPTER 11

Ten Lies We Tell Ourselves to Keep Hanging On

"Nobody can hurt me without my permission."

– Mahatma Gandhi

I'm checking in on you. How's the No Contact going? Still got withdrawals? Are you counting the days? Are you biting your fingernails off? Have you called him? Has he called you? Or are you finally starting to see the forest through the trees? Moments of seeming-weakness are your biggest strengths. A baby does not just start walking. She falls a million times before she can put one foot in front of the other with ease. There's still work to do, girl. Don't give up. Keep going and know that every day, you're one step closer to your superhero self.

I don't say that lightly. I know this might just be the hardest thing you've ever done. How do I know? Because I was there. And I quit. Many times. My undying love for Mr. Fill In The Blank made me miserable, I wasn't getting what I wanted, and I was in deep, emotional pain. Red flags were all over the place and yet, I wasn't paying attention to any of them. Sound familiar? Sometimes No Contact can be so horrifying that we run back to our person. The pain of dealing with our ex seems so much easier than the pain of being alone. Right? (Well, no). I know I'm beating a dead horse, but, here are 10 lies we commonly tell ourselves to remain anchored.

1. **I love him/her, or I've never felt this way about anyone before.** Love is like a sailboat. When it›s on the water, it carries you smoothly across the seas. But when it›s on dry land, it doesn›t do a damn thing for you. Love is an almost pointless, burdensome emotion when you feel it for someone who treats you like garbage and doesn't actually love you back. And that is why it is the number one worst lie we tell ourselves to keep hanging on. Focus instead on the actions in your relationship. What is actually going on? If you can't see it clearly, keep a journal of your feelings (today, I was angry, today, I felt good, today, we fought again). Make sure you re-read it after a few months and then read it with your brain, not your heart or your emotions. Gauge whether it is an overall healthy relationship or not. But do not base remaining in a relationship on love alone. Don't glorify the fact that you have a sailboat or not. Glorify the fact that you have a sailboat on the water that's taking you somewhere.

2. **He said he loves me.** So what? I love you too. And Taylor Swift loves her fans, each and every one of them. Love is action. Love is sharing the same values. Love doesn't feel like pain. The love songs are wrong. Love doesn't hurt. He can "say" he loves you all he wants, and even though it sounds wonderful and comforting, it's

his actions that matter. Does he show up when you need him to, does he want to spend a decent amount of time with you? Does he do kind things for you and love you the way you need to be loved? These are important questions you should be asking yourself.

3. **He needs me.** No he doesn't. He's a grown man. He's perfectly capable of taking care of himself. Or, at least, he should be. If he's really in need of an adult woman to take care of him, or keep him out of trouble, or whatever it is he can't do himself, then you're dating a teenager or worse, a "moddler," a man-toddler. Do yourself a favor. Don't get into the "mother" role. That's a weird dynamic that will end up feeling awkward down the road.

4. **I need him.** No you don't. You just think you do. You are also a grown woman. People need each other situationally, not in entire relationships. You might "need" someone to get a dish down for you if it's high up on a shelf (then again, you can use a chair). You might "need" someone to take care of you if you're sick; you might "need" someone to set you straight every once in a while. But you should not need anyone financially, or emotionally or to be "around" to give you what you lack or take care of your kids or make you look or feel normal. Being a grown-up entails learning how to make do on your own even when you are lacking. Sure, this sounds cold and shrewd. Hollywood and American culture have defined people who take care of themselves as icy and emotionless. But this is so not true. You can be independent, take care of yourself, not need anyone for anything and have a loving, warm, passionate relationship.

5. **We work together/we live together. I have to make it work.** Get a new job. Move out. These are excuses you use to keep you in a bad relationship that needs its proper burial. Getting a new job or finding a new place to live is extremely scary and disruptive. We all

want stability and we'll do darn near anything to keep it. But you have no right staying in a bad, loveless, or otherwise painful relationship just because you are afraid of change. Take a deep breath, open your eyes, and dive into the unknown. You both deserve this kind of freedom. And save yourself the burden of thinking, "He should leave, not me." I knew a woman who waited 10 years for that to happen. And for 10 years, she kept living and working with her ex, and stayed in a life of pain. You can choose empowerment. It's scarier than what you know. But it has a far greater pay-off.

6. **I'd feel like I was giving up.** Sometimes relationships bear the weight of struggle. There are phases couples go through, and having patience and working through those troubles is a necessary part of your commitment. But ask yourself two questions: 1.) Is my partner as committed as I am when it comes to working through this? And 2.) When I take a hard look at the quality of our relationship over its lifespan, what percent has been really good, as opposed to painful, and have I been able to maintain my values throughout? Be honest now. Giving up might not be giving up at all, when it comes to toxic. We quit smoking for a reason.

7. **I don't want to be single again.** Too bad. Not wanting to be single is like not wanting to go to the dentist to get a root canal. It's a part of taking care of yourself. Better yet, it's an unnecessary fear. There are 96 million singles living in the US alone. 12.2 million widows, 3 million widowers, and 25 million men and women who are divorced. It's time to change your paradigm about being single. It doesn't mean you're always alone. It doesn't mean you are unloved. And it certainly doesn't mean there's anything wrong with you (especially according to these stats). But being single does demand that you face yourself and learn to be independent. It means spending extra time getting to know what you like and

what you are capable of. If you avoid being single at all costs, you deny yourself a chance to experience life in a new, positive way. Still need convincing? Read Jen Shefft's book Better Single Than Sorry. As Jen says, "single doesn't equal lonely..."

8. **No relationship is perfect. I need to accept that.** Yup. You're right. No relationship is perfect. But «perfect» should not be the standard you hold your relationship to. Nor should it be the measure that allows you to shoot close to perfect and be OK when you don't reach it. In fact, perfect has no bearing on how to measure your relationship. But **health** does. Health is a lot easier and more realistic to measure. Take humans, for example. Say you have two friends: one smokes two packs of cigarettes a day, eats fried foods, never exercises, watches TV for five hours a day, has problems with obesity and was just told by his doc he has diabetes. The other friend is lean and fit, eats healthy, exercises every other day, educates herself and also just got back from the doctor. She gets a clean bill of health. She also manages her money well, volunteers in her community and is generally a happy person. Is she perfect? Nope. But she's healthy. She's living a less risky life, which could lead to a longer one. View your relationship in terms of health, not perfection. Health is something we can work towards, perfection is not.

9. **There's no one else out there for me.** If this is what you're telling yourself, you are in denial. I understand many people out there are in geographically challenged areas, maybe even isolated. I understand we all don't look like Beyoncé or Bradley Cooper. And I totally get the (faulty) thinking that there is only ONE soul mate out there for each of us (not!). I even get that the pool of available partners shrinks the older we get. But this kind of thinking is a.) hopeless, b.) negative, c.) mostly false, d.) limiting and e.) it ends up being prophetic if you really begin to believe it. Wipe it out of

your mind. It's an excuse to stay in a relationship that is poor and unhealthy simply because you are AFRAID to try again. Simply because you are afraid of taking a risk. Of course you want something better for yourself, but with this kind of thinking, you begin to believe that the risk of a better life is simply not worth taking. Why? We're scared and want guarantees. Well, there are none. You need to get out of a bad relationship despite not having another one to jump into.

10. **He'll/She'll change. He's/She's just not ready yet.** A tiger can't change its stripes, but it can change the direction it's walking. Humans can also change certain things about themselves but not others. We can change a like or dislike, or even a habit. But we cannot generally change a value--something we inherently believe in. We can change our minds about something, but we cannot generally change our inherent nature. My point? He's probably not going to change the fact that he neglects you. She's not going to change the fact that she doesn't really love you. You know how hard it is to change one little facet of yourself even when you try really hard? Well, imagine how hard it is for someone who has no inclination to change. It's pretty much impossible. Second point: YOU are not the one who will change him. Especially if you've been at it for quite some time now. Give up the fantasy. Your life is not *Sleepless in Seattle, Casablanca, The Notebook,* or any other cheesy love story told on the big screen. Move on. Change what you can...yourself and your situation.

PART III: REBUILD YOURSELF, GIRL

"Let me embrace thee, sour adversity, for wise men say it is the wisest course."

—William Shakespeare

When two people fall in love, healthy love or not, they begin to build. They come together and break ground and lay the foundation with whatever tools and materials they possess, and they build their love, they build a life together, they build a family. If they have the right tools, what they begin to build will be strong and enduring. If they don't, well, all sorts of structural fiascos occur. And the truth is, most people are not expert builders. They build their love with flimsy wallboard. They build without giving the relationship load-bearing walls and beams to sustain it. And often, what they build, they destroy. So it's no wonder many of us do not know how to love others or ourselves. We weren't built that way. It's no wonder our structure is flimsy in certain areas so that when it's our turn to build something we don't know how. Not that I want to blame the builder, but, in the real world if I engaged a contractor to build me a house and the roof caved in, well, guess who I'd blame? The guy I hired to build it. But you can't do that with your parents or caretakers. They built you the best way they knew, with whatever materials they had available at the time, and that's that. If your roof collapses, *you* need to fix it. No one else. There is no compensation for someone else's faulty parenting. So, what you can do, and what you must do, is rebuild yourself. And you can only rebuild yourself if you have the right tools and the right materials. This next section is composed of a sort of self-builder's kit. Each section offers an essential tool for your building process and teaches you how to use it.

By the way, a person who was raised in a "well-constructed" home, built with great care and the proper tools rarely moves into a poorly constructed shack that has a risk of falling down. Why? Because they know a good house when they see it. They recognize sturdy construction. And so, if you're trying to move from a less than ideal house to a strong well-built one, here's how.

Values

> *"Who looks outside, dreams; who looks*
> *inside, awakes. "*

–Carl Gustav Jung

As we work to transition from unhealthy to healthy, one of the most important tools we need, if not THE most important tool, is an essential set of
personal values. Creating values and sticking to them is the basis of all other
learning experiences going forward. Your values, or lack thereof, can and will
create your personal foundation with either brick and mortar or cardboard.
And so, if you want to change from unhealthy thinking and behaviors to
healthy, you must have a set of values, and they must be more important to
you than anything else.

To a love addict, the term "values" can be hugely confusing, because
we either don't know we have any, or if we do, don't consider them to be very

important. Case in point: have you ever broadcasted to all your friends that you have tons of self-esteem, self-confidence and self-love, and then stayed in a relationship with someone who degraded you, made you feel uncomfortable, or treated you poorly? This is an example of proclaiming your values, but not upholding them. If you love yourself, why hang around people who treat you badly? But…I am getting too far ahead. Let's start here:

"How do I figure out what my values are?" That's a very good question. And like I said, not many people even know what values are. I didn't really have an idea about my values until age 40 (late bloomer, remember?). I'll explain here.

First of all, a value is a thing (a principle, a belief, a standard of behavior) that we regard as essential to our being, so essential, in fact, that without it, we feel lacking or wrong or worthless. It's a MUST HAVE, not a want or a wish. A value (a MUST HAVE) is something we cannot live without and it's different for all people, save a few biggies. Being treated with kindness is a value. Believing that you should never be physically beaten is a value. Respecting others is a value. The trouble is, either we don't know what our values are, or, more importantly, we have a vague idea what they are, but don't stick to them, like in the example above.

One of those things we tend to give up our values for is love. To someone who loves with all their heart, who gives up everything in the process of loving, who holds on to a toxic relationship past the point of dignity, it can be said this person's highest value is "love" or "the relationship." But I would argue that that is not a value at all. Love, remember, is like a book. It is meaningless without a story. Love is an umbrella term for things like respect, kindness, care, closeness, availability, passion, chemistry, communication, willingness to work together, etc. More appropriately, this person's value is not based on love at all, but rather, an acute need to be loved, to be in a relationship, to be with someone. If we take a closer look at this person, we may find that he or she has forfeited some essential values.

In order to figure out what your real personal values are (or should be!) I would suggest you start with a list of your own personal likes and dislikes, as well as what you like or don't like in other people. Think of the people currently in your life and from your past. Did they have any qualities that really disturbed or upset you to the point where you said, "I cannot deal with this person at all!" For example, say your ex always "neglected" you. When you wanted to talk to him he wouldn't pick up despite the fact that you knew he always kept his phone on. The feeling of this crushed you. Consequently, one of your values might be "I cannot remain in a committed relationship with someone who ignores or neglects me." Remember, a value is a must-have. It's essential to who you are. And then, here's the hardest part: once you put this on your list, you stick to it. You don't bend. And the reason you don't bend is because this <u>value</u> is about maintaining who you are and what you're worth. This value is not only your way of protecting yourself, it is your way of raising yourself above the fray, refusing scraps, and making sure others know that your values are vital to your happiness.

What's not a value? Say you dated a guy or girl and they picked their teeth with a toothpick at the dinner table (funny, perhaps; but, this type of behavior bothers some people). Every time this person did this particular behavior it drove you nuts and you didn't like it. Is trying to avoid this kind of behavior a value? Probably not. It's more a preference. But the bigger value might be "I need to have a relationship with someone who has manners and conducts himself properly in public."

So you see, values are things, concepts, ideas that you recognize as being extremely important to you (must-haves) and once you know what they are, you stay true to them. By staying true to them, you only let in people who are good for your well-being. What is really important to you, might not be to me. Everyone's values are different. But when you find someone who shares your values, it makes the relationship feel good to you and work well.

Values are personal and often universal (don't hurt others; play nice, etc.) . But they rarely change throughout the years, unlike "preferences" (i.e. the guy picking his teeth at the table). More importantly, some values are very difficult to recognize. For the longest time, I thought I could handle a man who smoked pot occasionally. So, I kept dating men who did drugs socially. I thought I was wrong for being so critical of "socially laid back" behavior. And so did he. "C'mon, Tracy, lighten up! You're too rigid," an ex of mine told me over and over. And so, for many years, I thought the goal was to learn to lighten up. I was so wrong! The goal should have been to find people who thought like me, who also could not handle social drugs in their world. What a difference it made!

Here's a list of my values, as well as a list of my "preferences" in dating. See if you can see the difference.

My Values:

1. I will not remain in a committed relationship with someone who drinks heavily or does drugs.

2. I will not remain in a committed relationship with someone who lies.

3. I will not remain in a committed relationship with someone who cheats.

4. I will not remain in a committed relationship with someone who cannot take care of himself

5. I will not remain in a committed relationship with someone who does not treat my children or his with decency and respect

6. I will not remain in a committed relationship with someone who hurts or abuses me mentally or physically.

7. I will not remain in a committed relationship with someone who does not enjoy physical affection and sex. 8

8. I will not remain in a committed relationship with someone who doesn't allow me my space 9. I will not remain in a committed relationship with someone who is an avoidant 10. I will not remain in a committed relationship with someone who is not willing to fully commit to the relationship (this sounds like '*duh*' but it actually isn't).

My preferences, on the other hand, are:

1. I would really like him to be intelligent and teach me things.

2. I would really like him to be musical and play guitar.

3. I would really like him to have a great sense of humor

4. I would really like him to be a good listener

5. I would really like him to be great in bed

6. I would really like him to enjoy travel

7. I would really like him to be financially stable

8. I would really him to be open-minded about religious views and tolerant of all religions

9. I would really like him to like spending time indoors and out

10. I would really like him to enjoy my family and friends.

Do you see the difference? Remember your values need to be written in stone, whereas your preferences can change. So, how do you know if something should just be a preference or it should be a value? Say for example you met a guy you found to be cute, friendly, kind-hearted, but not well-educated. Because of his lack of knowledge of the world or a college education, you start to feel a rift. Maybe you even start to disconnect. How does that make you feel? Is it a situation you can overlook and live with and accept because his kindness outweighs everything else? Or do you feel as though it is something you simply cannot handle? If it's something you can live with (and be tolerant of and ultimately happy about) then this is a mere preference. If it's something that begins to agitate you and you find yourself constantly handing him a catalog of college courses, then "higher education in my partner" may be a value.

An easier approach to understanding values is the act of having things in common. I'm not talking about the same color hair, or the same birthdate or you both went to the same high school twenty years ago and now you're the perfect match. I am talking about shared beliefs. When two people share the same beliefs about things like religion, money, sex, intimacy, family, it tends to be easier for those two people to co-exist and have a healthier relationship. Why? Because those things tend to be value-based. And again, when two people share similar values, the relationship has a better chance of working. It's no wonder that eHarmony is so successful. They pair you with matches who share your values.

But I was initially confused over values. I thought if we both liked the same music, or we were both dumped by our exes, it was a sign that we had stuff in common. I was so wrong! I didn't realize that those were shallow similarities. Profound similarities, like I said, are found in your belief system. What you believe about money, religion, family, sex, and even politics is far more important than whether you share the same taste in music (though that doesn't hurt!).

Finally, when you don't know your values, you do not know how to discriminate. When you don't discriminate, when you forego choosing a partner based on your value system and let people with very different values in, you are basically throwing spaghetti against the wall and hoping something will stick. Knowing your values and using them to seek out partners removes a lot of randomness and helps you sift through literally millions of choices. And that is the ultimate goal of values. They work as little caretakers that weed out the bad, and let in the good.

i. **Putting Your Values to Work**

When we decide to make an emotional and/or physical commitment to someone, we get all the baggage--good and bad-- that comes with that individual. That means that we not only inherit a potentially fun, charming or good-looking partner, but we also inherit all his or her idiosyncrasies, habits, fears, neurosis, behaviors, skeletons in the closet, past relationships, and even some childhood insecurities that still might be lingering. We get it all.

So the object of dating is to determine what you might inherit, before making an actual commitment to someone. Because let's be real, once we make a commitment to someone, be it marriage or co-habitation or even a promise to remain together, it's a very difficult bond to break. This is where using your values comes into play. It's your job to know what you can handle and what you can't. And before I had a clear idea of what I really wanted and what my values were, I always seemed to mess up. I thought I could handle anything. Oh, how wrong I was.

Take Mark, for example, a guy I was crazy about and had amazing chemistry with. He only had a few issues. Trouble was, those issues bothered me to the point of near-complete frustration and pain. He was a very poor communicator. We had almost no shared interests. He lost his job due to drug use and theft (although it was in his past and he was clean). And, he was cheap. He never paid for anything and worse, he would ask for personal things and expect me to pay. There was no concept of "dutch" or halfsies in his mind. "Let's go out to dinner," I might suggest. "Sure, if you're paying," would always be his reply.

Ugh.

When I looked at these issues on their own, it seemed like a no-brainer. There was no reason I should stay with this guy. But instead of leaving him, I focused on his positives and shut my eyes to these other issues. I mean, I didn't want to complain about a few little problems. Mark was, after all, great in bed, always available, really into me, and a great friend--all things that were also important to me.

And yet the issues, no matter how much I tried to ignore them, kept rearing their ugly heads. They wouldn't go away. And I certainly couldn't change him or inspire him to change (despite trying!). In fact, I found myself using an old cliched line: "*If you really loved me,* you'd try to communicate better," or "*If you really loved me,* you would be more responsible with your own money."

Eventually, as is usually the case, those seemingly inconsequential problems became bigger than his good qualities. Mark's few negative issues outweighed all his positives. But I still couldn't figure out why I would stay if I was so miserable.

And then, one day, I learned about values and it hit me: *I had none.* Well, I did, I just didn't use them. I knew I needed to be with people who communicated well, who were financially stable, and didn't have a past life of crime (!) But then, I threw all that out the window because I thought I could handle anything (I couldn't). If I had known my values ahead of time, things would have been a lot different. In other words, I would not have chosen to date him! But back then…having a relationship (any relationship) outweighed the idea of living a healthy life or being alone. Having *any* relationship no matter how painful or inconvenient, was more important than my own well-being.

I did this often. I would date men that had addictions or shady pasts. I married a man who could barely speak English. When I could finally take care of myself financially, I dated guys who were so strapped for cash that two of them borrowed a combined total of three thousand dollars from me (that I never got back, by the way). None of this would have happened if I had known and used my values .

When you don't know your values, you think you have no choice. You think you have to inherit junk.

When you have no values, you don't know what you can and cannot handle.

Mark's issues and G's and all the other past partners of mine ultimately became the foundation for my personal list of values. And when I began dating after I had this list, I had a road map. I let my values be my guide. I knew what qualities, behaviors, or idiosyncrasies to stay away from and I knew what qualities I needed.

Most importantly, by defining my values, I knew how to place a boundary around myself when I encountered someone who did not share them. This was hard to do. It takes a few dates to know if someone shares your values. And oftentimes, after I had started to feel an emotional intensity for someone, I would have to give them up because I learned they did not share my same values.

Value-honoring also meant I had to change ingrained habits. It meant staying home alone when all my friends were going out to bars to try and pick up guys (I didn't want to find someone at a bar if one of my most important values was to find someone who didn't drink). And it meant I could not have a relationship with just anybody, simply because we "clicked." I would, after all, be inheriting more than just a "click." So, I learned to be patient and not invest my heart so quickly. I learned that dating is not about immediate gratification, but rather, deferring gratification, and simply enjoying people by learning about them before getting hot and heavy.

And lastly, I learned that absolutely everyone has issues, shortcomings and drawbacks. I can handle some of those problems, not all of them.

My husband, for example, is sometimes overly sensitive and I have to watch my "tone" around him (no Italian-style, arms flailing, screaming). That's a problem I can handle. He sometimes forgets to call the repair guy, or he'll set his alarm for a conference call at 3 a.m. instead of 3 p.m., or he'll forget to take out the trash, but he never forgets my birthday, he always cleans the snow off my car, and he does the dishes every night. He complains sometimes. And yet, he is aware of the bigger picture and grateful for our life together. He's sometimes very wasteful when it comes to food, water, electricity or other resources. And he probably fools around on his cell phone more than I'd like playing Scrabble. But I can handle ALL of those problems because he shares my core values. He does not drink or do drugs, he's healthy, not afraid of commitment, very passionate, never neglects me, I love the way he dresses, he's available, responsible, caring, a family man, and so much more.

Do you see how one set of problems can be handled, and another set cannot? And we are all different too. Different values will show up on each person's list. In Chapter 29, there's even more on values, including an exercise to help you assess yours!

Self-Esteem

"In youth, it was a way I had,
To do my best to please.
And change, with every passing lad
To suit his theories.

But now I know the things
I know And do the things I do,
And if you do not like me so,
To hell, my love, with you."

–Dorothy Parker,
The Complete Poems of Dorothy Parker

Somewhere in my late thirties, between bad boyfriend #32 and no good boy-friend #33, I remember hearing on a podcast on toxic dating that the reason I was still going out with inappropriate characters was because I didn't have enough self–esteem. Really? That old line? I had heard it so many damn times in my life that I had given up. No one has 100-percent perfect self-esteem! And yet, somehow, we all get by. In fact, I know women who hate themselves and are in long-term relationships. I was convinced that "liking myself" wasn't relevant when it came to finding a partner. I couldn't have been more wrong.

Let me be perfectly clear. At the time of writing this book I cannot say that I am anywhere close to having the amount of self-esteem I believe I should be filled with. You heard correctly. I don't always think I am attractive. I don't always feel confident. And I sure as heck don't always feel as though I fit in or belong. Sometimes I lose sight of my purpose in life, and sometimes I feel so broken and fragmented that I just want to curl up and hide in my house and not come out. Sometimes, in the days I'm in the car line picking up my kids from school, I feel like I just don't stack up to all the other power moms who, in my mind, know parenting like an astrophysicist knows her space mission. Sometimes, when it's that time of the month and I feel bloated and crampy, I don't want to even go out in public because I feel ugly. And many times I avoid speaking engagements because I just don't possess the confidence to speak in front of a crowd. And yet, I'm married to a confident, accomplished, respected and loving man. I have a strong network of beauti-ful, successful, loving friends. And my children, now 19 and 21, are growing up with confidence, self-esteem and aspiration. How on earth did any of that happen if I have such low self-esteem?

Here's a secret: I may not have had boatloads of self-esteem, but what I did have was the right kind. And it was enough.

You don't have to check all the boxes when it comes to perfectly loving yourself. I don't think people—women in particular—can love everything about themselves without feeling narcissistic. We all know we have faults.

We all know that there is always room for improvement. And we all know that it is nearly impossible as humans to live without the doubt, fear, sadness, frustration and feelings of failure that we tend to heap on ourselves. But you don't need to be perfectly happy and content with yourself to find a healthy relationship. You just need a decent amount of self-worth.

Self-worth is key. I may not be perfect. But I am worthy. That's really all you need to understand when it comes to self-esteem. When you place value on yourself, when you believe you are worthy, you tend to not accept abuse, scraps, and neglect as part of your relationship because you simply believe you are worth more than those things. You believe you deserve more. There's no secret to believing you are worthy. You say it. You feel it. And you live it. In the next section, we'll discuss an important tool for letting in the good and blocking the bad. Because when you believe you are worthy, you work hard to maintain a healthy environment, filled with people who respect you, accept you, and treat you with kindness. And sometimes, believing in your own worth means you sometimes have to let people go.

CHAPTER 14

Boundaries and Self-Control

"Givers need to set limits because
takers rarely do."

–Henry Ford

Most of us tend to lock our front doors and put our valuables in a safe place as a means of protecting ourselves and our possessions. We even lock our car doors when we park. Heck, I lock mine if I run into the convenience store for five minutes. I also keep my old jewelry and important paperwork in a safety deposit box at my local bank. A friend of mine who lives in Wyoming and likes to hunt always keeps his rifles in a locked gun case, bullets removed, in a part of his garage that also locks. And another friend, who has a rather valuable art collection, keeps it in a fire-safe art box specifically built for large canvases, and holds an insurance policy on it, as well. When we value things we protect them. And that's what boundaries are, a way we protect what is valuable to us. My house, my car, my possessions, my children are valuable to me, so I keep them close, I lock my doors, I don't walk down dangerous streets. Healthy boundaries in relationships work in the same way. A healthy boundary is like a locked door, or an imaginary wall you place around yourself so that others don't "come in" and hurt you; or, conversely, so you don't get out and hurt others. Here are some examples of a healthy boundaries:

- Not accepting phone calls or reading texts from someone who is repeatedly harassing you (for example, an ex who constantly sends you long, drawn-out texts to say how horrible you are for breaking up with him. I.e. "You'll never find anyone who loves you like I do…") .

- Not getting involved in or trying to solve someone else's drama.

- Not allowing yourself to "stalk" an ex on social media sites or in real-life.

- Not allowing yourself to become intimate with people who might live a lifestyle that makes you uncomfortable (someone who does heroin, for example).

Of course, not everyone has safe and healthy boundaries. Al Capone, Jesse James, Adolf Hitler, and Attila the Hun didn't. Your local prisons and jails are filled with men and women who lack them as well. But, you don't have to be bad or do something illegal to be accused of crossing boundaries. Children lack healthy boundaries until they're taught otherwise (*Look with your eyes and don't touch anything in the store!*). And people from other countries often cross cultural boundaries without even knowing they're doing so (if you've ever been to a Muslim country, avoid using your left hand lest you insult your host). For the greater part of society, though, social boundaries are well-maintained by most.

There are, however, less obvious kinds of boundaries that many in romantic relationships cross. And that's what I want to talk about here.

Take a look at the people around you. Is there anyone who brings you down, or sucks the life out of you, uses you, or treats you poorly? How do you interact with them? How do you deal with their behavior? When I think about people with boundary challenges, I think of Jerry, a friend of my father. Not only did he have a drinking problem, but he'd also come to our house unannounced, and let himself in without knocking. He would snoop through our cabinets, eat our food, and ask to borrow money that he'd never pay back. As a little girl, I remember coming down on Sunday mornings and finding Jerry crashed on our sofa, passed out from the night before. His behavior became so disruptive to our family and home life that I often heard my mother arguing with my father about the situation, imploring him to tell Jerry that he wasn't allowed back. It wasn't until the morning we found Jerry wading in the mucky waters of the swamp at the far end of our property that my father finally told him he wasn't welcomed back. This inexplicable, bizarre behavior—a grown man, presumably on drugs, splashing through a mosquito-infested, stagnant body of water—was simply too much for my parents to handle. And, even though my mother and father crossed boundaries all the time, this was a line they weren't willing to ignore. If Jerry could swim in a swamp, what else was he capable of? The higher goal, then, was to protect themselves and their children. And it worked. I never saw Jerry again.

But in romantic relationships, boundaries are much harder to institute and police. Here's an example of a relationship boundary fail.

Brigid was a single, 28-year-old ski instructor who lived in Salt Lake City, Utah. From time to time she would call me with her dating woes because she fully believed she was a love addict. Her problem, she said, was that she had abandonment issues from childhood, which, when they emerged, would drive her to go out to bars, where she'd get completely drunk, and try to pick someone up. The one-night stands that resulted made her feel miserable and ashamed the next morning. But she would hope and pray that the guy she hooked up with the night before would call her the next day, even though, when she was with him, she'd played it off like she didn't care. When he didn't call, she would spiral down into an even deeper depression. Brigid's behavior is not necessarily love-addict behavior. Without diagnosing her, I'd say this is probably a far better example of impulse control, mixed with (slightly) delusional thinking. While she did work with a therapist who would help her with these issues, my goal was to help her realize stronger boundaries.

Boundary #1 was to help her recognize that she was most likely going to a bar for the wrong reasons—to pick someone up because she was lonely. Knowing this, she could have rerouted and chosen a healthier alternative. Yoga, a hike, meditation, a run, time with friends for coffee, writing a novel... the list is endless! Her boundary, therefore, would be "refrain from going to bars just to get drunk and pick someone up." This actually never helped her loneliness and, as long as I've known her, she's never had a long-term relationship with anyone she met this way. Eventually, she recognized this and replaced this behavior with safer, healthier choices.

Boundary #2: Whenever Brigid had the option to go to a bar with friends, for example, she'd still need to work on boundaries. At the bar she could, for starters, tone the drinking way down. Like many of us, when she drinks, she makes exceedingly bad decisions. If she only has one drink, for example, I can pretty much guarantee she'll make better decisions, or even meet someone she could have a genuine connection with.

Boundary #3: In her original scenario, Brigid ultimately chose to sleep with someone she knew nothing about. The chances that someone you've met at a bar and hooked up with will call back the next morning are slim. Why? Because no connection is made. Instead, the unspoken agreement (once in the bedroom) is sex only. Her third boundary would be to wait and not sleep with or bring someone home.

We break less obvious boundaries as well. We let completely inappropriate people into our lives and when they cause us pain and suffering we wonder why. We agree to have a relationship with an avoidant. We jump into a relationship with someone who does drugs, hits or neglects us. And by letting unsafe people close to us, we lose the opportunity to protect ourselves.

By putting up boundaries (i.e deciding to not allow certain people into your life) you are blocking them from further disrupting your life (go bother someone else now). You are protecting yourself from a chaotic and unmanageable situation and you are choosing YOU first. Where once you felt out of control, the boundaries you've set now help you feel *in* control. And that's the whole point.

There are three "levels" to creating healthy boundaries with people. They can work together or separately. But the main gist is this:

1. **You can block someone completely from your life.** Some people are toxic and they need to go. Period. This is what NC is all about. No contact! Friendship over. Affair over. Don't even bother picking up the phone. The End. Years later when you are stronger within yourself, you may want to break this boundary. But to undertake this kind of severe action usually means that your relationship with this person is toxic and will always be. Side note: I had an extremely toxic friend. She was supposedly my best friend, but she was narcissistic and was always attacking me for not "being there" for her. She would scream at me to do as she said, under the threat that she would never come back. I felt so manipulated, used and bullied by her, that I finally made the decision to cut off the friendship completely. I never looked back. This is a good example of when to block someone completely from your life.

2. **You can block someone emotionally and mentally, but still maintain a "business-like" relationship with them.** This is the kind of boundary to establish if you work with someone or will still need to encounter them from time to time in mixed company (mutual friends, father of your kids, etc.). Do

not take calls, texts or other forms of communication from this person. For all intents and purposes, the relationship is over. When you see them, you can be cordial, but emotionally, you need to keep your boundaries up and avoid engaging in any kind of deep conversation. A good friend of mine has to maintain a relationship with her ex-husband because they share two children. But for the longest time, he would send her nasty, intrusive texts berating her for divorcing him. He would call her names and threaten to keep the children away from her and even threaten to take away her alimony and child support. For the first year she tried diligently to engage him and respond to his texts and let him vent. But his words were ranting and abusive. She felt constantly sick and beaten down, mentally and emotionally assaulted until, finally, she enacted strong boundaries. She stopped reading his texts. If he had something to tell her about the kids he could leave a hand-written note in the kitchen when she came the next day to pick up the kids. She enlisted the service of an attorney. If the ex needed to communicate with her, he had to do so via his own lawyer. They also both decided that seeing each other was out of the question, so she only picked up her kids through a caretaker, after he'd gone to work. Her new boundaries felt awkward at first, but then, as the stress and suffering of dealing with his constant harassment began to fade, she actually started to feel herself again. She could breathe!

3. **You can create a partial boundary:** A partial boundary can be employed, usually between friends or exes that you are no longer obsessing about. For example, if you enjoy spending time with a girlfriend, and she doesn't hurt you in any direct way, but she's, let's say, a bad influence (every time you go out with her she drags you to places you'd rather not go, or you end up smoking, drinking or hooking up), then you might want to practice boundaries with her. If she wants to hang out, tell her "no clubs, but maybe we can do lunch." If that doesn't work, avoid meeting her past a certain hour when there's no opportunity for her to "drag" you out somewhere. I have a friend like this. She is an amazing woman, but is prone to drama and she can

sometimes emotionally wear me down. I'm an introvert and she's clearly an extrovert and if I spend too much time with her I feel exhausted. I choose not to cut her off completely, but I do keep boundaries up when she's around. I pick and choose, very carefully, when I see her, and I always keep my time with her to a minimum.

We don't make boundaries to protect ourselves from others because we don't have the courage to stand up to them, or because we are "push-overs." A true boundary isn't you putting your head in the sand and avoiding. It's actively participating in our well-being because we care enough about ourselves to maintain a safe, peaceful environment of respect and civility. We deserve those things. And just as we deserve them, so do others.

Which brings me to the idea of placing personal boundaries around yourself so that YOU don't cause harm to others, which happens more frequently than you may think in matters of love. The truth is, some of us never learned healthy boundaries when we were children. And that's OK when we're young. But it's not when you're an adult. Here are some examples of when you should impose a boundary around yourself:

- When your anger turns from healthy expression of your disapproval of someone or something to screaming at the top of your lungs in someone's face for the purpose of intimidation or to hurt them.

- When you have feelings for a married man or woman and want to act on them.

- When you need to stay away from an ex after he or she has ended the relationship, or has moved on.

- When you find yourself getting involved in someone else's life to the point of trying to "fix" them or take care of them when they are capable of fixing or caring for themselves.

Healthy boundaries are an essential part of healthy living. They are not only a way you take care of yourself, they are also proof of how much you respect yourself and others.

CHAPTER 15

Growing Up (responsibility)

"We do not grow absolutely, chronologically.
We grow sometimes in one dimension, and
not in another; unevenly. We grow partially.
We are relative. We are mature in one
realm, childish in another. The past, present,
and future mingle and pull us backward,
forward, or fix us in the present. We are made
up of layers, cells, constellations."

–Anaïs Nin

Peter Pan: "Forget them, Wendy. Forget them all. Come with me where you'll never, never have to worry about grown up things again."
Wendy: "Never is an awfully long time."

–J.M. Barrie, Peter Pan

One of the greatest challenges so many of us face is actually not the actual breaking up with our partners or finding someone else who is healthy for us. While those things can be challenging, there's another task that's far more grueling. It's called growing up.

We definitely take growing up for granted. We think because we physically get bigger, become more intelligent, graduate high school, go on to college, find a job and raise a family, follow that linear movement toward old age, we've grown up. I thought that because I had a caretaker-style personality, I had grown up too early and too fast. I had gotten married, raised two wonderful kids, paid my bills, and for all intents and purposes, was a functioning adult. But, in my mid-thirties, I completely fell apart, practically kicking and screaming, because some guy I dated for seven months broke up with me. This is what would happen to me every time I found myself alone. And it was the direct result of never learning how to manage being a big girl, and being on my own. It was the direct result of never growing up, emotionally, to the point where I could have trust in myself and the world that I would be OK.

We often get stuck in our past. We arrive at a certain point, and emotionally, we hover there. It's known as stunted growth. This happens a lot when we avoid facing harsh realities by numbing and avoiding. We basically give up the extremely important developmental process of learning how to cope and manage life on life's terms. Instead of figuring out healthy ways to cope, we avoid our problems. We cover them up with fantasy thoughts of our Prince Charming. We cover them up by getting so involved in loving our partner or fixing our partner that we don't have to focus on our own issues. Depending on the degree of avoidance that we've practiced, by the time we are 30 or 40 years old, , we could possess the coping skills of twelve-year-old!

In analytical psychology the part of us that refuses to grow up—our childlike self—is often referred to as our "inner child." Susan Peabody, the co-founder of Love Addicts Anonymous, once said of our inner child, "Give her love, attention and care, just don't give her the keys to your car." In other words, many of us still operate as little children. We act out when we don't get our way. We cry when we don't get what we want. We demand immediate gratification. We act on impulse. We threaten or manipulate. And we don't always use mature, adult judgment when it comes to seeking out a partner or making adult decisions (like who to marry or who to have sex with). This screaming, kicking, tantrum-throwing inner child not only needs a few time-outs, she needs to grow up! But how do we emotionally grow up later in life? Isn't there a specific window of time for learning certain behaviors, and haven't we missed it?

Well, yes, and no. You can't go back. That's for sure. And you can't exactly rely on anyone to adult for you. But you can teach yourself to grow up. Just because we grow "unevenly" doesn't mean we can't work hard to play catch up. We *do* have the ability to teach ourselves growth strategies as adults. And it's easier than you think.

For starters, assess your own behavior. This list of Not-So-Grown-Up Behaviors of Adults will make this task easier.

1. Impulsivity is the number-one biggest not-so-grown-up behavior. Do you make a lot of impulsive decisions? What drives your decision-making process? How soon are you willing to jump into

a relationship? Have sex? Say I love you? Expect commitment? Mature adults, for the most part, take their time to make important decisions. They do this because there's usually a lot at stake and they recognize the benefits of waiting.

2. <u>Lack of self-control</u> is another biggie. While it's often very hard for even the most grown-up person at the table to resist an extra scoop of French vanilla ice cream over their warm brownie sundae, self-restraint is maturity's finest asset. It's what keeps loving partners loyal, and regret and shame out of the picture. We often make our biggest mistakes when we lack self-control. We blurt out things we regret, we have relationships that bring us shame, and we make bad decisions when we do it from a place of no self-control. How does your self-control stack up? If you strongly believe you're in love with your best friend's husband, what do you do? Do you have the ability to stop yourself when you think you might be making a mistake?

3. <u>Manipulating, threating, whining, crying, throwing a tantrum or otherwise acting out</u> to get attention or get your way is not-so-grown-up behavior. When you string all these traits together, it sounds like you're talking about a toddler. But, when you look at each behavior one at time I can guarantee you're guilty of a few (I know I am). Who hasn't cried a time or two to get the boyfriend to come back? Who hasn't threatened to leave if things don't change? Who hasn't acted out—maybe hopped in your car after too many drinks to roar out of the driveway in a rage when you saw your partner with someone else? And who hasn't tried to manipulate their partner to achieve some desired outcome by perhaps denying love or intimacy? Try to write down a list of ways in which you have done any of these behaviors. How might you have done them differently?

4. Codependency as a not-so-grown-up behavior can be a little less obvious to discern. When we "take care of" adults who are otherwise perfectly capable of taking care of themselves, we do so not out of a sense of altruism or love (although we may very well love them), but rather, so we can control their behavior to suit ourselves. We try to control the chaos and by doing that, we sometimes enable bad, destructive behavior. Melody Beattie's Codependent No More is an excellent read if you have a tendency to "try to please others instead of yourself," "think and feel responsible for other people," or "feel compelled almost forced to help people solve their problems."

5. Avoiding, giving up, or hiding from your goals, your problems and your responsibilities is not-so-grown-up behavior. Grownups are scared of what they don't know or what they don't understand. And yet, they know from experience and from a deep sense of trust within themselves, that facing these things head on and trying to understand them beats avoiding them hands-down. I have given many examples of ways we use our relationships to avoid or hide. Write down how you avoid. What do you think you're hiding from? What are your biggest fears? Try to create examples of ways to face things that scare you.

CHAPTER 16

Facing Your Fears

"A kind of light spread out from her. And everything changed color. And the world opened out. And a day was good to awaken to. And there were no limits to anything. And the people of the world were good and handsome. And I was not afraid any more."

–John Steinbeck, East of Eden

When it comes to relationships, most of us fall on one side of the connection spectrum or the other: we either fear closeness (enmeshment), or we fear distance and abandonment (avoidance). You will never fully extinguish these fears, as they are so deeply engrained in your psyche you don't even know they're there. But that's OK, because the object of the game is to try to balance out your fear and not fall to one extreme or the other.

For individuals who suffer from fear of enmeshment, our typical reaction to intimacy is to run, or push away. Intimacy scares us. It's not something we learned to accept or deal with in a healthy way because chances are, we were smothered by it--not real intimacy, mind you, but neediness disguised as love and attentiveness. So, we learned that intimacy means loss of freedom, emotional incest, crossed boundaries, and too much of the wrong kind of attention. In order for us to learn how to deal with our fear of enmeshment we need to:

- Trust that we can set our own boundaries, and that others do not determine the level of intimacy we can handle--we do.

- Believe in our own sense of autonomy and that love does not have to feel overwhelming or claustrophobic.

- Date people who don't smother us, demand too much attention from us, or make us feel closed-in, over-analyzed or overwhelmed. When that happens, we are more apt to not be so afraid, and thus, can open up and get a little closer to those we ultimately want to become intimate with.

- Surround ourselves with people who allow us our alone time. When we are with people who recognize our need for this, it sets a safe boundary for us. When we feel safe, we are able to come out of our "shell" so to speak, and feel rejuvenated and clear-headed.

- Avoid love addicts. People who suffer from feelings of enmeshment are attracted to love addicts (the parent who raised them???) but need to date someone who has a far greater understanding and tolerance for space than love addicts possess.

- Explore healthy levels of deeper intimacy with someone who does not threaten our freedom. What that means is even though you may be scared of deeper intimacy and more involvement, try to take baby steps to closeness with someone you feel comfortable with. If you feel safe with someone--generally, speaking--but an argument or an intimate moment makes you want to run, sit with it for a bit. Go into a separate room. Get some breathing time to think and be alone. Ask yourself if your trigger is a real or imagined threat. When we give ourselves time to be alone and figure things out, we are able to deal with situations in a more healthy way.

For individuals who suffer from fear of abandonment, our typical reaction to real or perceived intimacy is to latch on for dear life and never let go. Intimacy also scares us, but for different reasons: we do not trust that it will last, so the more doubt we have, the tighter we hold on. We were raised by an avoidant mother or father (or both) who may have neglected us, or at least, did not do a very good job of making us feel as though we could depend on their presence and love. We learned that intimacy is something that feels physically and emotionally wonderful when you have it, but it's something we can't rely on. In order for us to learn how to deal with our fear of abandonment we need to:

- Trust that we are loved, important and valid, if for no other reason than we exist.

- Learn that we have control over ourselves, but not others and that we cannot force love upon someone else.

- Understand that fear of abandonment is an illusion. Children can be abandoned, but adults cannot. The reason we think we can be abandoned is because we are still "thinking" like a child who has not yet grown and learned that he or she can take care of himself or herself, and thus, feel secure.

- Date people who live close, have a reputation for being stable, reliable and trustworthy, and do not trigger feelings of abandonment (i.e., avoid people who tend to go out and party all night with friends of the opposite sex, and don't feel as though they should have to check in).

- Avoid avoidants. People who suffer from feelings of abandonment are attracted to avoidants (the parent who raised them???) but need to date someone who has a far greater understanding and tolerance for closeness than avoidants possess.

- Explore healthy levels of autonomy with someone who doesn't threaten to leave the second we stand on our own or do something alone. What this means is learn to enjoy time alone without feeling threatened by it. Baby steps. Take walks in the park alone, take a class. Learn to build trust moment to moment with a new partner who is willing to allow for your personal growth. More importantly, start to build trust by refraining from love addict behavior (in other words, like checking text message or emails constantly). If, however, you start to feel threatened or the sense of abandonment creeps in, try positive self-talk like, "If this is meant to be, it will be. I cannot control it. I can only watch it unfold. Everything will be revealed whether I look for it or not."

i. **The "Void" We Think We Need To Fill**

There's a hole in a donut. There's a hole in a car tire. There's not a hole in you.

I need to come out and say this right from the start, because I believe it's one of the most important lessons we can learn in order to fully accept who we are and who we may choose to become.

Many years ago, I believed in the void. I believed I had a hole in me. That aching, empty, bottomless pit inside—the "hungry heart," as Susan Peabody calls it—was often the driving force behind my need to stuff myself with something, anything, so as to keep from feeling incomplete, alone, worthless.

Many people who suffer from depression, anxiety, addiction, or stress tend to fill that void with toxic substances, processes, and behaviors. We latch onto destructive people, get involved in inappropriate relationships, take drugs, have meaningless sex, smoke too much pot, spend too much money, overeat, or drink excessively, all the while believing that if we found the right stuff to fill ourselves with, that empty feeling will go away.

But it doesn't.

At some point, believing I was making healthier choices for myself, I filled the void with actions I thought were proof of self-love: I allowed the aching inside me to guide me to friends, healthy food, positive affirmations, exercise, and hard work. I took up painting. I wrote more. I joined a book club. Like all the self-help books taught me, I cultivated a "law of attraction"; what you seek is seeking you became my motto. I thought, "If I seek more, do more, become more, the void will go away."

It didn't.

No matter what I did, where I went, or who I was with, it was there. It was part of me. Or rather, it was a missing part of me.

The truth is that for anyone who has ever suffered, ever lost a loved one, or ever had their heart broken, there is a real, physical feeling of emptiness. If you pay close attention, you can actually feel a hollowness. Like the Tin Man knocking on his chest, it's almost as if we can hear the clanging echo of our vacant heart when we are sad.

And yet, I ask you to believe that there is no void.

What if that empty feeling was not an actual empty space inside you that needed to be filled? What if that empty feeling is just part of you?

What if you sat in a room with it and experienced it instead of trying to stuff something in it, hide it, or cover it up with healthy stuff or unhealthy stuff? What if you just accepted it like a dimple or a slight indentation in your skin, something that makes you, you? Something you cannot get rid of, but rather something that simply exists, and needs only to be acknowledged, not analyzed?

I asked myself these questions at my lowest point. I was experiencing deep suffering after a devastating breakup and I remember literally crawling on the floor, clenching my stomach, red-faced from crying for two days straight. I begged the universe to give me something to make this horrible feeling go away—a pill, comfort food, a cigarette, a drink, my relationship back…anything. The void was eating away at my insides.

It was at this point that my aching brain threw me a lifeline. I quickly realized that this pain was too painful to cover up. This pain was too deep to be filled. No friend could make the void disappear, no drug could mask the emptiness. Even if the man I loved had come back and said he made a mistake, that he wanted me back again, even that would not have kept me from feeling incomplete and worthless.

There was only one thing left to do: I needed to just sit with it.

For the first time in my life, instead of curling up and rocking, trying to avoid the emptiness, or running out and trying to find someone else to replace the loss of my love, instead of shoving food in my face, or shopping away all my sadness, I let it in—the pain, that is. I told myself, "This is part of me, so I will experience it, know it, and accept it."

And I did. And it was excruciating. Like giving birth without an epidural. And every time it crept up on me, the pain, that feeling of being hungry for something, anything, I said, "Bring it on." I can handle this. I wanted to handle it. And I did. And guess what, like boot camp, it made me stronger.

Our powerful human ability to visualize creates the sensation of a void. And so, our powerful human ability to visualize can take the void away.

Eventually, I started to be okay with the idea that, even if it felt like there was a hole, there really wasn't. I started to understand that nothing was missing. There was no void. I am actually whole.

And once I got that, It stopped hurting so much. I stopped trying to fill myself with garbage, or for that matter, so-called healthy distractions. Suddenly, there was no point. I was full.

I came to realize that this acceptance of emptiness and acceptance of the void was the basis for Buddhist meditation. The spiritual teacher Osho writes about it perfectly:

"There are only two types of people in the world: those who try to stuff their inner emptiness, and those very rare precious beings who try to see the inner emptiness. Those who try to stuff it remain empty, frustrated. They go on collecting garbage, their whole life is futile and fruitless. Only the other kind, the very precious people who try to look into their inner emptiness without any desire to stuff it, become meditators"

Today, while meditation is still not something I practice on a regular basis, I will sit with the empty feeling. I have gotten quite good at experiencing it, allowing it in in all its unpleasantness. The trick is to trust. Unlike before, I now trust that I have no void. I am complete.

Cultivating a belief in my own completeness has changed the way I perceive the world and the people in it. I no longer depend upon others to feed my hungry heart—I either enjoy people or I don't. Emptiness is no longer the driving force behind my behavior, which makes me less needy and far more willing to share and give of myself.

And while habit dictates that stuffing the void with toxic crap is immediate and far easier, I quickly remember that that's a temporary fix. I remember, I'm already full.

CHAPTER 17

Choosing Dignity

*"What's that?" "The laundry basket?" "No,
next to it." "I don't see anything next to it."
"It's my last shred of dignity. It's very small."*

–John Green, The Fault in Our Stars

In CHAPTER 5 we talked about the fact that you need to believe you deserve better than scraps. Now, we need to talk about what drives that belief: dignity. I think the concept of dignity is a very hard thing for many people to grasp. So many of us who settle for scraps tend do so because we are starving. We are so starving for love, attention, kindness, and comfort that we're willing to sign up for a relationship with someone who offers very little of any of these things. Our hunger turns us into bottomless pits of need at the height of our painful relationships—and this, sadly, leaves us without much use for dignity. Dignity is not high on our list of must-haves when we can't even meet our basic needs. And so we live, instead, like an animal chained to a fence post, feeding on scraps our owner tosses on the ground. Not a very dignified existence.

Dignity, when you're in pain or starving for love is not something you think you need. It almost seems like an entitlement intended for the rich and famous. Why do I need to eat off a gold plate when my ceramic one is just fine? What point is there in dignity when you're satisfied with less? But let me be clear. Dignity isn't a gold plate. It's not an entitlement for the rich. It is the ability to care for yourself, like eating an apple versus eating a bowl of Cheetos. Dignity is the nutrient-rich life-force that is a requirement of self-love.

"Dignity: the state or quality of being worthy of honor or respect; a sense of pride in oneself; self-respect. "*it was **beneath his dignity** to shout*," synonyms: self-esteem, self-worth, self-respect, pride, morale"—Webster's English Dictionary.

I actually heard the word dignity a gazillion times growing up and as an adult, but I never really understood what it meant until much later in life. And when I did, I was humiliated to learn how little I had of it, and how little I'd given it value. What the heck was I thinking when I chased after unavailable guys? Oh wait, I wasn't thinking. I certainly wasn't operating with any amount of dignity. I was operating out of hunger. Sending off emails to someone who didn't want a relationship with me…chasing after someone who gave so little in return…wasting valuable, unrecoverable time that could have been spent pursuing a career. Where was the dignity in those actions? Non-existent.

The importance of dignity came much later. But I had to learn what it was. I had to feel and know its value before I could grasp the idea of wanting more of it. Dignity meant nothing to me until I assigned it value. What do I mean by that? Well, when I finally stopped chasing after my ex and didn't respond to what little attention he gave me, it at first felt awkward, even painful, but then…it felt empowering. And when I gave up undignified behavior like waiting around for some guy to call me when I could have been out doing something for myself, it felt strange and uncomfortable at first, but then…it felt emancipating. When I made my writing and my career my priority instead of "date night," it felt cumbersome and unwieldy, but then it became liberating and passionate. And the more time and effort I put into those things, the more I realized I was building a sense of dignity for myself. That dignity was earned through right action and self-love. Dignity was not eating off some gold plate I couldn't afford. Dignity was something I had access to, that I could make, build and create myself. Its price was in direct proportion to the amount of value I assigned it. And, the more I practiced dignity, the better at it I got.

One of the greatest benefits of practicing dignity is that you receive it back from others. You teach people how to treat you, and if you operate on the notion that you deserve dignity, you teach people to treat you with dignity.

But what if you suddenly start demanding that your current partner treats you with dignity? We cannot force someone to change their behavior. But we can teach them that we don't accept anything but dignified treatment within the relationship. How do we do that? We must be willing to walk away from anyone who can't live up to our new standards. That teaches the lesson that we are unwilling to put up with anything less than the decent behavior we deserve.

Part of the process of rebuilding yourself must include an awareness of the value of dignity. And it must include action that leads to it. Dignity is not a given. We must choose it to see its value and its power.

Exercise: Write down examples of undignified behavior—yours, your ex's, a friend's, whoever, and then write down how you can change yours to reflect more dignified behavior.

And if you're thinking, I can write about dignified behavior, but how do I quiet the anxious voice in my head that berates me for every undignified thought or impulse? Read on.

CHAPTER 18

Positive Self-Talk (removing negative talk)

"In those days I used to talk to myself as if reciting poetry."

–Haruki Murakami, Blind Willow, Sleeping Woman

Negative thought-stopping and Cognitive Behavioral Therapy are more strong resources that you'll need to rebuild yourself. The more you turn negative thoughts into positive ones, the less stressed you'll be. It's really as simple as that. And yet, if you're anything like me, it is at times impossible to do. I'm slightly neurotic by nature. I worry about planes crashing and bridges collapsing and pianos falling on my head. I worry constantly about my health. There is a low, persistent hum of negative thoughts that buzz like bees around a hive inside my brain and it takes enormous effort on my part to silence that hum. In order to do that, I repeat over and over that worry will not change my circumstances. And that my fears are unrealistic (A piano? Really? What are the chances?). I breathe, I refocus, and I switch to my happy safe thoughts—*I'm in a white house in a tiny village in the south of Spain overlooking the Mediterranean sea*. Soon enough, a calmer me appears and onward I go. But it's usually not that easy.

If thought-stopping were easy, it would resolve ninety-nine percent of our problems. For some of us it seems impossible. How do we stop obsessive thinking when it is such a lifeline? When it seems so far beyond our control? The good news is, it's not impossible and it's not beyond our control. But it is a challenge and it does take time and practice.

I am reminded of a woman who writes to me often and tells me she cannot stop the negative thinking. *I'm not good enough, I'm ugly, I'm old, I'm fat, my teeth are crooked, I don't have enough money, I have too many hang-ups, no one wants me, no one loves me, I'm a failure.* When she first wrote she asked, *How can I love myself if I hate myself so much?* That's a whole book in itself. But, in a nutshell, you have to start somewhere. And the place I tell people to start is inside your brain.

Lie to yourself if you have to, but start by changing the negative thoughts to positive ones. Right now. Do it. Say, "I'm pretty," even if you believe you're not. *Shhh*, I won't tell. Now do three things: 1.) Write down all the people that your lie will hurt; 2.) If "me" is the only person on your list, cross it off. Lying to yourself in this capacity won't hurt you at all; and 3.) Write down the negative impact stating that you are pretty will have on the world in general. In other words, if you believe you're ugly, but you tell yourself you're pretty, what are the negative consequences of that?

If you've written down anything, anything at all, I can pretty much guarantee it is the true lie you tell yourself to remain anchored to your negative self-image. And I will tell you why. Even if you were the most hideous person on the planet (you're not), even if you were half werewolf and half human (you're not), even if your presence alone made crowds of people hurl themselves off cliffs to get away from you (it definitely doesn't) it wouldn't matter one iota if you *told yourself* you were beautiful. It wouldn't matter to anyone, but you.

But, perhaps, understanding that your negative thoughts and obsessive thoughts have a purpose will help instead. At some point in your life you've gained some kind of benefit from your negative or obsessive thinking. Only you know what that benefit is, but chances are, it's similar to this example.

Ashley was a 44-year-old divorced woman whose husband left her for another woman. She blamed herself for his leaving, and spent years fighting back a negative self-image and general negative thinking about who she was. She couldn't "hold down" a relationship; she always "attracted losers;" her marriage failed because she wasn't "good enough;" she didn't think she had what it took to be a "good catch;" and worst, she was "too old to date," again. And so she spent a lot of time alone, at home, reaffirming these negative beliefs by either obsessively following her ex-husband's new life on Facebook, or turning down dates with men she met through dating sites because, she believed, once they got to know her, they'd dump her.

Ouch!

The truth is Ashley had a very good reason to think negatively. Her negative thoughts protected her. They kept her safe from actually doing the hard work of living and dating and possibly getting rejected, but also of experiencing joy and happiness.

Her obsessive thoughts and obsessive behavior protected her too. Obsessing over her ex-husband didn't leave time for much else. Even if she were all those negative things she believed she was, well, wouldn't she want to work on herself to change? To become healthier? To become "good enough"? But no, that wasn't Ashley's goal. Her goal was to remain safe in the bubble of her own negativity. And while it caused her a horrible amount of shame and pain, at least it was familiar.

Most negative thinking starts innocently enough, with a parent or care-taker's ridicule, the rejection of a partner, childhood bullying, to name a few instigators. We not only question our worth when we are rejected, ridiculed or in pain, but we also incorporate that false belief into the story we tell ourselves of who we are. We become that false belief. Jay Shetty, a former monk and award-winning mental health podcaster, calls these types of neg-ative thoughts "weeds." And believe me, negative thoughts are weeds. They grow rapidly and can take over every crevice of your brain.

A perfect example of this type of weed-like thinking is my long-time belief that I was unstable. I don't know where I picked up that belief but it used to be one of the words I readily used to say about myself. Until one day, a very good friend who heard me describe myself that way said, "What are you talking about? You're one of the most stable people I know!" I was actually taken aback by her words and asked her to explain, and she proceeded to give dozens of concrete examples of how stable I was! I had maintained the same residence for over 12 years, I'd paid off my mortgage completely, I had a very strong, stable relationship with my family and friends, I'd graduated college with high honors, I was incredibly punctual, dependable, reliable, and so on. It was at that moment, at age 40, that I saw myself in an entirely new light. For some odd reason, I had never taken any of these facts into account when thinking of who I was. My age-old description of myself came from a place that no longer existed.

Negative and obsessed thoughts work to imprison you in a world of depression, pain, fear and apathy. They do their job with exquisite precision and will continue to do so until you pluck them up and pull them out so that healthy thoughts can grow. But I have news for you, until you decide to face your life and stop running away from your problems, you will always need your negative and obsessed thoughts because they are masters at helping you avoid.

i. **Dialectic and Cognitive Behavioral Therapy**

Once it becomes habitual, negative thinking seems almost impossible to stop. We don't feel like we control where our thoughts take us, whether it's a joyful place of peace or down the rabbit hole of gloominess and despair. And while there are a myriad ways to help break the habit of negative thinking, two of my favorites are Cognitive Behavioral Therapy and Dialectic Behavioral Therapy.

Cognitive Behavioral Therapy is explained well in *Feeling Good, the New Mood Therapy*, by David D Burns, MD:

> The first principle of cognitive therapy is that all your moods are created by your 'cognitions,' or thoughts.... you feel the way you do right now because of the thoughts you are thinking at this moment....The second principle is that when you are feeling depressed, your thoughts are dominated by a pervasive negativity. You perceive not only yourself, but the entire world in dark, gloomy terms...The third principle...is that the negative thoughts which cause your emotional turmoil nearly *always* contain gross distortions. Although these thoughts appear valid, you will learn that they are irrational or just plain wrong, and that twisted thinking is a major *cause* of your suffering. (Burns, 2009)

Cognitive therapy is based on a system of learning that can help you respond immediately to symptoms of depression and moodiness. It can teach you self-control over thought patterns that lead to depression, and help you gain a clearer understanding of why you think the way you do. *Feeling Good, the New Mood Therapy* is in fact an excellent book and it is on my reference list as a must read.

Another very effective modality called Dialectic Behavior Therapy is an off-shoot of cognitive therapy. VeryWellMind.com has a good definition:

Dialectical behavior therapy (DBT) is a type of cognitive behavioral therapy. Its main goals are to teach people how to live in the moment, cope healthily with stress, regulate emotions, and improve relationships with others. It was originally intended for people with borderline personality disorder but has since been adapted for other conditions where the patient exhibits self-destructive behavior, such as eating disorders and substance abuse. It is also sometimes used to treat post-traumatic stress disorder.

In a nutshell, Cognitive Behavioral Therapy helps you manage your negative thoughts (the environment going on inside you), while Dialectical Behavior Therapy helps you to learn how to better handle your emotional responses to people, places and experiences (the environment going on around you). To be honest, I have used both at the same time and found that they are super-helpful. In fact, I heartily recommend *The Dialectical Behavior Therapy Skills Workbook for Anxiety: Breaking Free from Worry, Panic, PTSD, and Other Anxiety Symptoms* by Alexander L. Chapman, Kim L. Gratz, and Matthew T Tull. Working in a workbook not only encourages you to read about and learn better technique for thinking and managing situations, it also inspires you to participate in your learning through writing exercises and taking action. And *ahem*, speaking of action, it is the missing ingredient to success. It is the flavor that out-flavors all the rest. And we talk about it next...

CHAPTER 19

Taking Action and Aligning Your Actions with Words

"Never mistake motion for action."

–Ernest Hemingway

For many, many years (too many to count), I was the smartest failure at relationships around. I had read every single self-help book on the planet, picked up some of the best advice on how to date, and learned many lessons on how to have a successful, loving, intimate relationship. I also knew extremely well the concept of loving myself—that I had to do this in order for others to love me, and that I was unique in the world. I knew all about forgiveness, and the importance of self-esteem and that if I wanted anything in life I had to go out and get it myself. I also knew all too well that when I was sick and tired of being sick and tired of a bad relationship (or anything for that matter), I would change.

But change never occurred.

The same problem kept rearing its ugly head over and over and over again. I would "say" that I was worth a lot and deserved better, but then I would date men who treated me poorly. I would "say" that I just don't want to deal with avoidants, but then I would date yet another avoidant. And so I was stagnant, stuck in one bad relationship after another. And when I picked up that gazillionth self-help book that told me everything I already knew, I threw it across the room after reading just a line or two, and yelled, *I know all this crap.* I felt defeated.

Why wasn't I a changed individual if I knew everything there was to know?

And then it hit me…

Sure, all these lessons were sinking in. And sure, I was learning them. But I wasn't putting them into action. I was still remaining in my head, hoping my outside environment would change so I wouldn't have to. I was waiting for the "right" guy to show up on my doorstep. I was waiting for the current guy to change his behavior and be my dream guy. I was waiting for the perfect job to appear out of nowhere and beg me to work it. But the truth is, the only time in my life real change ever happened was when I took action. When I actually got up and made some physical or mental change that could be measured in comparison to my previous actions.

In other words, a job never "appeared" until I actually went back to school, got my degree and applied to companies in my field. My current guy never "changed," so I left him. And when I was ready to date again? My dream guy never showed up on my doorstep. Instead, I became my own dream girl and well, when I did find someone, we both put in a lot of work on ourselves and on the relationship to make it a strong one. I also began to support myself financially, I dressed better, I improved my overall appearance.

I learned the meaning of gratitude and applied it every day. I was happy being me in a state of action.

OK, so it's time for some self-assessment. What phase are you in now? Are you in limbo, waiting for something to happen? Are you learning, training, gathering information to help you take action in the future? Or, are you already taking action? And if so, what actions are you taking? Are you trying to control the outcome of your current relationship? Are you care-taking? Or are you moving toward a positive action plan that includes aligning your words with what you ultimately choose to do? If you are taking actions, what are they? And most important, are you repeating these healthy actions, or are you trying them once and giving up?

If you're stuck…

Wondering how to take action when you've been in a state of non-action your whole life? Well, here's a good way. Remember the values we discussed a few chapters back? You start taking action by setting an important goal based on your values.

Just one goal! Don't overdo it. For example, you want to get that guy off your mind, but yet, continue to dream of him, think of him, and maybe even check his Instagram feed from time to time, despite not having seen him for three weeks. So…think of a value; something that is very important to you; something like this: *I do not want to be the kind of person who is controlled by negative or pointless thinking.* Now, create a PLAN OF ACTION to achieve that goal. For example, if you do not want to fill your head with "pointless" (and trust me, stalking this guy's Instagram page is pointless) meanderings, make a list of FIVE things to do that will help change that. Like these: get busy and fill my time with something more productive like starting a journal, deleting my Instagram app, at least for a little while, or unfollowing the ex, and when the urge hits me to check his page, count to 100 first and see if I can't find something else to do…

Actions are the vehicle that transports you to where you want and need to be to become healthier.

Lastly, a clarification. Actions and beliefs must be in perfect alignment if you want to feel like you're changing. What do I mean by that? Well, if you believe you are a smart person, then go get a degree if you don't have one. If you love yourself, then stop polluting your body with toxic substances or polluting your mind with toxic thoughts. If you believe you are strong, pull yourself off the sofa, out of the house, and go for a run. Beliefs need to equal actions for a balanced life.

Here are a few more things you can try that personally helped me get off my arse and start doing:

1. Challenge yourself to think in terms of action as necessity. Start to change the way you think about the importance of the task you want to accomplish. Do not settle for just thinking about something.

2. Write a list of things you want to accomplish. And further, give yourself a time-frame to complete those tasks. Where do you see yourself in six months? One year? Five years? Write out every detail of your plan of action.

3. Practice taking action with baby steps. If your goal is to change careers, start with baby steps. Update your resume. Research a new career, talk to someone in that field.

4. Start doing something and KEEP DOING IT. Forming healthier habits takes repeating and ritualizing. Do it 10-20 times before deciding if it's not for you. You have to get past the awkward phase as that is often what makes us prematurely quit.

My favorite quote on action comes from Zig Ziglar. He said, "You don't have to be great to start, but you have to start to be great." The actions you take determine who you are. Stop waiting. It's time.

CHAPTER 20

Aligning Logical Brain and Emotional Brain

"What I dream of is an art of balance."

–Henri Matisse

Somewhere along the line, I don't remember where, I learned that you think with two brains: your emotional brain and your logical brain. This isn't exactly science. But the more you think about it, the more obvious it becomes. For example, someone who makes impulsive decisions with their "heart" is often said to be ruled by their emotions. Others who make well-thought out, calculated decisions tend to be ruled by their head. And yet, any healthy individual must be ruled by both—by a shared balance between the two powers, whose rationale are democratically taken into consideration in decision-making.

In the case of obsession and addiction, there is almost always an imbalance. Most love addicts, for example, are ruled almost entirely by their emotional brains when it comes to love and romance. You might be asking, why *wouldn't* you be ruled by your emotions when it comes to love and romance? What's so wrong with that? And the answer is, nothing. Except that we should not <u>make all decisions about someone or something</u> with our emotions only. Logic must step in and do its job too. But, back to my point. Most love addicts are almost entirely ruled by their emotions. And what's worse is that their emotions are not very healthy to begin with. Neediness, shame, rage, anger, sadness, fear of abandonment, and fear of enmeshment are all emotions that typically fuel the love addict's heart. And so a purely emotional approach to a possible relationship can't always be trusted if your emotions or your subconscious motives for wanting to be in a relationship are not healthy. When your emotional goals are, "I don't want to be abandoned" or, "I don't want to be alone," chances are you won't make the healthiest choice. This is why it's essential that your logical brain becomes part of the decision-making process. The logical side of you isn't worried so much about being alone. The logical side of you is gathering other kinds of data—*How many red flags does this person have? Do we share similar values? Do I feel safe with this person? Does this relationship make sense?*

So, the conflict comes in when the two brains are not in alignment and desire different things. I am sure most of us can relate to this scenario: you're dating an unavailable person, someone who has been causing you a great deal of pain and frustration. Part of you refuses to give her up because you love her (the emotional part), whereas the other part (the logical part), is driven to find ways to get out of the relationship because you rationally know you need to move on. This type of little war happens inside us all to varying degrees. A healthier approach is to utilize both logical and emotional thinking to make decisions over a reasonable amount of time. An unhealthy approach is when we recognize the logical thinking but ignore it, and move forward as dictated by our emotions. We can go back and forth in a state of ambiguity for years. When that happens, the logical voice is suppressed until it can't take it anymore and screams, *you need to get out!* And so you do. But then, the emotional voice screams in retaliation, "I can't be alone; I need him!" And so, you go back. You cannot be ruled by rationality alone, just as you cannot be ruled by your heart alone. Your emotional brain and logical brain must work together. You have both. Use both.

Part of the process of grappling with the emotional brain versus the logical brain is knowing the difference between want versus need. We may want the donut (emotional response), but we need the apple (logical response). We may want the "bad boy," (emotional response) but we need the "nice guy" (logical response).

Want and need are wrapped up in several things, the first of which is the concept of **immediate gratification versus deferred gratification**: *I want the pain to go away immediately, so I will call him and break my promise of no contact (NC) even though it's not in my best interest.* We place a higher value on feeding our emotions and getting what we want right at the moment as opposed to putting it off until there is a more appropriate (but often more difficult) way to deal with the pain. When you think of immediate gratification versus deferred, think of saving money versus spending it. When you hold off on buying stuff you want right when you see and you save your money instead, you are able to buy bigger and better things that have more value. My son learned this lesson the hard way. He had saved over $2,000 for a new car. He needed only about $1,000 more to get the used car he wanted. Instead of waiting and working a little harder, he ended up blowing almost all his savings on t-shirts, games, food, and other stuff over the course of a summer. When school started, and everyone was driving their cars, he had no transportation of his own and had to ask for rides. His deferred goal was a car and freedom. He didn't get it. Instead, he settled for his immediate gratification goal of having instant fun.

You need to see yourself as an investment. You need to see that the more you invest in yourself, the more hard work, love and education and experience you put into yourself, the more rewarding life becomes for you. The more valuable you become. Not only to yourself, but to others.

Know that when a decision is right, both the emotional brain and the logical brain come together. They are on the same page, acting in alignment. The reason for this is because, ultimately, they want the same things for you. Your happiness is in their best interest.

The trick is to see value in your logical brain and start to take it a hell of a lot more seriously than you have been doing. Many of us over-glamorize emotional and creative thinking and tend to put a very ugly spin on "logic." We often see logical people as cold, rational, unfeeling, unemotional humans who have no heart, and we see emotional people as the salt of the earth, as well as warm, passionate, loving, artistic, driven, and fun. Not only is the kind of black and white thinking grossly inaccurate, it is detrimental to your health. You were given logic AND emotion and it is important to use both. Using only your emotional brain causes a huge imbalance. "Want" wins out over "need" and the price becomes evident in the fact that you are not investing in yourself or caring for yourself properly.

I do want to clarify that I do not think emotions are bad. But I do believe that during this rebuilding process we cannot and should not trust or depend on our emotions—at least for a little while. During this time, try leaning more heavily on your logical brain, until your emotional brain learns healthier ways of feeling.

So, in a nutshell, to rebuild Emotional vs. Logical Thinking:

1. Recognize the importance of deferred gratification. Oftentimes postponing pleasure as a way of achieving something of more value is the better option.

2. Turn off your emotional thinking. Temporarily. Exercise your logical brain! Give it more decision-making power and follow through with actions. Choose an option based not on how it "feels" but on

its logical benefits. This is how you train yourself to align emotional thinking with logical thinking.

3. Pull back on responding to your desire for immediate gratification. What does waiting look like? Are you a run-away train that just can't be stopped? A victim of your desires? Grow up! Remember that you can take your time about making decisions. Remember who's in charge. You are.

4. And speaking of growing up…Stop empowering your demanding, needy inner child by giving her free rein. Put her in a time out. It's not all about her. Besides, she can't make healthy decisions anyway (has she ever?!). And recognize that *want* is temporary; *need* is permanent. Lots of things in life are worth waiting for…especially *you*.

CHAPTER 21

Say Goodbye to Fantasy

"Oh, how I wish I could shut up like a telescope! I think I could, if only I knew how to begin." For, you see, so many out-of-the-way things had happened lately, that Alice had begun to think that very few things indeed were really impossible."

–Lewis Carroll, *Alice In Wonderland*

There's an underlying core belief many of us share that needs to shift in order for us to stop chasing after someone who is no longer fully available to us. This belief is very hard for me to describe here, but I'll try via a story:

When I was in high school I fell in love with this kid named B. He was marginally invested in me as a potential girlfriend. I think he was flattered but didn't exactly like me to the same degree I liked him. Nevertheless, I chased after him, sent him love letters, bought him stuff, and even wrote him a poem and had it read over the loudspeaker during lunch (ugh), until finally, we hooked up. I was in bliss. One night of bliss that is. Because the next day, when I saw him, he went back to ignoring me. I used to describe his behavior as hot and cold, which went on over the course of a year, but the truth is, his behavior towards me was mostly cold with a slightly elevated enthusiasm for me when he was bored or wanted to get laid. To me, that was everything. And so, when he'd call, I'd be out the door in minutes to meet him.

One day, before or after we had sex, I can't remember, I had read him a story I wrote about "us." He listened attentively, then laughed, and in an extremely rare, uncharacteristic moment, he looked at me and said, "you're a really good writer." I was flushed with joy! Finally, a compliment where there was usually an insult. Within nanoseconds my brain created an entire world built on the notion that we were in love and soon to be married (yes, nano-seconds). But two seconds after that, my hopes were dashed and the world I'd created crumbled. He asked me a question that would change my life. He said, "Tracy, why don't you date someone who *really* likes you?"

Huh? What? You mean you *don't really like me?*

At first, I felt anger. How dare he tell me who to chase after, or how to feel. Then came shame. I was mortified that he rejected me. What made it even worse was that he started to date another girl, who was, in my estimation, not nearly as fabulous as I was. I mean, she was the kind of girl who beat other girls up in parking lots. She smoked in the girl's bathroom. I'm pretty sure she was missing a tooth. What I couldn't wrap my head around was that on the one hand, my brain and my heart seemed to be telling me that he was absolutely perfect for me, but on the other, he was telling me he wasn't. And it took many, many months to understand that Reality was also telling me that he was not perfect for me, but I wasn't listening.

And that's what fantasy is all about. When we refuse to look at and listen to what is really happening and instead, create a world that makes more sense to us, we are denying ourselves a true present. And we will have an extremely difficult time finding a healthy partner.

Here's another story from one of my readers. Fantasy thinking was also responsible for Hannah's failed marriage. Hannah met her husband Corey, the way so many of us do, through an online dating app. She searched through hundreds of profiles and came across a guy who seemed to share her interests. In his profile, he was good-looking, lived close, and seemed to check all the boxes. When they started up an email conversation, she immediately felt a sort of chemistry between them. They talked about their love of travel, their careers and home life. Mostly though, they talked about how much they liked each other and how they would be the absolute perfect couple. Months went by, however, before they actually met. Any image she had of him was only through photos he sent. Any understanding of who he was came from writing, and occasional phone conversations that often continued into the night. And it took him nearly seven months to finally ask her out. She chalked it all up to the fact that he was shy. Prior to their meeting, however, they had both admitted they'd fallen in love. They had never seen each other, smelled each other, or touched each other. They had no idea if one or the other had any weird idiosyncrasies, dressed a certain way, acted socially acceptable in public, ate peas one at a time with a fork, and so on. To them, love was love. And what they shared was so deep, little things didn't matter. And while there was no mental, emotional or psychological ability to evaluate each others' character or behavior, they both figured that anything could be overlooked, as long as they were in love. Also, in the seven months prior to meeting, Hannah would use her fantasy-thinking to "fill in the gaps" about anything she didn't know about Corey. She made assumptions. She didn't do it intentionally. But, without conscious thought, she imagined he was big and strong and could lift her up and carry her into the bedroom, and that his voice held a deep tone, and that he moved a certain way. She would even imagine certain facial features she particularly thought were handsome, and pretty much convinced herself he had them.

When they finally met, while she still felt very much in love with the man she had connected to over the past seven months, she also felt a slight betrayal. Not only was he not as big and tall as she'd thought and didn't have the features she'd imagined, she soon learned he hadn't been very forthcoming about the fact he had very poor dental hygiene. She soon noticed he wasn't showering every day. And she even started to catch him in little lies via his body language, something you can't do in text and email. But she felt as though she was so invested in him that when he asked her to marry him she felt like there was no turning back. She figured she would learn to love the idiosyncrasies she didn't particularly like. And besides, she was getting older. She didn't have time to start all over again. And, well, she loved him.

Sadly, the marriage only lasted two years and Hannah ended up having to "start all over again" anyway. The huge disconnect between the man she thought she had married and the man she really married was too wide to reconcile. The two of them had virtually nothing in common but the desire to fall in love and be with someone. This is yet another example of fantasy thinking, or wishful thinking.

Healthy people don't "fill in the gaps." They don't commit to someone based on what they "think," "hope" or "wish" he or she should be. They are not afraid to see the reality of people. And, when you're not afraid to see the reality of someone, it means you're willing to accept certain people may not be for you. It means you don't get the easy fantasy, and you may have to be willing to "start all over again" and walk away.

i. **Fixing Something that Isn't Broken**

I often wondered why we stay in unfulfilling, broken relationships, obsessed over fixing them. And then it hit me. They're not broken! They're perfectly functional dysfunctional relationships. And the longer we stay, and try to fix or change or heal the dysfunction, it becomes even more dysfunctional, and thus more functional. It's a paradox. That's because we're not fixing anything. And we're not fixing anything because nothing is broken. The relationship is a painfully dysfunctional one, true. But that's its job and it can't be fixed. It is serving several important purposes, including:

- Keeping us from facing our fears of being alone
- Keeping us from facing ourselves and fixing our own problems
- Keeping us from real intimacy, because, let's face it, we're not emotionally grown up enough to handle this (if we were, we wouldn't be with an emotionally unavailable partner in the first place).
- Keeping our partner in a distant, dysfunctional relationship, possibly with no strings attached, because he/she is not capable of real intimacy either
- And it's keeping us both dependent on drama, obsession, avoidance and pain, because we both thrive on those things.

It's quite telling when those are the components of a relationship we refuse to leave.

ii. **Inventory Time!**

It's time to take stock of your progress! Take a moment to delve into all the ways you have changed since you began this rebuilding process.

1. What are the top five most valuable lessons you've learned?

2. What are your top five newest values?

3. What are your top five negative or self-defeating behavioral traits that you'd like to work on?

4. Did you dig deep? What do you think your relationship/love obsessing is saving you from? What is it you're trying to avoid?

iii. Needs and Expectations

You may have noticed the word "need" appears frequently in this book. For years, this word was almost always present in my thinking. Need is a love addict's currency. It's how we do business. We either desperately need something, or we assume others desperately need something and we're planning on providing it. Either way, as love addicts, we tend to do business with the wrong clients, ie, people who simply cannot afford the price we put on our needs. Let me explain this way…

I need you to love me. I need you to make me happy. I need you to take out the trash. I need you to feed the dog. I need you to make love to me. I need you to support me. I need you to be faithful. I need you to be nice to me. I need you to pay more attention to me. I need you to respect me. I need you to ravish me. I need you to stop lying. I need you to love me more than you love her. I need you to make a decision. I need you…I need you…I need you…

To a committed relationship, need is like foam to a cappuccino. You can't have one without the other. Needs must be met. And we hear it all the time: *I have a right to be loved. I have a right to be respected. I am in a committed relationship, which means my partner should meet my needs.*

All of those opinions and beliefs are true. You DO have a right to be loved. And you DO have a right to be respected. And you DO have a right to have your needs met in a committed relationship.

But you do NOT have the right to demand those things from someone who is unable or unwilling to give them to you.

That's the sad disclaimer of an unhealthy relationship. We get into relationships with unavailable people and then impose our expectations of need upon them. When they don't give us what we want and need, instead of leaving, we badger, beg and bitch about it.

But, are we too needy? Do we expect too much? There is an ongoing serious debate that women tend to set their expectations too high or too low. My response to this is always the same: we can have high expectations, but only from people who can meet those expectations.

We must always expect a certain set of decent basic treatment from all people: to be treated humanely, to be treated with kindness and respect. And to receive honesty and decency in our communion with them. Above that, we are not owed anything from strangers, or even people we date. In fact, unless we have some sort of agreement or understanding in place (*I expect these things from you, and you have agreed to give them to me*), our expectations need to remain at the very basic level. That means you cannot expect your date to call you back for date two. You cannot expect that he or she will text you heart emojis. You cannot expect sex or commitment or moving in together, or a future from anyone too early on, or ever, if the person is not willing or capable of meeting those expectations. And yet, you don't want to lower your expectations. You simply want to try a little harder to find someone who can meet them.

Your expectations equal your values. You have a right to have them, and they should be as high as you'd like to set them. But remember, you can't expect everyone you date or fall in love with to be able to step up to the plate. That hurts, but, it's a lesson worth knowing.

I want to throw in a few examples here about distorted expectations. I too grappled for years trying to understand if I should have high or low expectations. And believe me, it wasn't easy to figure out. One of my best examples is my first husband. As I've said before, we married young, within months of knowing each other, and so we didn't know each other very well at all. He's Spanish and I am American, and as an American I had certain expectations of how to run a household, how to look for work, how to raise children, how to communicate, and basically, how to be married. One of my expectations, which I thought was extremely basic, was that you give your wife a card, or flowers or a small gift on Valentine's day, Christmas, or her birthday. Seems like a perfectly reasonable expectation, right? Wrong. He never bought me any gifts or cards the first year or two of our marriage. After crying hysterically each time my expectations weren't met, I would have this big long talk with him that "in this country, we give each other cards." All my pleading barely made a dent, until it occurred to me that he wasn't indoctrinated into our Hallmark culture. They barely sell cards in Spain. This is an example of what seems like a reasonable expectation, applied to a situation where the expectation is actually unreasonable.

Managing expectations takes time. It can be tricky. Write down some of your must-haves (i.e. values) and see how they coincide with your expectations. Also, write about your expectations in dating. What are they? Do you think they're realistic? Think of the individual you are asking to meet those expectations. Do you think he or she is up to the task? And if they fall short what does that mean to you? I think after several months of relatively serious dating, you can and should talk about some of your expectations, though not all. In other words, after six months of dating, you want to bring up the goals you both have for the future, what the "next level" of your relationship might look like and possibly even the fact that "someday" you want children. Expectations not to bring up at this time? Marriage, wedding plans, baby names, moving in together, and things like combining finances. Don't put the cart before the horse. Those expectations come much later. Eventually, though, you will need to know and feel secure that your expectations are being met. And, if you're having trouble figuring out a timeline of when you can expect some of your expectations to be met, as I've mentioned before, Judith Sills' "A Fine Romance" is an excellent book. Baby steps.

Which leads me to the next rung on the self-responsibility ladder: behavior. Tired of relationship drama?

CHAPTER 22

Lose Your Bad Behaviors (drama, manipulation and venting, oh my!)

"Come on, say it again. I'm a perfect devil. Tell me how bad I am. It makes me feel so good!"

–Anne Rice, *The Queen of the Damned*

Most of us, in that very human, very egocentric way, are inclined to look outside ourselves when we want to identify a source of distress. This is especially true when it comes to difficult or toxic relationships. We look at our partners and we can clearly see what they're doing wrong. *She's an avoidant. He's a liar. She doesn't give me the attention I need. He's not doing his fair share.* While we may have a vague notion of our own faults, we generally try to say those faults are the direct result of our partner's behavior (*Yeah, sure, I'm a nag sometimes; but, I wouldn't be if you just took out the trash!*). Look, I'd like to say I was created a perfect, faultless human being and any trouble I incur comes from outside myself. Unfortunately, I don't have the luxury of being perfect. And truthfully, part of the problem of this line of thinking is that, well, it's a big clue to one of my many imperfections: I don't always take responsibility for my own actions. I blame. Whether you, personally, are guilty of blaming others for your problems too, I don't know. What I do know is that "blaming others" is one of a long list of self-defeating behaviors we all need to work on if we want to be better at relationshipping.

I think when we consider the idea of "working on ourselves" we often assume it means psychoanalysis. Digging into our past, analyzing our behavior, things like that. Although that is a hugely beneficial undertaking, I learned the more I hunted around my past, the more I found more questions than answers, and that what mattered in the end was the action I was willing to take in the here and now, to change my behavior. Dr. Phil said once, "It's one thing when you've suffered as a child from abuse or neglect; it's another thing entirely when you drag all that suffering into adulthood." So, instead of me encouraging you to go out and book a $300 session with your friendly neighborhood Freudian psychoanalyst (though I don't want to discourage you either), I thought perhaps I could steer you towards some basic self-defeating behaviors you can work on on your own.

- **Avoiding**: We've pretty much established that avoiding reality and responsibilities is one our biggest self-defeating behaviors. It comes directly from fear. If you want to psychoanalyze anything, psychoanalyze why you avoid. Chances are, it comes from your childhood, as we talked about in earlier sections. But here's the thing: if you don't "fix" your tendency to avoid, you will continue down the path of the bad relationship. Why? Because when we are avoidants, we simply look for ways to avoid stuff, and so our goal when looking for a partner is, will he/she help me continue to avoid. Don't confuse the term love addict and avoidant here (*Well, I can't be an avoidant if I'm dating one!* Oh yes you can). Love addicts are self-avoiders.

- **Manipulating**: In my many years on this planet I've determined that manipulation is probably the saddest, most desperate attempt to get what we want. At its fundamentally simplest, it is *I'll do this for you, if you do this for me.* At its ugliest, it can look like this: *I will kill myself if you leave me.* And, at its subtlest, it can be silent but very powerful: a partner who withholds sex, love, kindness, attention, etc. in order to get something in return (sex, love, kindness attention). We manipulate because we need something that we aren't getting by simply asking for it. I think at my lowest point of marriage to my first husband, I wished I would just fall down the stairs or get into a car accident so that he would pay me some attention and feel sorry for me. We need to stop this behavior and ask for things. If we repeatedly don't get what we ask for and need, it's time to find someone else who can give us what we need so we don't fall into patterns of manipulation. When we don't get what we want we either have to accept it, or realize we will probably never get it from this person and move on. And, we definitely have to assess our own personal needs to determine if they are reasonable or toxic. If you're asking your partner for 24-7 care, love, attention and praise, this is not a reasonable need, unless you're a baby.

- **Drama-Seeking**: I used to think I was drawn to drama. I learned much later in life that I was not "drawn to it" but had became so used to it I felt bored without it. What's the expression? Idleness is the devil's playground? For many of us who thrive on drama, we are not only drawn to it, we create it. Of course, we don't think we do this. *I swear, it's not my fault that the dog needs to be rushed to the vet for a splinter in her paw!* But we create mountains out of molehills, respond to neutral occurrences with over-the-top emotional responses, or worse, cause trouble. We crash our cars, we make ourselves sick, we throw the first punch, we cause a scene. Drama is a life force for some. Is it for you? And if it is, ask yourself what it gives you. Ask yourself too, what would it mean to you to have a drama-free existence? Do you equate drama with adventure? Or are you able to see that drama is negative, whereas adventure is positive?

- **Lying, Cheating, Stealing and blah, blah, blah**…We point the finger, we rage, we scream, and we feel completely incensed if our partner lies or cheats on us, and yet, are we free and clear of this behavior ourselves? Are we lying right along with our partners or are we innocent victims? I can't tell you how amazed I was when I heard that a married friend of mine who was cheating on her husband with another man, was outraged to learn that her lover had cheated on her with a younger woman. But, wait?! You're married! And yet, her being married wasn't the point. The point was her affair guy had pledged his undying love to her, had vowed to be loyal, and then, completely betrayed her. She was only faintly aware of the possibility she herself, by virtue of her own betrayal to her husband, was communicating to everyone that she was OK with betrayal. Like attracts like. Water seeks its own level. Improve your own behavior, hold yourself to higher standards and the karmic wheel of love will give it back to you.

i. **Venting**

I would like to address the topic of venting and complaining in a section of its own. But really, it's yet another of the self-defeating behaviors you gotta lose. Venting is a necessary part of the figuring-out process. And it's definitely a necessary part of the healing process. Urban Dictionary even has a term called vent art; "Art that someone makes to let out a feeling, usually a negative feeling like anger or <u>sadness</u>, which can be hugely constructive and restorative. Yet, there's a line that when crossed can turn otherwise healthy venting into a destructive force far greater than the initial problem you were venting about to begin with. At the least, it becomes a continuation, a dragging out of the toxicity of the past.

Many years ago I dated this guy. I'll call him Jack. All I wanted to do was spend my time with him. When I wasn't with him, all I wanted to do was talk about him. But here's the thing; I wasn't really talking about him. I was complaining about him. Well, at the time, I didn't think it was complaining. I thought I was analyzing our relationship and trying to figure him out. What that consisted of, however, was a steady outpouring of how wronged I was by him, how much he hurt me, how much I knew I needed to get out of the relationship, and ultimately, how I went back and fell madly in love again. I vented to my friends over and over and over until the inevitable happened: I burned a lot of bridges and lost some friends. People didn't want to hear about Jack anymore. If I wanted to get out of the relationship so badly, why didn't I? Why did I actually keep getting back *into* the relationship? Eventually, instead of stopping the venting, I started hanging around others who were also in miserable relationships. We could vent together. Misery, after all, loves company.

Looking back, this process of venting was not part of the solution. It was not healing or cathartic, it didn't help propel me forward. It was a continuation of my own toxic behavior. It was part of the way I obsessed. When I was not with Jack, I would summon him any way I could by thinking and talking about him. It was the flip side of the same coin. And when my mother, for example, would tell me to stop venting, I would get angry and defensive. Eventually, I would start to avoid anyone who called me out on my venting.

"They didn't understand!" I thought. I figured I was simply trying to "work this out in my head" and needed a sounding board, and support. And yet, I wasn't working anything out, so there was not much to support. Months and years went by, and I took no action. I was merely venting.

It wasn't my mother or my friends who didn't understand—t was me. The more I obsessed over my situation without doing anything about it, the more the act of "venting" and the toxicity of the relationship controlled my life.

When I realized this I started to change. It became clear that the solution to my obsession was not only to let go of the relationship physically, but let go mentally and emotionally too. And that meant giving up the venting.

To a love addict, our drug of choice is not only who we love, but our obsessed thoughts and fantasies of that person. So, each time we analyze our relationship or the person we are addicted to, or act out, or "vent" about how we can't stop loving this person, we are taking a hit of the drug.

When we enmesh others in that fantasy and that drama, we are validating our suffering, we are validating our pain, we are securing "partners in crime," so to speak, as we take another hit.

Letting go of venting is extremely difficult. The way we think, the way we communicate and the things we talk about all day is who we are. To stop venting feels like you are giving up a part of you you've built over time. Habits are hard to break, and the more hours you devote to the habit of venting or complaining, the harder it may be to stop. That's why you probably won't stop venting completely. A co-worker got the position you wanted, a neighbor's dog won't stop barking, the dress you just bought for a cocktail party you don't even want to go to has a tear in it and it's only Monday. Feeling run-down and beaten up by the world makes us want to commiserate with those closest to us. *Just let me get this off my chest so I feel better.* We want others to listen to us and support us, whether we are up or down. But your goal moving forward is to really cleanse yourself of much of your complaining.

In order to rebuild yourself, you have to question whether your venting is part of the problem or part of the solution. Analyzing your own behavior and questioning the validity of the relationship is very much part of the solution if it leads to a resolution of sorts. Analyzing your partner's behavior or the impossibility of the relationship, then doing nothing about it is part of the problem. Rebuilding yourself means recognizing that while a balanced amount of "talking it out" about your ex or partner with friends or family can help you, you have to always be aware of crossing the line into venting hell. Your clue? The amount of time you vent, the quality of the venting, and whether you are taking any actions towards resolving the problem. Let's do the exercise below.

Exercise: Write it down. What are you complaining about? Is it one thing or many things? How often are you complaining? Is it all day long, once a day, once a week? What actions are you taking so that you no longer have to complain about a certain problem? Are you seeking a solution, are you confronting the problems, or do you simply feel helpless and unable to take action? One of the biggest reasons we vent is because we feel out of control. See your answers above. What is and isn't in your control?

CHAPTER 23

Managing Stress Now That You Can't Hide Behind Your Defense Mechanism

"I am not what happened to me,
I am what I choose to become."

–Carl Gustav Jung

Whew! If you made it this far you're a soldier! OK, even if you jumped ahead and missed a few parts, you're still amazing! But, if you've been following along, you will have noticed part of this whole rebuilding process entails removing some of your defenses and support strategies. When we take away our defense mechanisms, those ingenuous, but often destructive coping tools like avoidance, fantasy, alcohol, drugs or hiding behind a relationship, we can feel raw and exposed. We immediately want to grasp for some sort of protection, and all-too-often, it's not good or safe. This reminds me of a blog follower who told me about the time she tried to give up her dependence on drinking. Alcohol was the only thing, she believed, that helped her feel comfortable meeting people. And so when she went to bars or clubs with her friends, she'd always get drunk and meet guys. Completely inappropriate ones who also drank too much. She knew she had to change, so she quit drinking cold turkey, and she couldn't be prouder of herself. But, when she went out sober one night, thrilled with her new approach to socializing, she walked into the place and quickly became so overwhelmed that she had a panic attack. The crowds, the men who approached her, even her friends made her head spin with such confusion and anxiety that she left the bar without telling anyone. She refused to go out for months after that, believing that alcohol was her only tool to help her meet people. It wasn't. But at the time, she didn't know this.

So what's the solution when we don't want to pull the proverbial rug out from underneath ourselves? When we still need some sort of coping device or crutch to get through a situation, but don't want to turn to our old destructive ways? And, no, it's not called Xanax. It's called creativity! We invent super-cool, healthy, stronger behaviors that help us cope in tough situations. Because we are not the sum of our coping strategies. We're so much more. I'll show you how.

Golfers have a handicap. Banks offer loans to help people buy homes and cars. We have family or friends to help us through rough times. We're not super-human. Sometimes we need help. Managing stress without the "protection" of love or obsession can be daunting. Managing stress without defenses can make us feel fragile, exposed, vulnerable. Many us have no idea what life looks like without our defenses. And so right here and right now may be the first adult time some of us will face stress in a healthy way after many years of avoiding it.

Stress can be anything from dealing with the death of a loved one, to managing work, family and finances all by yourself, to the fairly simple task of paying your phone bill online. It's all relative. Stress means different things for different people. I've felt like pulling my hair out over a cold sore at certain times. At others, I've deftly maneuvered my way through the pressure of running a company when the president, vice-president and marketing director all quit within the span of a month. We're not going to get into a discussion about how much stress is piling up on you. I get it. I've been there. My point here is not how much stress you're going through, but how you manage that stress in a healthy way, without self-destructive behaviors. So to do that, you have to understand how stress comes at you. There are three ways, in time, space and through order/disorder.

1. **TIME: Stress comes fast and furious**, seemingly out of nowhere. Someone dies, your partner rejects you, your stove catches on fire. These are the stressors that hit you when you least expect it, and you're totally unprepared. You're going about your day, la, la, la, and then, boom. You have to deal with *this*.

2. **ORDER/DISORDER: Stress is disorganized**, as disorganized as any 4000-piece jigsaw puzzle some mean, mischievous kid tossed on the floor. Examples: the dog just pooped on the new carpet, dinner is burning in the oven, a bill collector is calling, your partner just stormed out, and your son needs to be picked up from T-ball practice in ten minutes. *Calgon, take me away!*

3. **SPACE: Stress, builds, multiplies and divides** Like a hoarder's thrift store finds, stress can be insurmountable, cluttering, and dangerously impeding. You've just lost your job, which means you'll have no income, and you didn't make enough to squirrel away into savings for emergencies like this. Your medical bills are multiplying and so you opt to miss your doctor's appointments, and your

health and well-being begin to take a nosedive, which means your
relationship goes down the tubes, and…*Enough already!*

Stress typically doesn't go away by itself. It usually needs a push. So
how do we create healthy defenses against all those types of stress? Here's
some ideas:

1. **Organize the chaos in your life**. Organization is my most favorite
   defense mechanism. It wasn't always that way, but eventually, I
   realized that organization equals control, which equals empowerment. The more you have your ducks in a row, the more prepared
   you are for the chaotic events beyond your control. Being prepared
   feels good. Let me give you a scenario. My friend Jill is a successful
   creative person, and newly divorced. She spent most of 20 married
   years allowing her husband to control all their finances and bills
   and taxes, and once she was on her own, panicked at the thought
   of having to do it all by herself. She didn't even know where to
   begin. She would get a bill and throw it in a pile, or leave it in her
   purse. Occasionally, she would try to organize. She'd go online
   and try to use accounting tools. Or she would go to the bank and
   ask them for budgeting advice. Whatever the case, she made more
   piles and added more chaos to the heaps of chaos already there.
   This led to depression, which led to a slump in her creativity.
   It affected all aspects of her life. And then one day, most likely
   pushed along by an invisible sense of urgency, she finally took the
   time to sit down with all her bills and put them in order. She found
   five that weren't even paid! Once she faced this overwhelming task,
   however, the burden of procrastination and disorganization lifted.
   The more you organize your home, your closet, yourself, the easier
   it is to exist. And while I completely understand that disorganization can be part of a creative process, I also understand that if

you're reading this book you are looking to ease your suffering and rebuild yourself. Declutter. Organize. You can still be creative. *Previous defense mechanism:* avoid the bills, ignore the collectors, drink, spend more money, etc. *Management mechanism:* organize paperwork, set up payment plans, create calendars and reminders for things you need to remember, put things in order.

2. **Take care of your health as best as you can**. My mother always says, "Make sure you always have a few extra pounds on you. This way, in case you get really sick, your body has some fat to get you through." I'm not sure I'm willing to add a few pounds for that rationale, but I see where she's coming from. The importance of keeping yourself healthy is up there with breathing and existing. Health, if you have it, whether you realize it or not, is one of your greatest gifts. And maintaining your personal health and well-being to the best of your ability is paramount to helping you heal, rebuild and deal with stress. I don't want to make recommendations for any one diet or exercise routine, except to say that at least 30 minutes of cardio 3-5 times a week, stretching and some muscle building will not only help keep you in shape physically, it will do wonders for you mentally. Throw meditation in there along with a healthy diet and loads of omega-3s (proven to help curb depression, anxiety and stress) and you're doing more than the average Jane or Joe. It's an awesome idea too to set up an appointment with a naturopathic doctor. They specialize in a more natural approach to health and can really help you focus on diet and exercise routines unlike medical doctors. Bottom line: the more you take care of yourself physically, the more you will be able to handle stress. *Previous defense mechanism:* emotional eating, eating too much or too little, overeating to self-soothe, remaining sedentary, not exercising. *Management mechanism:* Eating a balanced diet, healthy

eating to self-soothe, exercising, meditating, yoga, participating in physical activities that help build cardio and muscular strength.

3. **Stop avoiding problems; stop procrastinating**. We all need to avoid stuff on occasion. I can't tell you how many times my mother said to me, "pick your battles; let the rest go." The trouble comes in when we avoid not only our problems, but our responsibilities, and our lives. Obsessing over someone, hiding behind a relationship, and being addicted to your partner are all not-so obvious ways we avoid. A more obvious way is procrastinating. Don't think for one second that procrastination is some innocent and occasional laziness. While there are a gazillion instances of small time procrastination—putting off getting a haircut, waiting too long to sign up for a class, not paying a bill on time—there are also larger-than-life examples. It took me 16 years to graduate from college and get a degree. It took me longer than that to start my career as a writer. Procrastination (a.k.a. avoidance) can ruin your life. So what's the solution? I'd like to tell you to just get off your ass and start accomplishing your goals. All of them. But, it's not that easy. Procrastination is so deeply imbedded into who you are and how you view yourself that it takes some work to figure out what is holding you back. According to Ken Christian, PhD, author of *Your Own Worst Enemy: Breaking the Habit of Adult Underachievement,* procrastinators or "Delayers" are one of the top 15 personality types known to have a self-limiting style that leads to what he calls adult underachievement. Chronic procrastination can even postpone becoming an adult, which includes having healthy, adult relationships. When we delay, we waste valuable time living. And all that we put off becomes an albatross around our neck. *Previous Defense Mechanism:* avoid, procrastinate out of laziness, fear or perceived inability. *Management Mechanism:* Learn

to make decisions, learn the value in taking action, face your fears to the best of your ability, little by little, so that you begin to chip away at your tasks. Stop avoiding pain and suffering by blocking action. Experience pain and suffering so that you are better able to manage it.

4. **Go at your own pace and don't forget to ask for help**. When you've spent a lifetime avoiding problems or hiding behind your relationships, you have very little knowledge of what you can and cannot handle. Everything seems overwhelming. What's more, stressors that pile up can seem even more intimidating. And that's why it's so important to tackle stress at your own pace and to ask for help if you need it. I learned that I could give myself permission to go at my own pace in the oddest of places—during a workshop in creative writing headed by Stephen Dunn, who won the Pulitzer prize for poetry for his book *Different Hours*. He was telling us the story of how he wrote his poems and emphasized that he couldn't have done it without help or if he were forced to abide by someone else's timeline. He had to go at his own pace, and he had to have help. That kinda blew me away. It made me realize that we are often under the false assumption that individuals who achieve greatness, let alone those of us who just need to check a few tasks off our list, do so completely alone, in a vacuum. And that they do it in some rigidly defined timeline. They don't. Humans help each other. And humans go at their own individual paces. It took Victor Hugo 12 years to write Les Miserables. It took Thomas Edison 1,000 tries to invent the light bulb. It takes me 25 minutes to walk a mile. We can't be so hard on ourselves. We need to honor our own pace. We need to learn, through trial and error, what that pace is. And, we need to ask for help if we need it. I didn't say we should allow someone else to do things for us. I said we can ask

for help. There's a difference. *Previous defense mechanism:* trying to do things alone, or expecting your partner to do things for you that, as an adult, you are capable of doing yourself. Not addressing issues at all; or, expecting issues to be addressed immediately. *Management mechanism:* Go at your own pace. Try to do things you can do yourself. Ask for help if you need it, but don't expect others to do things for you.

i.   **Responding to Conflict**

Back in the day, when I was running around rampant and impulsive under the spell of love, avoiding my real responsibilities, it was so easy to say or do virtually anything I wanted. I had no awareness or care of consequences. Like a child, if I felt wronged in any way, I could easily insult someone right to their face, I would speak my mind regardless of hurting anyone, and put someone in their place without so much as an insincere regret. While that might be considered confident behavior, I ultimately considered it to be careless, immature egocentricity. I still recall getting in trouble with my boss when I worked in the marketing department of a vitamin supplement company as a manager many years ago. He yelled at me for "lashing out," at one of my subordinates. His advice to me was, "You need to think before you act, otherwise you lose your credibility." Credibility? I didn't even know I had something as glamorous as credibility! But I didn't want to lose it, that's for sure. I figured silence was the answer.

And so after a lot of work on myself trying to be a better person, the pendulum swung in the opposite direction. I retreated. If someone wronged me or I felt unfairly treated, I would simply bite my tongue and walk the other way. My fear of hurting someone's feelings or saying the wrong thing was so overpowering it stopped me dead in my tracks and rendered me silent.

And that's how we approach learning sometimes. Our solution to dealing with conflict is often lashing out or staying silent, as if behavior, conflict resolution, or problem solving were only black and white. It took another few years to realize there's a lot of gray in between these polarities, and conflict can be resolved in a balanced way. I learned, for example, that it's perfectly OK to call someone out on their behavior if you simply do it with respect. I had to remember I was in control and could use my words and the tone of my voice to set the mood of any confrontation. I learned that talking "down" to someone doesn't empower you, and is never a good tool for negotiating your way through a conflict. And that silence, while important at times, can render you powerless. Use your powers for good! Make yourself heard, but listen as well.

Managing life is hard when you don't have a lot of practice. When provoked, we tend to either fight or run. But what I've learned is that true problem solving is best done when you confront issues and work via respectful communication to resolve them. The more we do this, the better we become.

ii. Falling Without a Net

When the light bulb moment comes and we snap out of our fog and recognize how to finally change and better our lives, a period of heroic courage seems to effortlessly propel us forward. We break up with our toxic partner, we stop all of our noxious, self-defeating behaviors, we interrupt the pattern of repeated harm we do to ourselves and others, and we give up all those deplorable, defective, useless defense mechanisms that got us into all this trouble in the first place. The light of clarity and newness shines down upon us and we think, ahh…the promised land. But, wait! Not so fast. All those pesky little defense mechanisms that you just got rid of? They served a huge purpose. They protected you and kept you safe. At least that's what you thought. And, yeah, I know, you've grown up and you're way cooler and way more responsible than ever before. You don't need to hide behind anything. Not you. But here's the thing. You know when a tsunami hits, it's usually a good idea to run for cover? Well, it works the same with stress. We will probably always need some sort of protection to help us. We may be superheroes.

But we're not super-human. Without some sort of coping strategies to help us through rough times, we feel like we're falling without a net. And the second that happens, the second we lose our balance, boom! we go right back to our old toxic ways. We may not choose the same defense mechanisms as before, but trust me; they'll come back.

So know this. Defense mechanisms are super-important. The toxic ones, no. The healthy ones, very much so.

Being a strong, healthy individual doesn't means you must exist without any sort of comfort or protection. It means you have to pick and choose healthier forms of protection. And oh! The choices you have. But understand that toxic ones, even though they serve a great purpose, impede our growth or hurt us. Take avoidance, for example. A person who avoids growing up, or avoids facing life's challenges can delay the pain that growth and facing life might produce, but at the same time, this choice also eliminates access to all the undeniably beautiful and necessary parts of growing up and facing life. Using love, fantasy and relationships to effectively avoid your life ends up being a rather disastrous defense mechanism. Yeah, sure. It feels like you're truly living at the time. But true love and growing up, facing life's challenges, paying the bills or being responsible is not mutually exclusive. They can and should happen at the same time.

CHAPTER 24

Gratitude & Mindfulness

"Consider the sunlight. You may see it is near, yet if you follow it from world to world you will never catch it in your hands. Then you may describe it as far away and, lo, you will see it just before your eyes. Follow it and, behold, it escapes you; run from it and it follows you close. You can neither possess it nor have done with it. From this example you can understand how it is with the true Nature of all things and, henceforth, there will be no need to grieve or to worry about such things."

–Huang Po, *The Zen Teaching of Huang Po: On the Transmission of Mind*

I would like to end this section with two extremely important concepts that I believe will help you move forward. These tools can easily change your life when you truly grasp them and begin to utilize their gifts.

But a word of caution. There has been so much written on gratitude and mindfulness lately, especially when it comes to social media, that these very real, very powerful messages can easily be overlooked, or worse, ignored after being faced with too many of them scrolling past our eyeballs. My Pinterest board is filled with affirmations. My Instagram feed often feels like one huge meditation. And Facebook, forget it. Every one of my friends, as wonderful as they are, floods my newsfeed with their feel-good memes. If I read "Enjoy the little things" one more time, I am going to detonate. If someone tells me to keep yet another gratitude journal, I'm going to…you get the point. It's too much.

But gratitude and mindfulness, whether everyone and their mother are posting about them or not, are super-important. So you must let a little of their message in. You must allow yourself to focus on and try to grasp the meaning of these two ideas, not necessarily together or even at the same time, but try to understand each completely. More importantly, if you catch yourself trying to read a million cute little gratitude memes with bears and rainbows, but you're simply swiping over each one quickly to get to the next, STOP. Your brain will become saturated with bears and rainbows instead of the real meaning behind those words. And that's what you want to avoid.

This is one of those things I struggle with, and I must keep renewing my vow to appreciate each without getting too overwhelmed. In order to do that, I usually turn to Viktor Frankl, a man who lived through and survived the death camps of Auschwitz, lost nearly every family member and lost his homeland. By today's standards he had every right to be a bitter, depressed, ungrateful person, but he was anything but..

In his book, *Man's Search for Meaning*, he said:

"The one thing you can't take away from me is the way I choose to respond to what you do to me. The last of one's freedoms is to choose one's attitude in any given circumstance. Regardless of what happens to you, you can always choose to be <u>grateful</u> by imagining how it could have been worse."

Another huge inspiration of mine is Nelson Mandela. In his autobiography, *Long Walk to Freedom*, he writes about his 27 years in prison and what ultimately led to his freedom. His gratitude is in the form of optimism:

"I am fundamentally an optimist. Whether that comes from nature or nurture, I cannot say. Part of being optimistic is keeping one's head pointed toward the sun, one's feet moving forward. There were many dark moments when my faith in humanity was sorely tested, but I would not and could not give myself up to despair. That way lays defeat and death."

Lastly, Elie Wiesel, author, winner of the Nobel Peace Prize and a survivor of Auschwitz, writes in his novel *Night*: "No one is as capable of gratitude as one who has escaped the kingdom of night." To me, this says that if you have escaped suffering, you are probably more likely to recognize the possibility of gratitude.

Mindfulness, unlike gratitude, is not how you look at things, rather, *that* you look at things. Period. The best way mindfulness was ever explained to me is this: you've hiked to the top of a very high mountain and at the summit, which you have never been to before, what do you do? What is your reaction? For most of us it is to simply look in awe of the view, as it is, not as it should be. We don't think about the climb up. We don't dwell on the inevitable climb down. We don't say, "this view would look so much better if that mountain were over there instead." We just take in the very moment as it exists because we know it will not last. We know our time with that view is limited.. That is mindfulness.

Sylvia Boorstein puts it this way: "Mindfulness is the aware, balanced acceptance of the present experience. It isn't more complicated than that. It is opening to or receiving the present moment, pleasant or unpleasant, just as it is, without either clinging to it or rejecting it."

It's often easy to be mindful on mountain peaks or in the depths of dark, mysterious canyons. I know I try to breathe in every detail of the ocean when I am standing at the shore. But the power of mindfulness traverses awe-inspiring moments as well as the mundane. And that is the true trick. To be mindful and fully present in front of your partner, your children, your boss, is not nearly as glamorous as standing on top of a mountain. But that is when mindfulness works wonders! Jon Kabat-Zinn, a biologist who created a mindfulness-based stress-reduction program (MBSR) and is the author of *Full Catastrophe Living: Using the Wisdom of Your Body and Mind to Face Stress, Pain, and Illness*, wrote, "Look at other people and ask yourself if you are really seeing them or just your thoughts about them."

We so often make stuff up about people. We fantasize about who they could be or should be. We imagine a future with them. We try on their last name even before we've had a third date. We "fill in the blank" with information we don't know. Stop. Don't do that. Don't create a person you wish for. Just be present and see the person as he or she exists in front of you. It's hard work. It takes practice. But mindfulness along with gratitude can change how you perceive the world. Mindfulness can help you see people for who they really are, even when you don't want to. But you have to, in order to grow. And once you do, gratitude is there to support you.

PART IV: DATING, THE NEW YOU

"Wisely and slow; they stumble that run fast."

–William Shakespeare, Romeo and Juliet

Vibe check complete! You did it. Pat yourself on the back. You've come a long way. In section I you demolished your old, outmoded self by learning about love addiction, obsession and self-avoidance. In section II, you tossed your dysfunctional relationship out after reading (and believing) that you deserve better than scraps. In section III you rebuilt yourself by using tools such as getting rid of old defense mechanisms, learning your values, and building healthy boundaries. You're a machine! Now it's time to put all your training to good use and get out there and date!

Bzzzzzz!!!! (That's the sound of a game show buzzer signaling the wrong answer).

I'd be a horribly bad life coach if I led you to think your process is that linear and perfect. It's not. I truly hope it happened that quickly and seamlessly for you. But, in actuality, learning doesn't happen that way. In my process, I had good days and bad. I would have ah-ha moments and learn a ton, then seemingly forget it all. I backtracked. I even ran back to the very guy I swore off. You too might keep repeating the same mistake until you get it. But! I have news for you. This is normal. You are far closer to figuring things out after having read the first three chapters than if you had read or learned nothing. So, not only pat yourself on the back, give yourself a break. This next section is to be read when you're ready. Ready to date, ready to be single, ready for whatever. You may think you're never ready! Remember, dating is NOT the goal for everyone. That's so important to know. Rebuilding your-self is the goal. And while this section on dating is definitely for those of us who want to test out our newfound strengths and want more info on dating in general, it can also offer invaluable insight on intimate relationships with family, friends or other platonic partnerships. Note too that this section is filled with lots of exercises, more than any other. The reason for that is to prepare you for taking action toward this next phase of your life, with or without a partner. And since we can all agree that healthy relationships—platonic or not—are in our best interest, let's keep learning...

CHAPTER 25

Are You Ready for a Healthy Relationship?

"AM TALL, stylish, blue-eyed, blonde, live in eastern state, wish to correspond with gentleman living west of the Missouri, poor or rich can write, all answered: am not wealthy. Box 821, Lincoln Neb. "

–Omaha World Herald personal ad (Omaha, Nebraska), 14 January 1900, page 10

"For those of us accustomed to sailing through life effortlessly, real relationships present unaccustomed demands. It takes more than social contact, good times, clever conversations, interesting stories, and lively exchanges to make a friendship. Profound relationships develop over years and involve all that it means to be human."

—Kenneth W. Christian, PhD, author of *Your Ow n Worst Enemy*

As badly as most of us want a healthy relationship, we sometimes opt for the fiery, passionate, drama-driven, chaotic version instead. Sure, that's fine. There's a time and place for everything. But the crazier, wilder, and more intense a relationship is, the less able it will usually be to outlast the desire and heat it's built upon. What goes up must come down, and the more extreme the altitude, the more drastic the crash back down to earth. And then what are you left with? A flattened blob of yourself on the pavement of life.

But the alternative is a completely different beast. Healthy relationships tend to look, feel and be different for many different reasons, mostly because the participants have created it that way. So are you ready for a healthy relationship? Many of us aren't. Many are not long out of one relationship before diving into another. Or we don't have a decent model of a loving relationship, and so we grab whatever comes our way. Or maybe we still think we want drama and intensity versus the secure, loving comfort of intimacy.

Here are a list of challenges and solutions that will help make you stronger and more receptive to healthy love:

- **No model of a healthy relationship**: If you witnessed your parents fighting all the time, or your dad ignored your mom, or your mom was an alcoholic, or your parents hated each other (you get my point), these are not the best models to follow. And yet, we go out into the world and find mates based on how we learned to love as a child.

What to do about it: Learn to follow a new healthier model. As an adult, we can teach ourselves the type of love we want by watching and imitating couples who inspire us! It was one of the most life-changing things I've ever done. Observing well-functioning couples made me feel as if I had been riding a bike backwards my whole life. No wonder it had gotten me nowhere. When my mother re-married seven years after divorcing my father, I was able to witness a truly beautiful and healthy relationship, unlike the one I had grown up with. If you don't have access to a healthy relationship model, go find one! Ask around. Look around. No one has a perfect relationship, but millions have healthy loving relationships.

- **No proper grieving period**: When a relationship is over, whether you called it off or not, you need to grieve. Period.

What to do about it: You need to spend a decent amount of alone-time trying to put your life back together, figuring out who you are and finding your center. Without this period of coming to terms with the end of *that* relationship and self-centering, you risk choosing a new relationship based on flimsy things like loneliness, neediness and sadness. A partner is not supposed to "be" in your life, he or she is supposed to compliment your own awesomeness. And here's something to really pay attention to: not grieving could be a sign you were not in the last relationship for intimacy with the person, per se, but rather, for the intensity of the relationship, *any* relationship. This relates closely to the next point...

- **Jumping into a new relationship before the old one is officially over**: Like I said above, when you do not have a healthy amount of alone-time in between relationships, it tends to be a sign that you sought intensity, not intimacy in your past relationship. Almost anyone with chemistry can create that intensity, so replacing him or her is relatively easy.

  What to do about it: The healthier option is to spend some serious time looking back at the person you broke up with to see where YOU might have gone wrong. What you might want in a new partner and what you might want to avoid are key things you need to learn before heading into relationship number [fill in the blank].

- **Choosing the same unhealthy person over and over**: My mother used to say, "You will get the same problem over and over again until you learn to fix it." For me, my biggest gripe was, "Why are the same kind of guys always attracted to me? Why can't I attract healthy guys?" In following my mother's advice, I never figure out I was allowing these types of guys in. *Duh*. That it was in my power to start to be more selective. That being said, if you're dating the same "type" over and over (especially ones who tend to hurt you, frustrate you, or create suffering) you have not learned to "fix" this problem.

  What to do about it: Read more about love addiction, even if you think you're not a love addict, build your self-esteem, learn what your values are. Learn what it takes to change. These are all ways in which you can grow out of repeat patterns that hold you down. Oh, and one other thing: learn to love differently, learn to accept love differently. When we repeat the same toxic patterns, it's because we are looking for the same way in which to love and be loved. There are other ways. Keep reading to find out.

- **Not being a healthy person yourself:** How do you expect to attract a healthy partner if you, yourself are manipulating, lying, cheating, acting out, abusive, angry, miserable_and so on? You can't do it. Well, you might be able to attract a healthy partner, but you will not be able to sustain a relationship with a healthy partner if you possess these qualities. Why? Because, forget what you were told about "opposites attract." Not in this situation. In this situation, like attracts like. Water seeks its own level.

  What to do about it: You need to be the healthy person you want to connect with. You know the Gandhi-ish quote you see on bumper stickers? *Be the change you wish to see in the world.* Same thing when it concerns love. In fact, Gandhi's real quote is somewhat more applicable: "If we could change ourselves, the tendencies in the world would also change. As a man changes his own nature, so does the attitude of the world change towards him... We need not wait to see what others do." Changing yourself as a love partner means building self-esteem, being able to take care of yourself mentally, emotionally, financially and physically, and being able to enter into a relationship as an equal partner, not someone who is looking for a fix or a hole to fill. When we can create within ourselves a healthier individual, we no longer need to fight so hard to "find" a healthy partner or create a healthier partner. Others' perception of us will have changed.

- **Expecting too much from dating:** I've added this in because let's be honest, dating well is a skill we need to learn. It's not exactly something we all inherently know how to do.

  What to do about it: For most of us who tend to set expectations way too high when it comes to dating, reading a book or two on how to date can be helpful. I talk about what we can and cannot expect from a date in the sidebar, "Tips for Healthy

Dating," in section 34. Judith Sills "A Fine Romance," will also put dating into perspective if you want a deeper look at the life cycle of dating to marriage.

- **You're not looking for a healthy relationship:** *Hello?!* I know this seems obvious, but you don't know how often people *say* they want a healthy relationship, but *do* something completely different–like, chase after an unavailable person, fall in love with a bad boy, settle for someone who is not their equal, or who remain in a relationship with someone they aren't remotely in love with. Say what you mean and mean what you say. Your words, hopes, dreams, wishes must be in alignment with your actions. We do the same in so many other arenas of our life too: we *say* we want a better job, but we *do* nothing about it. We *say* we want to go back to school but we don't apply. We *say* we want to make changes but we don't budge.

- **What to do about it:** Quit settling for less than what you deserve. Stop selling yourself short by dating someone who's only interested in booty calls. Dump the guy or girl you're not into so you can finally make yourself available for the someone you truly love. And read and re-read the parts of this book about availability. Know that if you're dating an unavailable partner, chances are YOU are also unavailable.

i. **Are You Available?**

By this point, we can pretty much conclude unavailable people are really poor choices when it comes to healthy relationships. We now know many of their traits: they don't want to be in a relationship, or they're married, or they have other commitments that seem to keep them from coming around, or they're in prison, or whatever. You get my point. When we look at these types of traits in others, it makes sense. We can clearly begin to see their unavailability.

But what about us? What about someone who continuously holds on to an unavailable partner? What about someone who is seemingly locked into a relationship with a partner who is not fully…*there?*

Newsflash: they are unavailable too.

Yeah, I hear you. *But! They were totally available when I first met them.* But, they're not available now. Now what?

Think about it. Are we truly available and ready for love if we stay with partners who are unavailable, closed-off, not present? Are we truly available if we remain with people who are afraid of commitment, intimacy, and closeness? What does their behavior say about ours?

Here's where the extent of our denial makes itself known. The beliefs we use to convince ourselves of our own availability seem crystal clear: I *am* available; all I want is love; I'm the one in the relationship making all the plans and pushing forward. I do everything shy of begging him to be present and involved in my life.

But these are not signs of availability. These are signs of our own fear of commitment, our neediness, and a desire to control what we cannot control. Natalie Lue, blogger and author of *Mr. Unavailable and the Fallback Girl,* puts it like this:

> Like attracts like, so he masks his fear of commitment by just refusing to commit to an outcome and seeing what he can get en route, and *you* mask your fear of commitment by taking up with men who are the least likely candidates for giving you commitment…You're committing to *not* committing. (2008)

And this is the thing. When we try to have a healthy relationship with someone who either can't or refuses to, it makes us betrayers of ourselves. It makes us just as unhealthy. It makes us just as unavailable too.

When we are truly available for a committed healthy relationship, we pursue and stay with partners who want the same things we want. We pursue and stay with partners who are as willing as we are to step up to the plate and do the heavy lifting it takes to love and be together. And we do not waste our valuable time trying to convince anyone to love us, or be with us. We commit to people we can be our best selves with. Not our naggy, raging, angry, frustrated, disillusioned selves.

I remember my mother saying to me that dating unavailable guys was like "trying to get blood from a stone." But she failed to give me a metaphor for myself and my own issues with unavailability. How about this? It's like telling everyone you're a vegetarian while you're chomping on a steak. You're saying you're one thing, when in actuality, you're another. Even more disturbing, you're telling yourself that you're one way, when you're really not. You're something else entirely. That is self-deception at its finest.

So, here's how you fix this. You want to be available? Well then, make yourself available. Get rid of the guys you're not serious about. Get rid of the guys who aren't serious about you. Make a concerted effort to date men who are present and available. Then, be willing to let go of partners who can't make an obvious and honest commitment through their actions, not just their words.

CHAPTER 26

The Importance of Being Single

"You alone are enough. You have nothing to prove to anybody."

–Maya Angelou

If you possess even a shred of love addiction, you will see the word "single" and immediately skip over this section or close the book. Don't do it! Take a deep breath. Let's just explore the idea of singleness, nice and easy, as if you were doing research, "for a friend."

Being single, to some of us, is like being in solitary confinement on Riker's Island. It's a prison sentence. It's worse than a medieval torture chamber. Worse than being eaten by a crocodile. Worse than sitting with your married/coupled friends as they discuss how wonderful being together is! You get my point. And this horror or jealousy, or intolerance, or whatever you want to call it, comes from fear. Plain and simple. Fear of being alone, fear of the unknown, fear of failure. What's more, our fear of being alone is gender biased. It happens more to women than men. Writer and clinical psychologist Karin Arndt, PhD explains it like this:

> "I see this fear of aloneness in my female patients far more than my male patients, and I believe this mirrors a reality in the larger culture…For so many of my female patients, the fear of being alone has two primary facets. First, there is dis-comfort associated with being alone on a day-to-day basis. When alone they feel antsy, uncomfortable, lonely, or bored and employ a variety of methods to avoid feeling that way. The second facet involves a fear of being alone into their older years — the fear of being the dreaded "spinster." This fear should not be underestimated. It haunts the lives of so many women and oftentimes dictates a woman's life choices. Many women will often choose ANYTHING to avoid the imagined fate of the spinster." (*Psychology Today, 2018*)

My fear of being alone, indeed, was one of the driving forces behind getting married to a complete stranger after knowing him only six months online and about 5 weeks in person. My fear of being alone made me stay in a painful, toxic marriage long past the point of dignity. And my fear and hatred of being alone made me fall into a relationship with an avoidant right after I was divorced. The fear of being alone, in fact, outweighed any discomfort, anger, rage or frustration I ultimately felt dating an avoidant.

But in 2008 at age 40, after yet another emotionally devastating break-up, and facing what I imagined was a partnerless, solitary future, along came…another guy to save me…

Cue the sound of screeching brakes! Cue the record scratch! Cue the distant scream!

Actually, another guy didn't come along. Another guy didn't save me. I saved me. How? For the first time ever, I made peace with my singleness.

Aloneness was a sensation I had avoided all my life. But here I was faced with the inevitability of confrontation. And when you are faced with your worst fear you have a choice: you can either bury your head in the sand and avoid, avoid, avoid. Or, you can rise out of the ashes, dust yourself off and face the beast. I was done with avoiding. It didn't serve me. And so, I decided to face the beast.

I broke out my armor and my weapons, and I headed into the world. I.e. I didn't shave my legs, wax my eyebrows, or wear anything remotely alluring (*hello sweat pants and Uggs*). I think I only brushed my teeth once a day. And I certainly didn't bother putting make-up on (except lipstick. Can't live without that). And what happened? I had a whole new appreciation for the concept of liberation and freedom. What a burden it is to always be tuned into the world around you. To always be on the lookout for a potential partner. It's actually exhausting (something you only know when you begin to appreciate your singleness).

Of course, I had to dig deep to figure out what single women "do." I hadn't been truly single since before my marriage in 1996. And at forty, going out to nightclubs wasn't really an option, nor an interest. Are there even nightclubs anymore?

My first stop was the bookstore. I found myself perusing the shelves for books on being single. I soon learned that every jacket cover was pink. And worse, according to these books there's really only two types of single women you could be. You could be the one who lays on the sofa in her ugliest PJs, chomping on day-old pizza and watching re-runs of Sex in the City or Bridget Jones' Diary. Or you could be a Kardashian-type girl who shops the hell out of her singleness and serial dates as if she only has one week to live.

I was neither. Well, I was a combination of both. And a whole lot more.

And this is the point I'd like to make. Singleness is a neutral state of being that allows you to figure out who you are. It is neither good nor bad; right or wrong. It just is. And it's your job, it's your responsibility to figure out what to do with it.

Using your single time to wait for the love of your life is not what I mean. Waiting for the next in line and dreaming up the moment he or she appears can be detrimental. And I'll tell you why. Because when we wait for someone to come along, we are more apt to fling ourselves into relationship with *anybody* who shows up. Because the goal is not to click with someone, get to know someone and possibly fall in love. Nope. The main goal is to not be single. And we all know that 'discerning taste' isn't exactly an attribute if you're just trying to not be single.

My second stop was my own journal. I sat in front of the empty pages until I could come up with a list of things I've always wanted to do and become. Forget Bridget Jones. I didn't want to take my single life sitting down on my threadbare sofa in my threadbare robe. I wanted all the things I had given up all those years while I was focused on finding a relationship. The lightbulb finally went off and in its glare I realized that much of my life had been a waste of valuable time. So here's what I put on the list:

Publish something. Paint. Go rock climbing. Run. Start up your own company. Volunteer. Collect donations for the poor. Meditate. Train for a marathon. Go back to school. Take a road trip. Plant a garden. Throw a Dear Diary party. Take a cooking class. Direct a short film. Go to Morocco.

Note none of these goals entailed being partnered. When you live out your singleness and enjoy life, what you're actually doing is celebrating yourself. You are making peace with who you are. Because let's be real, if you aren't happy single, you most likely won't be happy in a partnership.

Finally, I stopped dreaming. I said goodbye to fantasy and I actually started to work. I worked at all the things on my bucket list, and I took action. Before, I was just Intention-Girl. I would dream up these things, but I never put them into action, because, thank God, a man would come around and I wouldn't have to. I could stay safe. When I was single, I didn't worry any longer about being safe. I worried that I wouldn't have enough time to enjoy this time alone, without distractions.

Yes, for the first time in my life, I saw dating and romance as a distraction. Something that got in the way of me being me and getting to work on things I loved. And that's the key. The story you tell yourself about your singleness is what will make your experience wonderful or horrifyingly lonely.

And don't get me wrong. I spent many nights alone and crying. I second-guessed myself. *Maybe this is all just an attempt to cover up my loneliness,* I moaned. But I reminded myself that love and relationships were more the culprit. They were my attempt to cover up the hard work of being me.

Being single is so important. You must learn to be single—at least a little while. In that space alone you can think. You can be. You can work. You can grow. You can get closer to the one person who will be with you through thick and thin, the one person you can always rely on: you.

i. **The Purpose of You**

> *"We begin to find and become ourselves when we notice how we are already found, already truly, entirely, wildly, messily, marvelously who we were born to be."*
>
> –Anne Lamott

It's time to find the purpose of you, and your single life is the best way to do it. We don't want this to be another six months of waiting for the next partner to come along. We want to squeeze the pulp out of every day that we are alone. And our goal is to figure out our purpose.

Years ago, when I went through this phase, I thought my purpose in life was to love myself. Isn't that the first bit of advice we all get when it concerns failed relationships? *Well, you didn't love yourself enough.* Ugh. I thought I was all right. I didn't completely hate me. And, while that was part of my purpose—to be more comfortable with myself while alone—there was a bigger one. Since I used relationships to hide behind and to avoid my own issues and responsibilities, I had to figure out what I was hiding from all these years. What the heck was I so scared of?

A therapist told me once that I was probably scared of being alone. But I wasn't buying that. If I was scared of being alone, what exactly did my aloneness mean? There must have been something buried even deeper. And so, I sat alone. And I felt the awkwardness of it. And I squirmed a bit. I felt panicky and uncomfortable. It occurred to me after I sat there alone long enough that when I was alone, truly alone, it meant that I was forced to create a life for myself. That a life wouldn't just be handed to me. When I no longer had the distraction of thinking about my relationships it was like a black hole opened up, a vacuum, and I had to fill it with something or get sucked in. And that was scary as heck. So scary, in fact, that I would continue to bear a torch for my past relationship, even if I was the one who did the breaking up, just so I didn't have to face the idea that in this emptiness, I had to work. I had to be responsible. And I had to take care of myself. Something in me still wanted to be a kid. Something in me was determined to never grow up. And for years, I didn't. I was a female Peter Pan.

And then I dug even deeper. One afternoon, I was reading the bios of writers who had their essays selected for publication in an online literary magazine called FreshYarn.com (If you get the chance, read *Diamonds* by

Jill Solloway from the first installment. It's fab!). The more I read the sicker I became. In fact, my stomach heaved and I was overtaken by a powerful sensation of nausea. Every bio I read was bursting with one achievement after another. Tiny lifetimes of success. This one, an executive producer; that one, the writer of three collections of short stories; another, an Emmy-award-winning writer for blah, blah, blah. Twenty, thirty successes each. Not one of the bios said, "Jane Smith, mom of two. Keeper of journals." You get my point. I took a wrong turn in internet land and ended up in a world unrecognizable to me. A world of achievers. It hurt. And the pain came directly from the thought, *What would my bio say?*

Of course, the over-dramatic version came to me quickly:

Tracy lived at home until she was 27, quit college in '95, married, had babies. She moved to the suburbs, changed a million diapers, attended horrifying Longaberger Basket parties and became highly skilled at no-fault divorce proceedings. She has written voraciously for most of her life but, to date, has only published one 4-page, double-spaced short story in an online magazine that earned her fourteen dollars and thirty-seven cents. She is, however, a great kisser and has fallen in love nearly 50 (count 'em FIFTY) times.

My relationship experience would put any of those writers to shame. And yet, I wasn't even good at that, apparently.

And so, I decided that my purpose was not exactly to be a success. But to achieve little successes, in my own way, of importance to me. My purpose was to be myself through my art and somehow figure out how to earn money doing what I love.

Exercise: What is your purpose? How deep can you dig? Forget that your parents messed you up. Forget your fear of abandonment. Forget your fear of being alone. What does aloneness mean to you? It scares you for a reason. What reasons can you find?

CHAPTER 28

Find a Better Model of a Loving Relationship

"Monkey see; monkey do"

–West African proverb

As I've said before, growing up, I never had a decent "model" of a loving couple. My parents' marriage seemed bizarre to me, to say the least, in that my dad did whatever he wanted and my mother let him because she believed he knew what he was doing (little did she know!). And little did I know that this relationship dynamic is very common. It can be labeled Narcissist (father) and Empath (mother); or, Addict (father) and Co-Dependent (mother); or Abuser (father) and Victim (mother). Whatever you want to call it, it was not a good model of love. The man my mother married after my parents divorced was a man who was present, loving, kind, respectful and hard-working—virtually the complete opposite of my father. They would go on to have one of the most beautiful, most healthy relationships I had ever seen. Their relationship, in fact, became the new model for what I went out and looked for myself later in life.

My mother's second husband has always supported my mother and stood by her. He never stopped buying her flowers or helping her do dishes. They wake in the morning at the same time, and go to bed at the same time. They work together, live together, travel together and eat together. They are very kind and loving towards each other.

They've been this way since 1989, when they first started dating. But for many years, I refused to identify with him or see him as any kind of father figure because I had my own father. And so, for all those years, I still used my father as a model of the man I wanted. I guess I did that because I was a devoted daughter. *Mom left you, but I won't!* And I didn't. I even dated men like him for many years past his death in 2004. Especially then. Something in me felt far too loyal to my dad to ever think of abandoning him by dating someone unlike him. How messed up is that?

The trouble was I didn't really like my dad. I didn't trust him or feel safe with him or feel comfortable when I went to visit him. Sure, I loved him. And sure, he was entertaining and exciting. And there was a great sense of danger and adventure when I'd see him. I never knew what kind of weirdness would be going on. In fact, his life was one of the greatest sources of storytelling for our family. And I did love telling stories. But I wasn't mature enough to recognize that using him as a model for a boyfriend was not the best idea. I didn't realize that I could love my father, be faithful to him as a daughter, but still seek out someone more compatible and felt RIGHT to me. I mean, heck, for many years I thought like my mother. That my father's way was the right way and it felt normal and good to be loved the way he loved us. While his way might have worked for my mom, it didn't work for me.

It took a lot of growing up to realize no one has a choice when it comes to picking and choosing a dad or mom or any parental figure. But we all have a choice when it comes to whom we choose as a partner later in life!

So…I guess it had been happening all along, but I wasn't aware of it until about 2004 (when I divorced) that I was starting to look at my stepdad as a better model for me. This was huge, because it meant realigning myself with a father-figure who was not mine by birth. It meant betraying my own father. And yet, I was willing to take that risk. My survival depended upon it.

So, even though I was not yet one-hundred percent convinced I could be dating from a better pool of men, I would ask my mother important questions about her relationship. The dialogue below includes my questions along with her answers. I think it's very important to share this so you too can start to reassess who your "teachers" of love are:

- **Me: "Do you ever get a sick feeling in your stomach when you're with your husband?"**

- **Mom:** Only in the beginning when I first started dating him and didn't know him. I felt a sense of doubt and dread and confusion in the beginning. This is normal. It comes from feeling hurt in the past and being scared of the future. But that went away quickly. I loved him and, it took time, but I trusted him.

- **Me: "Do you ever feel like you want to run away, or date someone else?"**

- **Mom** No.

- **Me: "Do you want to change him?"**

- **Mom:** I love everything about his core, who he is. He does, however, have some annoying traits, like he collects piles of magazines and holds on to them for years. If I had my druthers, I'd throw them out (the magazines). But no, there's nothing I would "change" about him. I love him as is and I can handle any of his less appealing qualities.

- **Me: "Do you hate him sometimes?"**

- **Mom:** Hate? No. He can get on my nerves sometimes, but there's always a bigger picture. Do you ever "hate" your kids? Or do they simply annoy you from time to time? It's the same thing.

- **Me: "Do you always trust him or do you doubt him sometimes?"**

- **Mom:** I always trust him. There is nothing he has ever done to prove otherwise.

- **Me: "Are you always happy?"**

- **Mom:** No one is always happy. But for the most part, I'm happy! More than happy, I'm grateful.

- **Me: "Do you think he would ever cheat on you?"**

- **Mom:** Years ago the thought crossed my mind. And of course, you go through phases where you always have to say to yourself, "Nothing is certain," but we've been together 30 years and he has always been true to me.

- **Me: "Were there or are there now any red flags with him?"**

- **Mom:** When we first started dating, I made assumptions. I came from a very bad relationship, so I didn't trust any man at all. That distrust led me to initially harbor suspicions about him (such as he was a liar, he was boring, he was hiding some big secret). It was like I was shell-shocked in those early days. Looking back, my suspicions about him, though they all turned out to be unwarranted, were my way of protecting myself. They also kept him at a safe distance until I could get to know him better BEFORE making an emotional investment. So, to answer your question, he had no red flags and still has no red flags (there are men and women without them, can you believe it?!) but at first I wouldn't believe it. I think to be suspicious and have doubts, at least in the beginning, until someone can prove they can be trusted through their actions, is a good thing.

- **Me: "What are your overall thoughts on your husband?"**

- **Mom:** That he is a gift. And that I have been very fortunate to have him after what I've been through.

From these questions and by observing their relationship over the years, I knew I wanted that kind of relationship too. I wanted a man who was decent and trustworthy and loving and affectionate. I wanted a family man who put family before anything else. I wanted a man who had no addictions, who didn't lie or cheat or embarrass me. I wanted a man who was stable and reliable and hard-working.

When we use our own fathers or mothers as models of the perfect man or woman, we do so subconsciously, instinctively. It seems a natural, biological manifestation of being human and passing on our genetic traits. And yet, for the sake of inner happiness, we sometimes need to break with tradition and find someone outside our circle of familiarity.

I think when we don't have a healthy model of a loving relationship, we too often turn to Hollywood, or romance novels. We also tend to think a healthy relationship is one and the same as "passion" or "hot, steamy sex" or drama-driven LOVE. It is none of those things on their own. They may be components, but they do not complete the picture of "loving relationship." I'm sure many of us know how to love. But how many know how to sustain a "loving relationship?" Passion, infatuation, chemistry; these are just first steps.

Rebuilding helps bring us to these realizations so that we may make better choices. And although changing our ways feels unnatural at first, you will get used to the changes you make, and then, they will work their magic on your life.

Exercise: If you haven't done this already, now's the time to look at your parents. Are they a good model of a loving relationship? What did they teach you? Do you keep dating your father or your mother? Maybe you continuously seek out a brother or sister figure. Whoever you may be drawn to, try to figure out why, and then, ask yourself if this person is a good match for you. Look at qualities like neglect or avoidance or unavailability. If you are always attracted to avoidants, for example, try to find the parent who was most avoidant. He or she is most likely the one who taught you to love that way. Then, go through your inventory of couples you know or are able to observe. Include an aunt and uncle or your grandparents, and coworkers. Who among them seem to have healthy, successful relationships? Hone in on how they communicate, how they resolve their problems. This is how you relearn to love in a healthier way.

CHAPTER 29

A Successful Healthy Relationship Looks Like...

"Once the realization is accepted that even between the closest human beings infinite distances continue, a wonderful living side by side can grow, if they succeed in loving the distance between them which makes it possible for each to see the other whole against the sky."

–Rainer Maria Rilke

Let's segue now into what makes for a successful relationship and examine its five basic components: values, trust, communication, respect and love. Remember, no relationship is perfect. But, you can come pretty close. It's just like trying on a pair of jeans. That perfect fit seems elusive. And then one day, in the "New This Season" aisle…you find the love of your life. The jeans, that is.

Values

Can anyone really be sure his or her relationship with a partner is a "success?" About 12 years ago the successful relationship I was in really wasn't. Sure, I loved the guy, and he loved me (or so he thought), and we laughed a lot, we had sex a lot, we communicated relatively well, and we never fought. Of course, I still fretted over whether or not he could be trusted. And I would catch him in little lies here and there. And there was that sense of dread I always had that he would go out with his friends and drink or do drugs (which was a big deal-breaker for me). But I stuffed those feelings and ignored them, because, in my mind, the bigger picture was that we were getting along so well. The bigger picture was to keep the peace and not sweat "the small stuff." Little did I know that lies, mistrust, drugs…those aren't examples of "small stuff."

And it worked, me not sweating the small stuff. Until it didn't.

When we split up, I was dumbfounded. How could something so perfect have failed? After a significant amount of time crying and mourning the relationship's passing, the obvious made itself known (as it always does). We, as a couple, liked each other, we were even extremely attracted to each other mentally, physically, even emotionally. But—and again, this is a reiteration on values—we did not share certain core values that, after time, started to betray both of us. The biggie? Drugs. He was a chronic pot smoker and wasn't able to give it up like he initially thought he could. It was a huge part of his life. I, on the other hand, felt that any drug when used in excess destroyed life and I didn't want to date or be married to someone who constantly smoked. The important thing to note here is that neither of us were right or wrong. Smoking pot is perfectly acceptable for millions of people, but it wasn't OK for me. Someone who plays video games 24/7 is perfectly acceptable for millions of people but it's not OK for me. And likewise, a woman who has two kids and lives in the suburbs is a perfectly acceptable partner for millions of people. But it wasn't OK for this guy. I was in a relationship with a man who didn't share my core values and I didn't share his. He could sense it. And I could sense it too. We were both betraying ourselves for the sake of the relationship. We were not honoring our core values. And when people do not share the same core values in life, or honor their own, the relationship has a much bigger chance of failing.

So what does any of this have to do with a successful relationship?

As I've mentioned before in Chapter 13, sharing **values** with your partner is the key most important ingredient to a healthy relationship. Sharing similar interests is helpful, but if you don't share similar values, you are building a rather shaky foundation for your future together. This means it is imperative to know what your values are *before* you go out looking for a life partner, *before* you accept just anyone into your life. For example, one of my values is that I cannot date men who do drugs or have a drinking problem. I realized this value late in life, but for the longest time knew I had an extreme aversion to even the most socially harmless recreational drug use. For years I tried to be like everyone else and just accept that other people didn't feel the same way. But each time it came up, it interfered with my emotional and mental peace of mind and literally put me in pain. I realized too that it didn't so much bother me when a friend drank or used drugs (because I didn't live with that friend), but it bothered me enormously if someone closer to me, like a boyfriend, did. His substance use had a greater impact on my life. Finally, I realized something very important: my aversion to drugs may not be balanced or healthy, but it's not going anywhere and I had to start making peace with it. I also had to start honoring my own spirit by staying away from people who didn't feel the same way. As soon as "no drugs" became a value of mine, I was able to look for someone who shared it.

Exercise: Write a list of your core values. It can be anything from "I need a partner who desires me physically," to "I will only date men who do not lie, cheat or steal." A value is stronger than a preference. "I prefer women with red hair" is not exactly a value, it's a preference. If you don't find it, you can live without it. A value, on the other hand, marks something you cannot live without. Once you have a clearer picture of what is most important to you, start stacking those values up against how well you hold yourself to them. For example, if you have "I only want to surround myself with people who accept my children and treat them with kindness and respect" on your values list, how well do you uphold that value? Do the people in your life adhere to this value of yours? Remember: values are in place to keep you safe and to allow you to honor your core self and help you maintain a peaceful, healthy life. Your values are what you're worth.

Trust

Equally important for a successful relationship is **trust**. Both you and your partner need to trust each other and be trusted in return. Without trust, almost any relationship will fall apart. If you are anything like me, a love addict who grew up in a family in which she was unable to trust one parent, then you will have a very difficult time learning to trust someone you've just met. And when you enter into a new relationship, you need to take it slow and spend a fair amount of time questioning its honesty and validity. It is your way of protecting yourself from diving into something too quickly, or possibly getting hurt again. Building trust is a slow and oftentimes awkward process. Even if your new partner is completely trustworthy, he or she still needs to earn your trust. Remember to have patience with yourself and ask for patience from your partner, and in time, you will learn to trust again. If you don't see yourself making progress and constantly find yourself doubting or mistrusting your partner, you need to be completely honest with yourself. Do you feel this way because there is reason to doubt? Do you feel uncomfortable trusting them? If this is the case, he or she may not be entirely trustworthy and your instincts are picking up on it.

Exercise: Think of all the people in your life, friends, family members, co-workers, etc. Is there anyone you spend time with whose presence makes you feel completely relaxed and trusting? If yes, this is the "feeling" you want to achieve from your partner. If you are not feeling that same sense of calm, trust your instinct. There probably is a reason that you're in doubt.

Communication

A third vital component to any successful relationship is **communication**. Body language is great. Physical attraction is great. Compatibility is great. But if you and your partner can't understand one another, and if there isn't a mutual platform of comprehension, then there is, in my opinion, no relationship. Communication embodies everything from, "pass the potatoes," to deep conversations about the meaning of life. It also embodies every emotion you possess and the way you express them. Do you scream when you don't get your way? Do you pout when no one understands you? Do you throw things during an argument? Do you close down and sometimes refuse to talk if you're angry? How is your ability to negotiate? Do you lie? Are you passive aggressive? Are you a poor listener? These are all examples of ways in which communication can be completely sabotaged. The key to good communication is the ability to get your feelings and thoughts across to your partner in a calm, respectful, adult-like manner. It is to negotiate peacefully and respectfully, and to realize you will not always get your way or be understood. It is also to be a good listener. When we work towards change within ourselves, we tend to need better tools, better ways of doing things. Communication is a prime example. Our old tools, our old ways of getting what we want or avoiding situations we don't want don't always work in healthy relationships as well as they did in toxic ones. Pouting if we don't get what we want doesn't go over very well with someone who doesn't communicate in that way.

Raising our voices and screaming to make our point is a form of aggression. Healthy communicators don't communicate that way. To have any hope of communicating with a healthy person, one must speak their language, which is based on give and take and mutual respect. There are entire books written on communication. I've included recommendations in the resources section.

Exercise: how do you communicate with friends and family members? Do you find that you communicate differently with a partner? If so, why? Is it because the relationship draws it out of you this way? Write a list of some of the faulty ways you have tried to get your point across. Do you think you would communicate the same way if you were with someone healthy, who was a better listener, and didn't judge you?

Respect

Respect for self and for others lays the foundation for love, tolerance, patience, pleasure, gratification and so much more. When you have self-respect you have dignity. And when you have respect for others, you have a deeper understanding of what it is like to be human. The value of respect in a successful relationship can be measured by the strength and empowerment it creates between two people. Think back in your life and remember the respect bestowed by a teacher or a parent. How did that make you feel? Was it loved, empowered, motivated to return the emotion? Respect begets respect. It's as simple as that.

Exercise: Research the definition of "respect." For our purposes, it is a "feeling of deep admiration for someone elicited by their abilities, qualities or achievements." How does your partner size up to that definition? Does he or she have enough admirable qualities to earn your respect? If your partner has cheated on you repeatedly, how does "respect" play into your feelings for him or her? Do you respect yourself? Do you respect your partner? If there is a clear lack of respect, you need to assess your and your partner's reasons for staying together. People who love each other respect each other.

Love

As I've mentioned before "love" is not one thing. It's an umbrella term for a whole slew of things. To a love addict, the word is complicated. But for starters, I can tell you that love is NOT butterflies in the stomach or lust or sexual compatibility. Love is generally NOT anything that comes during the first three months of a hot and heavy, passionate relationship. Love is not "attraction" or "love at first sight" or even "attachment, or "need." And though it is very closely related to all those things, it is none of them independently. From my own healthy experience I can say that when I first met my current husband I experienced curiosity. Then I experienced doubt. Then interest. Then lust, butterflies, need, want, and sexual compatibility. Then friendship and closeness, and so on, all the while building a more solid foundation of trust, respect and communication while maintaining all my core values in the presence of this person. Under that scenario, "love" is time. It is a thing that is built between two people. And, this commitment to time and building must be mutual.

I also want to add that two people can love each other very much, even after MANY years, but treat each other poorly, disrespectfully, coldly and neglectfully. This was the scenario of my grandparents. My grandfather would say of my grandmother, "I love her, but I don't like her." She'd say the same. Even though this kind of experience qualifies as "love," it is not exactly a sign of a healthy, successful relationship. If you just have love and you don't have respect or peaceful communication, or trust; if you lack values and allow your partner to treat you poorly or neglect you, it's time to rebuild your notion of love.

Exercise: many of us still believe that "love will save the day," and "love conquers all," and "if he loves me, then everything will be OK." While this is great for Disney and Hollywood, it is not realistic for an actual healthy real live relationship. Relationships are not as superficial as Hollywood makes them out to be. And love may be one thing, but a successful relationship is something else completely. The bottom line is this: a successful relationship is not based on love alone. It is based on two people who have a mutual interest in loving, trusting, respecting, communicating, and being with the other and building a relationship while maintaining their core values. Ask yourself if this represents your current relationship. Does it have trust but not love? Does it have respect but poor communication? ALL these things are important to the whole of the relationship. Also, love is subjective. What is your definition of love? Do you need lots of space, or do you prefer closeness? How often do you prefer to have sex? What level of intimacy are you most comfortable with? A lot or a little? How do you wish a partner would show you love? Do you like to be called every day? Do you need him or her to buy you gifts every once in awhile? Do you need to hear, "I love you" often? The more you know about how you would like to be loved, the better chance you have of finding someone who can love you in ways you like.

Healthy Relationship

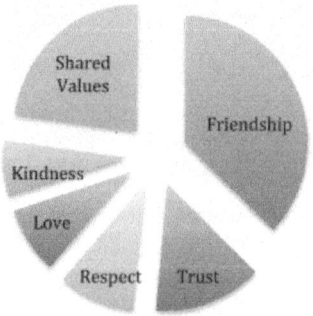

When we take a look at the Healthy Relationship pie, love is only one slice, not the whole darn dessert. So, in dating, push the idea of love aside, and see if you've got all the other things to build on. In my case, love was not what attracted to me to my husband in the beginning. And why should it have been? I didn't know him well enough! Love is the byproduct of mutual respect, chemistry, passion, friendship, trust and kindness, and these things take time. It's like a good stew, which needs to be cooked for hours in the crockpot. It is not something you get or feel right away.

So then what's that ravenous, crazed, yearning we feel, if not love?

In Helen Fisher's *Why We Love, The Nature and Chemistry of Why We Love*, she explains that love has three parts:

> Romantic love, I believe, is one of three primordial brain networks that evolved to direct mating and reproduction. *Lust*, the craving for sexual gratification, emerged to motivate our ancestors to seek sexual union with almost any partner. *Romantic love*, the elation and obsession of "being in love," enabled them to focus their courtship attentions on a single individual at a time, thereby conserving precious mating time and energy. And male-female *attachment*, the feeling of calm, peace and security one often has for a long-term mate, evolved to motivate our ancestors to love this partner long enough to rear their young together. (Fisher, 2004)

This process of romantic love can go off the rails if we are not in a healthy place. While I was acting out as a love addict I mistook intense emotions for love. The two are hugely different. Love is an umbrella term for passion, attraction, friendship, respect, and attachment shared between two people. Intense emotion for another person, however, is impulsive, chaotic and mostly irrational. It made me wonder if I was genuinely looking for a partner or if I was looking for just anyone to take care of me, to be with me.

In the early stages of dating it's so important to know the difference between unhealthy emotion and what the general population call love. I also want to clarify that the diagram above is not a "dating pie"; it's a healthy relationship pie. What's the difference? Love would not be on a dating pie, nor would trust or friendship (unless you both knew each other as friends for a long time). They are things the two people involved work to create. If these things are not created within the relationship over a significant amount of time, then you might have a relationship, all right, but it's not a healthy one.

Exercise: Make your own pie chart from a past relationship, and make a future pie chart of what you would prefer your relationship to be built on.

i. **Signs of a Healthy Partner**

Because I never knew what to look for in a good partner, I kept going after my "ideal." I looked for superficial things: looks, if they were sexy and good in bed, if they needed to be taken care of, etc. You know, important stuff! I also read too much into "signs" or Hollywood moments– if I had had a run in with an old friend in the rain and we both got stuck under his umbrella a la "Singing in the Rain," then he was the one for me. Or if we both have the same initials, it's meant to be. Not very mature or realistic standards to set for a relationship.

I never felt comfortable with apparent "good guys" either. They all seemed boring. It was the bad boy who made me feel like I had the potential to love and be "alive." I may have been attracted to bad boys, but sadly, I had a very immature notion of a good partner. When my priorities changed, my "ideal" man changed, and I quickly realize that "good guy" and "exciting guy who makes me feel alive" were not mutually exclusive! Good guys could actually be exciting too. Anyway, here is a list of things I believe are really good <u>indicators</u> of a healthy partner. But keep in mind, no one is "perfect" and no one will have all these qualities (or maybe they will!) but the idea is to have a sense of what you should be looking for when you are ready to date again. And to know a person's good qualities are not necessarily based on looks or "chemistry," but rather on the more concrete history of how they have lived their life up to the point of meeting you.

Above all else, know that it takes time to discover many of these traits in someone. You cannot meet a person and instantly know they possess all these things. If you think you can, you have a very shallow notion of getting to know someone. Likewise, there are good partners who do have skeletons in their closet, but they've honestly changed. It's your job to figure out of you can handle that. For now, here's my list...

He or she has....

- An honest nature
- A good reputation among his/her peers
- No history of cheating or fooling around
- No history of drugs or other addictions (unless it is in their past and resolved through their actions)
- A history of stability and commitment in a loving relationship, maybe even children and marriage
- An ability to express love and kindness to his or her children and other people
- Financial stability and security (knows how to handle his or her money).
- An ability to experience intimacy (not just intensity)
- A strong, loving family or set of friends
- Values, morals and beliefs that YOU agree with and respect
- An ability to be independent and take care of himself or herself
- Interests other than sex and dating
- Normal healthy behavior
- Is not just out for himself or herself
- A genuine sense of gratitude (is grateful)
- A genuine love of life (is happy)

- Compassion, sensitivity, kindness, hope and a positive outlook on life – A loyal nature

- A willingness to communicate and resolve conflict

- A willingness to compromise for the sake of the relationship

- Wellrounded and smart

- Fun, funny, can laugh at himself or herself

- Optimistic, but realistic

- Not afraid of struggling,

- Able to defer gratification

- Not avoidant of his or her responsibilities

- Able to give and receive

- Displays no abrupt or extreme behaviors

- Consistent

- Matches words with actions

- Open with you, not secretive

• We all come with baggage. And while some are still carrying theirs around and others are creating more, you want to find someone whose baggage you can deal with. There's no such thing as healthy baggage or unhealthy baggage. It's what an individual does with it that counts. And what's more, it's whether or not the two of you can deal with it. Someone who has a much-regretted minor one-night stand in their distant past is a lot different than someone who has a pattern of long-lasting extramarital affairs. What can you handle? We all have limits. Know yours. Check your values.

And, on that note, here's another slant on assessing a potential partner's deal-maker, or deal-breaker qualities.

ii. **Look for a Partner Who Does This, Not That**

Sometimes we lose sight of our priorities when it comes to dating. Or maybe, we toss our priorities out the window the millisecond we meet a really hot guy who lavishes a little attention on us. Hey. We all do it. Just like that, we forget what we're looking for, what we need and what will ultimately serve us well in the long run. Worse yet, we can easily get caught up in a fantasy of what we *think* we want and need. For the sake of immediate gratification, we forget all our values and fling ourselves into what we hope will be the relationship of our dreams.

For those of us who tend to lose all sight of ourselves the moment we're no longer single–as if being in a couple is the highest form of self–we tend to have an immature, superficial idea of love that is not so much based on health, stability, comfort and calm, as it is on neediness, desire, drama, and an urgency to fill an inner void . And, *tisk, tisk*, we even use people and relationships as a way to cope, or worse, to avoid the reality of our lives. As I've said, I did this for years until I learned to envision not only a healthier me, but a healthier partner.

I also learned that having a healthy relationship takes patience as well as the courage to say no to the wrong people. It takes a strong sense of self to be able to recognize good qualities in others, and not-so-good qualities. And above all, it takes the determination to love yourself to the point where you want healthy people, places and things in your life, not "Sure, why not. You'll do." Trust me. That never turns out well.

So, how can you tell good qualities from bad in a potential partner? How do you recognize healthy people versus unhealthy? Well, you look for people who do this...and not that. But be warned. Some of these points may seem sexist. I admit it. I'm old school.

- DOES THIS: **Asks you out on a date.** NOT THIS: Waits around for you to ask him out on a date

- DOES THIS: **Calls you and calls you back.** NOT THIS: Doesn't call you or call you back, and if he does, it's five days later.

- DOES THIS: **Makes time for you, wants to spend time with you.** NOT THIS: barely has time for you and when he does, it's usually in the bedroom, or on his terms.

- DOES THIS: **Lives a clean, healthy life.** NOT THIS: smokes, drinks to excess, does drugs, doesn't face or deal with his health issues, eats poorly, etc.

- DOES THIS: **Takes care of himself financially**. NOT THIS: Still lives with parents at 40, borrows money, in debt, gambles, doesn't work, or doesn't have a stable job that allows him to pay his bills and pay for a roof over his head without depending on others.

- DOES THIS: **Communicates well.** NOT THIS: Bottles everything up and won't talk, communicates only minimally, refuses to face emotional discussion, poor listener, manipulative, or bullies and screams to get his point across.

- DOES THIS: **Lives an honest, respectful life.** NOT THIS: Cheats, lies, is evasive and deceptive, dishonest in business, in personal matters or with strangers.

- DOES THIS: **Treats you (and others) with respect, care, kindness and dignity** NOT THIS: treats you poorly, ignores you, avoids you, is repeatedly unkind to you, controls you, etc.

- DOES THIS: **Enjoys you and likes you for who you are, not for what you could or should be.** NOT THIS: Expects you to be something or someone you are not. Tells you, "Maybe you should get a boob job," or "This roll of fat can definitely go."

- DOES THIS: **Is a genuinely happy person filled with gratitude.** NOT THIS: is a genuinely unhappy, angry, ungrateful person who whines and complains incessantly.

- DOES THIS: **Feels and acts passionate towards you.** NOT THIS: doesn't feel or act passionate towards you, withholds sex, love or affection, exhibits cold or inappropriate behavior, has a fear of intimacy that keeps him from trying to be close to you

- DOES THIS: **Is a grownup and acts like one**. NOT THIS: is immature, refuses to grow up, possesses classic Peter Pan characteristics and simply cannot get his act together.

CHAPTER 30.

Are YOU a Healthy Partner?

"You had the power all along my dear."

—Glinda the Good Witch in *The Wizard of Oz* by L. Frank Baum

We've been focusing so much on what a healthy partner can and should look like, but, what about you? You need to be everything you expect in a healthy partner. Perhaps the reason I spent so many years dating unhealthy men was because I myself was unhealthy. I was superbly pessimistic, whiny, needy, immature, impulsive, prone to living in a fantasy world, oversensitive, and had poor self-esteem. As if that weren't enough, I also suffered from ADHD, body dysmorphia, anxiety and depression. What a catch!

So where's the surprise when I went out into the world to look for my "second half," only to find avoidant, neglectful, pessimistic, egocentric, immature types who didn't have much to offer? In my mind, I was made this way, take it or leave it, and needed no changing. My "problem" wasn't me, it was that there were no decent guys out there.

So often, when I give support to people in the comments section of GirlRebuilt.com or answer their emails, I say things like: *You deserve better than that jerk*, or *You're worth more than someone who ignores you and treats you badly*. And, it's true. No one deserves to be treated badly. But, we need to clean up too before we begin to attract better quality people. We need to lose the labels we have created for ourselves and simply learn better ways to behave.

Trouble with most people is, we don't want to work on ourselves. And if we do, we want to do it within the safe confines of some bad relationship to keep us warm and comfy. So, basically here's the absurdity of what we really want: to keep a neglectful, immature, avoidant, unloving guy around (for sex, friendship and love) while we become mature, optimistic, loving, self-sufficient, confident individuals.

Make sense? Heck, no.

We want the impossible; we want the absurd. And that doesn't happen in real life. One of the hardest things to accept when you are on the path of rediscovering yourself is that "like attracts like." We may be–*gasp*– as messed up as the neglectful, immature, avoidant bad boy we're dating. That's horrifying. But it's one of the most important reasons I constantly advise people to stop analyzing their partner and turn inward. It's so much easier to analyze the faults and idiosyncrasies of others. Worse, it keeps you perpetually trapped in your own dis-ease of avoiding yourself.

So, see that list in the previous section? Well, your job is to rewrite it with you as the focus this time. And keep in mind, if you do not have one or more of the points on this list, now's the time to work towards changing that!

Owning your behavior is hard. It forces you to ask yourself over and over, *Whose fault is this?* And often our default response is, "It's not my fault!

It's someone else's." But let's lose the blame. At the end of the day what truly matters is you are doing your best to be your best. Have I said this already? If I have, my apologies, but keep your eye on the prize, girl!

CHAPTER 31.

How Healthy Might
Feel Awkward

*"We must be willing to let go of the life
we've planned, so as to have the life that is
waiting for us."*

– Joseph Campbell

Ready to get a little uncomfortable? Well, real change, like it or not, is going to force you to deal with a few growing pains, discomfort, and downright awkwardness. But, believe it or not, we humans are built to adapt to change. It's called evolution. So let's evolve…

When you spend years repeating toxic patterns of behavior, it is very, very, very difficult to just put on the brakes, stop what you're doing and start using healthier behaviors. A fish doesn't just jump out of the water and start walking. It takes millions of years for that little guy to evolve. Unfortunately, we don't have that much time; and luckily, we can adapt to new stuff for more quickly. But that's not without saying our changes and sensation of change won't, at first, feel unnatural. They will. And the first thing you'd most likely want to do when exploring a new behavior is give up and revert back to your old ways. This is the point where most people do give up and stop trying to change. Change is just too painful. Trust me, I know. For years, I would attempt to do things differently but it just didn't feel right. And hey! When something doesn't feel right, it's bad for you, yes? Heck no. Sometimes it's great for you. Lifting weights and training to run a marathon can hurt like heck sometimes. But exercise is very good for you. My point is, you can't just wish for a healthier partner, but refuse to change. It doesn't work that way.

Let's work together to understand this concept: almost all new behaviors feel awkward when you first learn them. Learning to ride a bike? It was once a new behavior you had to learn. Learning a new language? *Oh la la. Trop dificil!* How about learning to cook the perfect omelet? You certainly weren't born doing that. And here's the thing, kids learn new behaviors a lot quicker, and with a lot less resistance to learning new tasks than adults because, well, they're kids. They have less rigidity, shame and egocentricity than us adults. They're more malleable. And they are far less concerned with making mistakes and failing. And that's what this section boils down to. In order to grow and change and shed your skin (and evolve from a fish into a land animal) you have to be willing to get in touch with your ancient childhood fearlessness, which will help you let go of some need for control. You have to be willing to stumble and even fall. Most of all, you have to be willing to accept that a level of discomfort is a requirement of change. It's part of the process. At least until you get it. And then, guess what? When you not only change your behavior but repeat your new way of being and acting, over and over…you train yourself. You regrow. You learn a new, healthier habit. And then, you're back in the comfort zone. No more ickyness.

I'll close this section with this one quick memory. I was finally ready to change my behavior and stop reaching out to this guy I was dating. I was always the one to reach out, and because of it, I felt the relationship was one-sided (it was). Trouble was, when I called him, he'd respond. We'd talk, or we'd see it each other. So, I knew that every time I reached out, I would get some sort of response, a hit, if you will. If I didn't reach out, he'd almost never make an effort to connect with me, which meant I would have to let go of the relationship. This scared the heck out of me, even though it was so one-sided! And so when I first stopped calling him, I felt horrible. I felt I was denying myself something. I felt I was doing something wrong and I told myself every lie in the book to convince myself calling him was the right thing to do. It felt so awkward not picking up the phone that I slipped at least 100 times and called him anyway. At one point, I truly felt doomed. I felt there was no hope for me. And then, one day, I guess I just got sick and tired of being sick and tired. I had had enough practice not calling him, and I was able to do it. We never spoke again.

CHAPTER 32

How to Avoid the Avoidant

"Why did I come here? I thought. Why is it always only a matter of choosing between something bad and something worse?"

–Charles Bukowski

I always hate to suggest that anyone should stay away from an entire group of people with the same, stereotypical personality type. But I have seen what happens when you put a cat and a bird in the same space and it's just not pretty. I have also seen what happens when you put a love addict and an avoidant together in a relationship and it's equally unpleasant. As much as these two personality types are drawn together, they just don't mix well. And don't go, "Yeah, but, oil and vinegar!" No. Just no. An avoidant and a love addict do not make a tasty salad condiment. And I want to be firm on that. Because the moment I tell you that, yes, of course, there are those rare couples, a love addict and avoidant that get along just fine, you will no doubt say to yourself, "That's us! We're rare and special and we'll make it!" But the chances are slim. If you're reading this book, you are most likely in a painful relationship trying to get out. So trust me. I have seen the love addict-avoidant pattern repeat itself ad nauseum, and it just doesn't change. The love addict chases and the avoidant runs in the opposite direction. The cat eats the bird. The oil pulls away from the vinegar. And the more extreme these two personalities types are, the more extreme the highs and lows and the suffering. Of course, it's a little subtler than cat chases bird. Here's a real life example.

A friend of mine named Josh fell in love with his co-worker, Amber, while he was still married, albeit planning to divorce. His wife was controlling, manipulative, jealous and possessive and so, he (mistakenly) fell for a girl he thought was "safe." Amber was laid back, romantic, sexy, and super into Josh, everything his wife no longer was. And so Josh and Amber confessed their love right away, and had an intense affair. When he finally divorced his wife a year later, thrilled at the idea that he was finally free to be with Amber, things started to change. Amber suddenly became less available. Her romantic and sexual side seemed to turn cold and detached. She said, there's more to life than sex, and admonished Josh for being like a "typical guy" always wanting it. She didn't want to be touched anymore or spend time together, and at one point, she said to him, "I don't think I can really love you because you cheated on your wife." The more Josh tried to see and spend time with Amber, the less time she was available. Suddenly, she had three jobs and almost no time for him. Josh was crushed. And anything he tried to change within himself or within the situation, just wasn't good enough for Amber. He immediately saw the mistake he had made in choosing this new partner. Not only did he regret having had an affair, but by trying to choose someone he thought was "safe" and so unlike his ex-wife, he didn't realize he'd found an emotionally avoidant partner. He broke up with Amber, and this immediately changed the dynamic. Amber was almost miraculously in love again and wanted him back. Now, she was willing to do anything to keep him in her life. And it went on like that for several years until finally, Amber moved to California.

When one or both partners are avoidant, their unavailability is the key to their attraction. It's what keeps both partners emotionally "safe" from real intimacy. Josh's marriage was a built-in protection that kept both Amber and Josh from true commitment and everything that commitment entails. When that was gone, Amber created new barriers. When Josh broke up with her, he created a barrier, which made her feel safe again and so, she immediately wanted to get back together. This exemplifies the dance of the love addict and avoidant.

I always love using this couple as an example of "love addict and avoidant" because their relationship story is replete with all the subtle qualities of the paradigm. Both are avoiding a reality that they do not wish to confront. Avoidants will always blame their partners for making it impossible for them to love fully. Avoidants will even be sad when their partners don't have what it takes to be their one true love. Don't get me wrong. There's a huge difference between someone who's avoidant and someone who simply doesn't want a relationship with someone else. The difference is, the avoidant stays. And the love addict stays. And they drag out this pattern—the love addict trying desperately to change the avoidant or change himself to appeal to the avoidant, and the avoidant putting up walls to emotionally close herself off from any hint of intimacy—until one of them finally breaks off the relationship. Or not. The love addict, on the other hand, will take care of the avoidant, over-help them, and remain in denial about certain glaring red flags, while focusing only on positive qualities. "She said she loves me," "She's kind," "We laugh a lot." Meanwhile, she wants less and less sex, she says she can't "fully" love him because of his faults, and she is becoming more unavailable.

Love Addicts need to avoid Love Avoidants. Period. People who suffer from love avoidance are not good or bad, but they are NOT the best choice for a Love Addict. And Avoidants do have successful relationships, but NOT with personality types like ours. Need more convincing? Let's take a look at Pia Mellody's three main characteristics of love avoidants from her book, *Facing Love Addiction*:

1. Love Avoidants evade intensity within the relationship by creating intensity in activities (usually addictions) outside the relationship.

2. Love Avoidants avoid being known in the relationship in order to protect themselves from engulfment and control by the other person.

3. Love Avoidants avoid intimate contact with their partners, using a variety of processes [she calls] "distancing technique."

(Mellody, 2003)

The love addict, on the other hand is driven by intensity, and a need to feed what Susan Peabody, author of *Addiction to Love*, calls "the hungry heart," that painful, perceived void within us. Love addicts demand attention and closeness to fill this void. Love Avoidants evade closeness and bestowing attention because those things are too "intimate." So while love addicts and avoidants are naturally attracted to each other, they typically can't sustain a relationship because their coping mechanisms (one avoids, the other chases) are too incompatible.

If I took inventory of the personality traits of all my exes, whoa, they'd almost all be love avoidants, which is to say, I was attracted to one easily recognizable type; they said they loved me but avoided spending too much time with me, and always had an excuse for why they couldn't come over. Eventually, when I came to my senses, I was determined to avoid this "type" of character at all cost. I wanted to break the cycle. And that meant figuring out not only *who* this type person was that I needed to steer clear from, but *how* to stay away from him. Here's a multi-step action sheet I came up with to help me:

Step One: Make a list of your personal values: (ahem, if you have not done this yet, do it!). Knowing your values helps you determine what you absolutely cannot live with and what you absolutely cannot live without. And once you know those things, you can clearly determine if John, the hot guy at the coffee shop who just told you he loves to "party hard" on weekends, is an appropriate person for you or not. If you happen to have "I will not ever date someone who drinks or takes drugs excessively" on your values list, you know that you need to order that coffee from John and then move on. Quickly. I may have said this before but it bears repeating: when we choose our values over relationships or people, they guide us down a path of self-respect, dignity and peace, and help us meet our basic and higher needs.

But what does this have to do with avoiding the avoidant? Well, everything. Your list of values needs to include, "I will avoid dating partners who neglect or avoid me." That is the first step. Get clear about not wanting to date someone who exhibits avoidant behavior.

Step two: Understand that love avoidants typically don't start out avoiding you! Barring the occasional love avoidant type who treats you like crap and neglects you from the start, most love avoidants start out rather sweet, in fact. They can pursue you, be super flirtatious, fall in love quickly, and come on quite strong–for a little while, that is. And then, a few months into the relationship, when they begin to feel too overwhelmed, their avoidant nature kicks in. At this point, they still may "say" they love you, but the action is no longer there. You start to wonder how someone can be so in love for the first few months, then turn it off so quickly. You wonder how someone can say they love you, but not put any effort into seeing you, calling you, talking to you or spending any time with you. You even start to wonder what YOU did wrong. Well, by this point in the book you know that you most likely just fell for a Love Avoidant. But more than that, you bought into the idea that love can and should happen impetuously. Both love avoidants and love addicts are highly impulsive. This impulsivity plays nicely into addicts' and avoidants' defense mechanism of latching on quickly to someone–anyone–so as to avoid facing any more pain. So just because someone falls in love with you quickly, or pays you loads of attention for the first 6-9 months, it doesn't mean they won't eventually show their true colors. A good rule-of -thumb is the old cliché: if it started fast, chances are it will end fast. Your job, therefore, is to not assume that you're in the clear just because your partner is really into you. Take a step back. Ask yourself questions: Has he/she been consistent in words and actions? Has he/she been predictable? How long as he/she loved me with actions, not just words? Passion and chemistry can happen quickly, but turning over your heart in love to someone typically takes time. A healthy partner will not be so impulsive.

Step three: Get to know the stereotypical qualities of love avoidants. Yes, I know, you're not supposed to stereotype and everyone is so different and blah, blah, blah. I am the first to repeat that you cannot think in terms of *all men are this way* or *all women are that way*. But, let's consider for the sake of personality types, most people from any particular group share certain qualities. Not all, but many. And everything on this list in and of itself is not a sign of an avoidant. But the more boxes you can check, the more likely you are dealing with one.. That being said, here are some of the qualities to look for:

- Over the age of 40 and still lives with Mom or Dad.

- Over the age of 40 and never been in a long-term, committed relationship.

- Possibly drinks excessively, smokes pot, does drugs, or is addicted to a substance or process (gambling, sex, food, work, alcohol, etc.).

- Has not treated their partner(s) well in past relationships.

- Avoids responsibility in his or her life (financial, social and personal)

- Doesn't take care of himself or herself well (meaning, brushes teeth, wears clean clothes, grooms, etc.).

- A Peter Pan (someone who exhibits signs of wanting to remain eternally youthful and never grow up).

- Falls desperately in love with partner within the first weeks of the relationship.

- Not interested in or ambiguous about commitment of any kind.

- Uses excuses to avoid intimacy, closeness, sex or deep conversations.

Here are a few more personality traits on Avoidant Personality Disorder from the latest version of the Diagnostic and Statistical Manual of Mental Disorders, or DSM-V:

- Hypersensitivity to rejection/criticism

- Self-imposed social isolation

- Extreme shyness or anxiety in social situations, though the person feels a strong desire for close relationships

- Avoids physical contact because it has been associated with an unpleasant or painful stimulus

- Feelings of inadequacy

- Severe low self-esteem

- Self-loathing

- Mistrust of others

- Emotional distancing related to intimacy

- Highly self-conscious

- Self-critical about their problems relating to others

- Problems in occupational functioning

- Lonely self-perception, although others may find the relationship with them meaningful

- Feeling inferior to others

- In some more extreme cases — agoraphobia

- Utilizes fantasy as a form of escapism and to interrupt painful thoughts

Before you let your inner-caretaker take over and convince you, "this is a great guy! I feel sorry for him already," remember your VALUES. These are the types of qualities in people you want to avoid.

Step four: Use logic when you date. This is one of those things that sounds easier than it actually is. So often we meet someone, and whether we like it or not, our emotions take over. We feel like we're just along for the ride and that we've been "love struck," as if this relationship happened quite beyond our control. Well, get over it. Stop letting your emotions control your behavior. Your emotions are there for a reason: to tell you when you're hot, cold, angry, sad, etc. They are reflectors of the bigger picture. **But they do NOT have the ability to make critical, logical decisions that will guarantee your safety.** You need to enlist the expertise of your logical brain to help you figure out if this relationship is right. Please re-read Chapter 21 on Aligning Logical Brain with Emotional Brain.

Step Five: Take your time when you date. This means simply enjoying a person with no hoped-for outcomes. It means getting the whole "I wonder if he's the one" out of your brain. And it means giving up the notion that dating is love. It's NOT! You may be attracted to someone, and they may be attracted to you. But dating someone new is partly awkward, sometimes romantic, if you're lucky, and mostly filled with the unknown. I hate to take the thrill out of it, but it's work. It's the part of the relationship in which there really isn't a relationship yet. Why? Because relationships take time. Dating slowly and getting to know someone over months, not just days or weeks (and not just online, but in person!) is possibly one of the best things both of you can do for each other. Only time reveals a person's true character and allows you to see what they may initially want to hide, or things that naturally take time to come out (like their insecurities about intimacy or their fear of commitment). When you use dating as a guide to help you get to know someone as opposed to using it as a means to an end (we're in this relationship now!), it gives you both the freedom to come and go if it doesn't work out. And while this lack of security may horrify you, it also buys you time to protect yourself and know what you're getting yourself into. Time allows you to make an educated choice about someone and thus, love consciously, as opposed to just falling for someone recklessly, without thinking.

Step Six: Don't depend on chemistry. Love addicts are often attracted to love avoidants because, let's face it, we are opposite sides of the same coin. They seem to have what we lack, and vice versa. It almost seems like it should be the perfect match. Well, it's not. Love addiction and love avoidance are EXTREME personalities. Imagine a straight line. In the center is an (imaginary) perfect, healthy person. Love addiction would be far left of the line and love avoidance would be far right. Neither are healthy places to be. If anything, in a relationship, these two perpetuate the dis-ease of the other. So, just because there's chemistry, or a sense that you're clicking, that doesn't make it a good, healthy relationship.

And speaking of chemistry…The biological cocktail of chemicals that washes over you when you first meet someone you have chemistry with is part of the animal urge in us all to procreate, but it's not a determination that a relationship is safe, healthy, compatible or loving. And it won't tell you if your partner is respectful, attentive, or caring. We can "click" with darn near anyone. If you are older and wiser, you know this already. I clicked with so many people over the years, I've lost count. Imagine a teen's collection of selfies on their mobile phone. That's how many times I clicked with someone. I found out that clicking didn't necessarily mean that these men would make good boyfriends. Having chemistry with someone is a great precursor to a healthy relationship, and it may even be a good "sign" that you will get along. But by no means, and I repeat…BY NO MEANS does it signify the health of a potential mate or the health of the relationship you might have with them. You can click with an axe murderer. But you wouldn't want to date one, would you?

Step Seven: Understand that we are different with different people: Your avoidant partner may not necessarily be avoidant because he avoids everybody and everything. He may just be avoidant with you! **He may be an avoidant in response to your love addiction.**

Ouch!

But hear me out. We so often think our partner is the way he or she is with *everyone*. We believe that avoidant personality disorder is a static characteristic. This is not entirely true. Many personality traits we think are set in stone, are actually malleable. They exist in response to who we are with. We can be different with different people. I'm sure you know a few people who just bring out the worst in you. Others tend to calm you and make you feel alive and wonderful inside. Some people trigger really bad behavior in me, others do not. They keep me peaceful. Avoidance and love addiction, believe it or not, oftentimes tend to be situational. And more than that, they can be symbiotic and inter-dependent. One often does not exist without the other. I often call myself a Love Addict, but the truth is, I can also be a Love Avoidant, IF I am paired with someone who pursues me too aggressively. When I am paired with another Avoidant, I become a Love Addict. It's a balancing act, because, simply, nature seeks balance. And therein lies the key…until you become balanced within yourself, you will continue to find and attract more extreme versions of love addiction and/or avoidance within your partners.

iii. **How (Not!) to Attract an Avoidant**

The idea that someone is being avoidant simply because you are being even remotely love-addicty implies that if you just change your ways, your partner will suddenly stop being avoidant and finally love you the way you'd like to be loved. Not so fast. You cannot change your nature, and your partner can't change his or hers either. No matter how much you stuff your desire for more closeness, it won't feel right and the love avoidant in your life will not suddenly love you more. Love avoidants tend to be more successful with other avoidants. Other avoidants give space, place minimal demands of intimacy and do not threaten enmeshment. That's not you. You need someone with less intimacy issues who can step up to the plate and offer more. But! There are surefire ways to snag an avoidant if that's really your goal (let's hope it's not). Here's how...

1. **Be impulsive**–Love Avoidants love when people are impulsive. Why? Because when you're impulsive there's no room to take the time to understand and get to know people, places and things. And when there's no time taken to carefully consider if someone is right for you, your chances are higher you will lock yourself into a relationship with someone who is not a suitable partner. Avoidants know they come with a lot of issues; they're insecure and lack confidence. But they desperately crave the idea of love and sex. If you're impulsive, you're more willing to give them a chance.

2. **Fall in love quickly**: Along with being impulsive, you also need to fall in love fast. Because when you want to date an Avoidant, emotions need to run extremely hot in the very beginning because within no time, they will start to run cold. As soon as you are flying high in love, the avoidance can begin!

3. **Overlook red flags**: Red flags, despite their importance, need to be ignored. Avoidants come with a ton of them–they tend not to call you back right away, they often lie, they disappear for days,

they are chronically "busy" or occupied to the point of never being able to see you, they tend to not have a very stable history of long term relationships, they tend to avoid other responsibilities in their life, and the big one: they are emotionally stunted and have a fear of enmeshment. So…if you truly want to be with an Avoidant, just turn a blind eye to any and all red flags–especially those waving ferociously. Your Avoidant will be so grateful.

4. **Say one thing, but do another**: One of the best ways to seduce an Avoidant is to say one thing, like, "I'm going to break up with you because [fill in the blank]" but then do another, like, STAY in the relationship. You are not only seducing your Avoidant, you are teaching him your words mean very little. He will adore you all the more because, as you will see in #9, he does the same thing.

5. **Be controlling**: Avoidants need little pushes here and there to do things because they're like overgrown toddlers. They need to be told to take you out on a date, they need to be told to bring flowers, they need to be nudged into sleeping over, and they definitely need to be shoved full-force into any kind of committed relationship. God forbid we don't control, cajole, nudge and push Avoidants into doing stuff. If we didn't, we'd lose them immediately [Are you getting my sarcasm yet?!].

6. **Be insecure**: Avoidants are insecure, so you need to be insecure. And because water seeks its own level and like attracts like, you'll never find and hold onto an Avoidant unless you yourself lack security about who you are. A woman who is secure in herself is greatly intimidating to Avoidants and if you are that woman, they will break up with you. The same can be said for self-confidence and self-esteem.

7. **Never grow up**: Ever hear of the Peter Pan Syndrome? Poor Peter Pan suffered from severely stunted growth, a bit of narcissism,

and an intimacy disorder which kept him from being truly able to commit to anyone (Wendy). He was the eternal boy, unable to grow up, and that tends to mean one thing: he couldn't handle a grownup relationship that is built of responsibility, care, partnership, equality, communication, and other adult-like behaviors. If you're a grownup, and you're dating an Avoidant, chances are he will feel incredibly uncomfortable around your grownupness. Take it down a notch and kick and scream like a toddler. And don't dare ask him to be responsible or make a commitment to you. Way too scary.

8. **Have low expectations**: If you think your Avoidant will want to communicate with you regularly, spend reasonable amounts of time with you, love you maturely, and be a responsible partner, you're barking up the wrong tree. You need to drop your expectations way down. In fact, you need to get rid of your expectations and settle for scraps. Scraps are what you will get when you date an Avoidant.

9. **Accept words as truth, not actions**: Avoidants are big on words, short on action. If you already have experience with an Avoidant, you'll know the ole routine. They will *say* they love you, but they'll rarely make the effort to come over and see you. They will *say* they want you in their life, but they'll run away from you every chance they get. This confuses most people to the point of running in the opposite direction. Who doesn't it confuse? Two types of people: those who trust that words are valid proclamations, and have no need to wait around and make sure that right action follows or the job is completed (Ever have an electrician say, *Yes, I will fix your broken electrical outlet,* then, take your money and never actually fix the outlet?), and people who desperately want to be in a relationship with anyone and settle for words over actions. They are

not confused or put off by accepting words as truth, and not caring about actions. They are simply frustrated by it. Oh well. Small price to pay if you want to date an Avoidant!

10. **Be a caretaker**: Avoidants are attracted to caretakers like teens to angst. Like yin to yang. Like butter to bread. That's because Avoidants avoid responsibilities (because responsibility is too over-whelming) and caretakers are driven by taking on responsibility for others (because it means they don't have to take responsibility for themselves). That being said, this is a match made in Heaven if you are a natural caretaker. You will definitely be doing a lot of caretaking in this relationship, and your Avoidant will be able to continue to avoid. Ahhh....functional dysfunction!

Conversely, if you do NOT want to date an Avoidant, well, that's relatively easy to do too. Simply, DO NOT FOLLOW THIS PLAN!

CHAPTER 33

A Little Bit More About Red Flags

"Sometimes a man wants to be stupid if it lets
him do a thing his cleverness forbids."

–John Steinbeck, *East of Eden*

Most people know a red flag when they see one. Yet, no matter how healthy and grounded you are, overlooking them—at least for a little while—is normal. No one wants to throw away a perfectly good rug because it has one tiny hole in it. And yet, that's what sets healthy relationship seekers apart from unhealthy ones. A healthy person will ultimately choose to walk away from a potential partner if the "signs" warn of danger. If that one tiny hole in the rug, for example, is a sign of poor construction, forewarning that the second you get it home, the whole thing will unravel. An unhealthy person will most likely see these types of signs, but ignore them or say, "I'll fix them!"

The reason we do this is because being in a relationship–any relationship–is often more important than the quality of the relationship, and, being alone is perceived as far more unpleasant than being in a relationship with a mate who might not be good for us. That said, there's an element of willful ignorance within us. Healthy people, on the contrary, know the difference between a red flag and, let's say, a pink or white flag. Red flag: he's having an affair. Yup. That's a pretty big one. Pink flag: his brother's having an affair. He's not the one with the direct problem, but how connected is he with his brother? Do they share the same values? What is his overall opinion of infidelity? White flag: He's cheated on his girlfriend in 8th grade, but felt guilty about it and never did it again. See the difference?

That said, here are 10 warning signs, or red flags to look out for when dating. When you see, detect, notice or confirm any of them, he or she is most likely not the best catch. Be prepared to move on!

1. **They have one or more episodes of cheating in their past** Many people are on the fence with cheating. Some say, once a cheater always a cheater. Others say, people can change. I'm not sure which side I'm on. Personally, I'd like to know that the guy I am about to date has never cheated and has my same values. I think if they mentioned that they'd cheated in their distant past but have proof of a long-term stable relationship where no cheating took place, there may be hope. Keep an eye out on this one.

2. **They're married** If you meet someone who is clearly giving off "the vibe" only to find out he's/she's married, this is the reddest of all red flags. Honestly, unless there's solid proof (I say 'solid' because the whole "almost divorced" line is so common that it is meaningless unless accompanied by actual proof) that they've done something like moved back in with their parents, or have completely severed ties with their ex and a divorce proceeding is underway, this is one guy or girl you need to stay away from. Heck,

if he's interested and you think there's a chance, tell him, *When your divorce is finalized, then you can call me.* A note to the potential open-relationshippers among us. Some people think it is socially and ethically OK to have a relationship with a married individual. And to that I say, ask the wife first. Ask the other partner. Chances are the relationship isn't as open as the married person would have you believe. There may be some serious betrayal going on. If that's the case, just know that you are willingly participating in the suffering and betrayal of another human being. That's not a healthy relationship. It's a red-flag sundae with a cherry on top!

3. **There's more secrecy than you feel comfortable with** She said she'd be going away for the weekend, but wouldn't tell you where. You've never met her friends. You don't know where she lives or, for that matter, where she works. Red flag, red flag, red flag. People who are available are engaged in sharing and opening up to you. Maybe not all at once. But, enough for you to feel like there's definitely a willingness to be somewhat vulnerable.

4. **They do not speak well of their past relationships, and/or it was always the other person's "fault" that the relationship ended**. One of the things that I loved about my current husband when we were first dating was how kindly he spoke of his ex wife, even though *she* had left *him*. She was, in his mind, the mother of his children and even though he was hurt by her, she still deserved the respect of not being talked badly about. Granted, this hurt a bit. Sometimes we want to clearly be the center of someone's world and elevated while everyone else is demoted to *bitch*, or *monster*, or *most hated*. Some of us feel "safer" when our love interest speaks badly about others. It's as if we are the only one they love. And yet, the way your date speaks about people in his or her past is a direct clue into how he might speak about you someday. So, unless he is

putting his ex on a pedestal and bemoaning her loss all too much (yeah, that's not good), you don't want to date someone who trash-talks his ex.

5. **They continue to impose strange restrictions after a decent amount of time dating** (i.e. "Don't call me at the office," "Don't show up unannounced," etc.) People who like you typically want to be around you. And, unless you are coming on too strong and showing up unannounced all the time (not good), this type of restriction is a bit strange, especially after dating for a decent amount of time. Case in point: I was dating this guy for five months. By this point we had slept together, said, "I love you," and we were even leaving clothes and toiletries over the other's house. I had very clear boundaries (never showed up unannounced, never called his office, unless he specifically said it was OK). At any rate, one afternoon, I happened to be passing by his house and thought, "Let me just pop in." Bad idea. He opened up the door, barely let me in and I felt immediately uncomfortable. No, no one was there. He wasn't cheating on me per se, but he felt as though my presence was a threat to his personal space and that didn't bode too well for me. Anyway, you don't want to ever just "show up" unannounced right after you begin dating someone. Not a good dating move at all. But, you also don't want to date some guy who imposes those types of restrictions when it's not warranted.

6. **They fall in love with you almost immediately** Most people don't see this as a red flag, and yet, it's a biggie. People who value their heart and know the seriousness of commitment don't "dive in" so quickly. That's not to say they won't feel passionate or hugely emotional towards you. But they will refrain from things like moving in, saying I love you, proposing marriage, or even having sex until

they feel comfortable and safe. Likewise, you could be someone's "red flag" if you fall in love at the drop of a hat. Yikes!

7. **They've never had a long-term, committed relationship**. OK, so, anyone around the age of 25 might not fit this particular red flag. But, if you're dating someone 30-years-old or older and they have not had a somewhat serious, committed relationship this could be a sign of social anxiety, intimacy issues, avoidance, emotional unavailability and so on. Again, I want to stress, all people have baggage. All people have problems. Just because someone has social anxiety, that's not a reason to chuck the relationship. But one of the best signs of a healthy partner is that he or she has had healthy, relatively successful relationships, or it's something he or she is working towards. People are capable of change; there is hope. But, for love addicts, you want to try to dodge people who cannot or will not commit. It's too much of a trigger for the love addict personality.

8. **They say one thing and do another; they lie** This is a classic move of Miss or Mr. Unavailable and a red flag if ever there was one. It is essential that a healthy relationship is built on trust and honesty, and the only way for that to happen is if a person's words align with their actions. If you are detecting lies, then you are most likely consenting to a lifetime of distrust and distance from your partner. Always remember: when a person lies, they want to put distance between you and them. When a person tells the truth, they are seeking closeness.

9. **They do drugs; drink too much** Whether you partake in recreational drugs or drinking or not, you definitely want to stay away from someone who does these things to excess. What's excess? That's up to you to decide. But here's the bottom line: heavy drug and alcohol use is a relationship barrier. While "a few drinks" may

loosen you up and help you relax, a lot ultimately keeps you from experiencing true reality (especially the uncomfortable kind) and worse, true, deep intimacy. Not only that, but no one has ever had a serious conversation when they were stoned, drunk or on drugs. You need to see and experience people as they really are, and if your date is always drunk, then who are you dating? You'll never know.

10. **They treat people poorly, take pleasure in hurting others (including animals) or express an unusual amount of hate and anger toward people, places, or things**. Always be on the lookout for subtle clues of a potentially violent, sadistic or disturbing past. These are the types of red flags that, when ignored, can be very dangerous. Narcissists, sociopaths and psychopaths have a fairly well-known history of hiding their true intentions and these types can be extremely tricky to detect. According to the American Psychiatric Association a Narcissist might exhibit five or more of the following traits:

> A grandiose logic of self-importance
>
> A fixation with fantasies of infinite success, control, brilliance, beauty, or idyllic love
>
> A credence that he or she is extraordinary and exceptional and can only be understood by, or should connect with, other extraordinary or important people or institutions
>
> A desire for unwarranted admiration
>
> A sense of entitlement
>
> Interpersonally oppressive behavior
>
> No form of empathy
>
> Resentment of others or a conviction that others are resentful of him or her

A display of egotistical and conceited behaviors or attitudes

(American Psychiatric Association, 2013)

When our desire for a relationship, love, or sex overcomes our capacity to think logically, rationally, and to take care of ourselves, we must accept the sad reality that we're praying to a false god. We've made something very unhealthy more important than ourselves. And that usually doesn't have a good outcome. Take a look at the people you've dated in the past. Can you clearly see their red flags? What did you do when you noticed them? Ignore them, or leave? If you have a current partner, how do they sum up? Does he or she have red flags? Are you just "dealing with" those red flags in hopes they go away, or are you working toward getting out of the relationship? Red flags are warning signs. If a potential partner or date is waving a red flag, pay attention. You may have to take action. That doesn't mean work to change him. It usually means moving on to someone with no red flags.

i. **20 Reasons He/She Is Not Your Soulmate**

Back when I was still with C, I found myself constantly questioning whether or not I was doing the right thing by staying with him when so much of the relationship felt so wrong. I mean, he was "the one." I'd been with him for three years and loved him like I'd never loved anyone before, and he said he loved me too. But there were a few glaring issues that kept troubling me. And yet, I honestly believed I had to overlook them because, well, that's what you do when you are with your soul mate, isn't it? You overlook the bad and try to stay focused on the good.

Thing is, the longer I stayed, the more I realized his bad qualities, while acceptable to others, were not acceptable to me. That's when I became aware my idea of "soul mate" was a little flimsy. You can love someone deeply, you can even have a lot of things in common, but if certain criteria are not met (umm, he says he loves you he's taking someone else out on a date), you may have to reevaluate your definition of "soul mate." As I've said, you're not dating half a person. You're dating the whole shebang. That being stated...here are a few obvious signs that he or she might not be the one.

1. 1. **He/She left you.** Plain and simple. Your soul mate doesn't leave you, even if he/she insists he's never loved anyone more than you. Whatever the excuse, it's just that. He's not the one. When someone wants to be with you, when someone is right for you, they don't leave you. They want to be with you, despite their circumstances. Period.

2. 2. **You left him/her.** When we leave people, repeatedly, we do so because something's not right—with you, with your partner, with the relationship. It doesn't matter. What matters is why you leave and what you think might change if you go back. Ask yourself this: if the relationship is right and good, would it still inspire me to keep running away? Why do I keep leaving? What do I think will be better if I go back? Your repeated leaving might be a pretty strong sign he/she is not the one.

3. **He/she is with another partner** I have met so many women who fall in love with a married man (or a man dating another woman) and come to believe that the two are soul mates; that "he married the other woman because he hadn't yet met me." If that were the case, and occasionally it is, then you need to stay away from that man and his wife until his relationship is completely over and he is free to date you. Soul mates are not committed to other people. That's fantasy. And it's also wishful thinking. Wherever you stand morally or ethically on the topic of "affair," or whether you believe married individuals are free game or not, is not the point here. The point is, soul mates aren't "half" committed. They are fully committed.

4. **You're with another partner.** Oops! You finally met your soulmate but you're married or committed to someone else. That's OK. If you really think you've met your soulmate, get out of your current relationship FIRST (not impulsively, please, especially if kids are involved). Again, soul mates aren't "half" committed. They are fully committed. That goes for you too.

5. **Someone is cheating on someone else.** When a loving relationship is right and good, no-one is cheating, no-one is lying. Cheating and lying are both ways people distance themselves from one another. Cheating does nothing to bring two people closer. Cheating is an immature act. It is based on the concept of immediate gratification (I want what I want and I want it now and I don't care about the consequences). Adults can control themselves. Immature people can't.

6. **He/she neglects you, avoids you, doesn't call, doesn't write, text, etc.** Soulmates don't neglect you, avoid you, or have a million excuses why they didn't call. Not sure what that's all about. But you deserve better than that. Normal, healthy men or women who are interested in you, call you, want to see you and spend time with you. Don't think otherwise.

7. **He/she verbally, emotionally, mentally or physically abuses you.** If he/she is "the one," they are not abusing you in any way shape or form, and likewise, you are not abusing them back. Physical fighting and making up doesn't count, either. If he hit you once, chances are he'll hit you again. If you are in danger, get out. You are worth saving. Enough said.

8. **You've only met him /her online and haven't even seen him yet.** It takes a long time to know and love someone. You may "click" with someone relatively quickly. You may be attracted to them right off the bat via a photo. But attraction and clicking over

the internet are not signs of deep love. Those things are superficial, and though they are a great start to a possible relationship, they are not a relationship. Talking for hours with someone you cannot see, hear, smell or touch is not soul-mate-ish. Good partners need to fully commit, in person, looking each other square in the eyes so as to enjoy the reality of their closeness. When we invest so much of ourselves so quickly in an online romance, without giving ourselves the most important gift of face to face, we are doing ourselves a huge disservice. We are not being cautious or caring about the safety of our hearts. Take your time. Get to know someone.

9. **He/she lives too far away to have a normal, healthy relationship.** Long distance love affairs occur all the time. But in order for them to be healthy there must have been or will be a foundation of physical closeness for the relationship to take root. A couple who dates for a year, for example, and then one of them is sent overseas for military duty has a chance of success because the relationship has a foundation. But someone you met over a long weekend, who was in town partying with friends and plans to fly back to his home in…Norway? Probably not going to work unless one of you is willing to be a little closer.

10. **Either of you are heavy drinkers or drug users.** When someone is actively using drugs, or drinking, they are not exactly making decisions with a clear head (or heart). They are ruled by the drink or drug. And so, their ability to determine whether you might be a good catch for them or not is heavily skewed. Add that their drug and/or alcohol use is likely a way of numbing their emotions and reality, and you have a recipe for disaster. Falling in love under the influence, or remaining in a relationship with someone who is excessively under the influence is like falling in love with someone who constantly wears a mask. You're never getting the REAL

person. And no matter how long you invest in getting to know them, you know nothing about them because they are only showing you a disguise. And, I hate to be the bearer of bad new, but if and when they sober up? They are typically unrecognizable.

11. **He/she has a circumstance or situation which keeps him/her from connecting with you.** Soulmates may have skeletons in their closet, but they don't have circumstance which keep them from enjoying who you are and what you have to offer. They are available. Maybe not 24/7. But a good enough amount of the time that you two can healthily connect. If, for example, he has a son that for whatever reason takes up all his time or a job that calls him to work 90 hours a week, or a hobby that requires he spend every free moment he has on it, chances are he may not be emotionally available for you. Don't get me wrong. People have children, hobbies and work. But, if those things tend to be a constant reason or excuse for someone not to spend time with you? They are not your soulmate. People who love you make time for you.

12. **He/she only wants sex.** Sex is not love. If he/she is your soulmate, he will love you and want to make love to you all the time. But that should not be the ONLY thing he or she wants. You have far more to offer, and the right person will recognize that and love the whole package. And please! Don't be fooled by the sensation of hot, passionate, deep, meaningful sex. Any two people with chemistry and attraction can have that. If that's all you want, fine. But that alone is not the basis for "soul mate."

13. **He/she never wants sex.** If he/she is the one, that person will love you and want to make love to you all the time. Or, almost all the time. Or, better, as much as you both need so that you never feel starved for sex. Libidos are tricky things. Some of us have strong ones, some of us don't. In long-term relationships this tends to be

one of the biggest bones of contention. He wants more, she doesn't want it enough. Hormones ebb and flow through the years. The trick in knowing if your partner is right for you, is that he/she wants what is best for you as well, which includes pleasure. Again, we cannot please people all the time, even people we love. But communication and action is key.

14. **He/She comes right out and says, "I'm not the one."** (Or a variant of that, as in, "You're too good for me," or "We're not supposed to be together," or "I don't think this will work out," etc.) Listen to him/her. He's telling you something. Whether it's a game or a manipulation or not. Take EVERYTHING your partner says at face value. Why? Because not playing games or falling prey to them will teach your partner quickly that whatever he/she says, it had better be valid, because true communication is the only game you'll play. So, don't accept comments like "I don't love you," and think, "He doesn't know what he's talking about," or, "She doesn't know what's best for her…" Listen closely to what is being said and have expectations that it will be followed by right action.

15. **You have to chase and stalk him/her.** If you have to chase after or stalk or watch someone, they're not the one. This is harassment. It is trying to force a relationship with an unwilling or unavailable person. As one website explains: "Stalking is a form of mental assault, in which the perpetrator repeatedly, unwantingly, and disruptively breaks into the life-world of the victim, with whom they have no relationship (or no longer have)." [5]Stop stalking. You are better than that. Someone will love on your terms. But you must first put the energy and effort into loving yourself.

5   Lamber Royakkers "CyberStalking: menaced on the Internet". *sociosite.org. Retrieved 14 May 2013.*

16. **You're the only one giving 100 percent in the relationship, all the time.** Although good relationships are not always fifty-fifty, like we grew up believing, they're not hundred-zero either. They're not even eighty-twenty. But they do fluctuate more closely in a healthy range of give and take. Balance is the key.

17. **Every day seems to be fraught with suffering.** Love is not suffering, despite the examples set by Romeo and Juliet, Wuthering Heights, Doctor Zhivago or Lady Chatterley's Lover. Novels and movies may romanticize the pain and suffering of love, but in reality, there's nothing romantic about real suffering. Our lives are not little movies. We should never expect suffering for love to be normal or healthy. Suffering and pain are signals that there is something very wrong or that "desire" outweighs the value of a healthy relationship.

18. **You just met him/her and this is your first, second, third, fourth, fifth or sixth date.** You cannot possible know if someone is "the one" right off the bat. Sorry. Cannot happen. A deep, healthy, loving relationship develops over time. It's a process. And to know if someone is "the one" or not takes many months, if not years.

19. **After months of dating him/her, something doesn't "feel" right.** Or after a few dates, if something doesn't feel right, it probably isn't! Listen to your instincts. They are there for a reason. They help guide you. As bad as you want to be in a loving relationship, it's more important to listen to your gut.

20. **He/she comes with red flags.** I've said this before and I'll say it again: plain and simple: he/she is not the one. Keep in mind though, that a red flag is not "snores at night," or "constantly blows his nose" or even "doesn't dress in the latest fashion." These are not red flags unless you are completely superficial. A red flag is a sign of

danger. It is, "has a history of cheating," "lies consistently," "never calls when he says he will," "does drugs," and so on.

i. **Tips for Healthy Dating**

So, are you ready? No, I mean, are you *really* ready to start dating again? As a former love addict I had to take far more precautions than the average girl when I wanted to start dating again as a healthier individual. I couldn't just pick myself up again and throw myself back in the ring. I'd done that all my life and lost every match. I needed a different approach. And you will too. And just as a recovering alcoholic has to reconfigure the people, places and things in his sober life, we need to do the same. Here are some of my tips and lessons.

1. **Know when you are (really!) ready to date**. You may think you're ready. You may even fantasize about the hot guy or girl at the office who gave you a "look." But when it really comes down to it, and the question gets popped (*How about Saturday night?*), some of us are simply not ready, emotionally, mentally or physically. How do you know when you are? You know when the idea of dating doesn't scare the hell out of you. You know when the idea of dating might sound "scary" but it sounds exciting too. You know when you don't curl up into a ball and start crying hysterically after a first date because all you can think about is your ex. You know when you start to feel comfortable around strangers (maybe not 100 percent, but enough). And you know when being alone is not a bad thing, but you're ready for something new.

    Many of us who still mourn, analyze, fantasize or try to get back with our ex long after the relationship has ended do so not because we love them, per se, but as a form of self-protection. Think about it. If you are still emotionally attached to a person, it keeps you from having to date someone new, and thus experience the possibility of new pain and rejection. Also, there is the issue of diving from one relationship into another, and being "ready" for the wrong reasons. In this case, are you really ready to date? Or are you simply looking for your next "fix"? How do you know the difference between being ready and looking for a fix? See Tip #4 below.

2. **A date is JUST a date**. Learn to put dates into perspective. A date is not romantic, it is not your future, it is not love, it is not a dreamy Hollywood story of passion and ardor. And while a date may have elements of all those things IF there's chemistry and attraction, don't get too hung up on said chemistry and attraction. A date is a meeting. Someone finds you interesting (or you find them interesting, or both), and they want to get to know you a bit more. They want to talk to you, maybe they even want to kiss you at the end of the night. Maybe you want to kiss them. Who knows! Whatever the case, treat it like a meeting. It might be fun but it might be awkward; it might make you giddy or miserable, and it might make him or her want another date or never want to call back. Your first date will most likely not look like Rose and Jack's embrace on the bow of the Titanic with "My Heart Will Go On" playing in the background. It might, however, look more like Marge Gunderson's "date" with Mike Yanagita in the movie Fargo (YouTube it if you don't know the scene). My point is, when you meet up with someone for the purpose of getting to know you, and vice versa, you have to try and remove the romantic element, otherwise, you leave yourself open to fantasy and high expectations, which brings me to tip #3…

3. **Lose the** expectations. This is a repeat of a previous chapter, but I am going to drill it into you. If you go into a date looking for your soulmate, you will probably be sorely disappointed. Why is that?

Because your expectations are far too high for an unsuspecting stranger who doesn't know what you want or need and basically owes you nothing but a little common courtesy–that's about as much as can be expected on a first date. Any more than that and you're barking up the wrong tree. You see, understanding the concept of expectations is probably one of our biggest hurdles when it comes to dating. We have high expectations too soon, or of the wrong people, and then, once we see that our expectations are not getting met, we whine about it, but settle anyway. But go back to that simple formula I mentioned before: **we can only have high expectations of people who are healthy enough, interested enough and capable of meeting our expectations. And we also have to be willing to expect the same from ourselves.** You can't go on a first date and expect to be treated with basic human kindness and respect from someone who is not a kind and respectful person. You can't go on a first date and expect that a person will call you back for a second date, if that person is not interested. And you can't go on a first date (or a second or third) and start expecting that the two of you are automatically a couple. These are all unrealistic expectations and you are setting yourself up for a let-down. Expect NOTHING. And be happy. Don't expect a call back! Don't expect a text! Don't expect a second date! You are owed nothing. You didn't go on this date "expecting" a second or third date. You went on this date to simply ENJOY this person now (mindfulness and gratitude, remember?). That's all you get.

4. **Know the difference between dating and desperation**. Are you OK with just you? Or are you looking for someone to save you? Can you handle being alone? Or do you hate your life because it's missing a soulmate? Is it a combination of both of these things? Knowing what is driving your desire to date can have a huge impact

on WHO YOU CHOOSE to date. If you are OK within yourself then you can be far more discerning with whom you choose to date. Why? Because you have nothing to lose. You're not dating out of need or desperation to fill a void. You are simply dating because you would like to meet someone you can enjoy. Period. A love addict has to be on constant alert of their personal motives. If you feel a void within you, you may pick and choose prospective dates for the wrong reasons. You may be willing to overlook red flags, put up with abuse or neglect, or date "down," all for the purpose of stuffing that void within you. Remember, when we date, we are not looking for our second half. We are not looking to be "completed." We must begin to understand that we are complete already. And if we don't feel complete on our own, we need to bring ourselves there first. Healthy dating is about meeting other people who are also complete.

5. **Let things happen organically.** Letting things happen organically means removing the fantasy...100 percent. That means that when the date is over, it's over. You can think about the wonderful feeling of his touch, but do not try on his name and imagine the two of you on the beach in Cancun as Honeymooners. You can certainly enjoy the thoughts of her that pop into your head the next day, but don't imagine what your children will look like. Letting things happen organically means living in the now. If he hasn't called, he hasn't called. Gently push those wanting, needing and fantasy thoughts from your head and replace them with thoughts on your work, or what you are presently doing. Remove the ruminating! Remain mindful of what is right in front of you. The more you fantasize or obsess or play out how perfect the date was in your mind, the more intense and unrealistic it becomes. Whereas, the more you remain grounded in your daily life, the more the idea of

your date will simply be part of your experience, not what your entire life hinges on.

6. **Step away from the computer**. One of the most important steps any of us can take to be a healthier dater is to abandon the idea of online dating. Online dating sites are a petri dish of toxicity for individuals who are prone to fantasy and obsessing over dating. Why is that? Because they contain three very dangerous things: the hope of instant gratification (finding someone with one click), the promotion of fantasy-based exchanges (when you don't have a clear picture of someone you are free to "fill in the blanks" and create what you want that person to be), and the almost complete removal of the crucial human necessity to judge someone realistically, in person, BEFORE getting emotionally attached to them. Because love addicts need to learn to defer gratification, control their susceptibility to fantasy, and be able to judge people realistically, online dating is a bad idea. It's like an alcoholic hanging out in a bar after he has given up drinking. It's only a matter of time before he will slip. Online dating may be great for individuals with a healthier perspective on dating, but not for love addicts.

7. **Don't have sex on the first date**. Cosmopolitan magazine recently wrote that not having sex on the first date is "outdated." In other words, go ahead, girls, that rule is "antiquated and harmful" and produces "unnecessary anxiety and shame about something normal and natural: dating and sex." Unfortunately, they were NOT talking to a love addict. Like it or not, you need to play by the antiquated, SAFE rules from days of yore. I say this not just to the women, but the men as well. Sex to a love addict is never taken lightly. It *means* something. It usually means a full-blown commitment and an excuse to obsess over someone. That's why it needs to be put on the back burner for a significant amount of time

(three months? Six months? You decide. But not the first night. Please!). A love addict's job is to learn to defer gratification. To sniff out a person for red flags FIRST, before making any heavy-duty commitments, physical or otherwise. And here's something Cosmo won't tell you: what's the hurry? If you're into someone, and they're into you, and you plan to spend your lives together, why not wait? You've got all the time in the world. Why not make it about other stuff first? Sex on the first, second, third, etc., date is Russian Roulette to a love addict. Put it off. It can wait. He/she's not going anywhere. And if he/she does leave, they weren't worth it anyway. More than that, it might save you from obsessing more than you would if you *did* have sex.

8. **Do keep a journal**. The perspective and instincts we have before we get to know someone intimately are amazingly sharp. I am convinced that every red flag a person might have pops up on the first or second date, if we really pay attention. Trouble is, when we want something bad enough, we are willing to ignore the red flags, and ignore our gut instincts. Keeping a journal helps us to stay on track and remember what we felt and sensed in those first hours. Be sure to write down your first impression, if you noticed or felt anything funny, if something didn't add up. What was your logical brain picking up on, versus your heart (emotions)? While this may seem like overkill, it will help you in your process and ability to "learn" to date healthily. Looking back, we always see with perfect vision. Hindsight is, after all, 20/20.

9. **Don't trust your emotions**. I know. It sounds counterintuitive when talking about dating. But it's not. A love addict can't trust his or her emotions. Not yet, anyway. Why? Because we tend to be ruled by our emotions, and when that happens, our logic goes right out the window. I was very imbalanced in this way. My

logical brain would pick up on abuse, red flags, neglect, shame and general danger. My logical brain would scream at me to leave a bad relationship. But my emotions were screaming back, "Never! I love him!!!!" And so, I stayed. This is an extremely unhealthy way to make life decisions. You cannot be ruled by emotions only. You need a balance of both your head and your heart. Trouble is, because we have been off-balance for so many years, we need the pendulum to swing in the opposite direction before it can someday settle in the middle where it belongs. We need to depend more on our logical brain so that we begin to trust it again. Only after our logical brain has determined that we are safe and secure are we able to allow our emotions to "speak up." . So, all those emotions that howl at you, screaming that they are convinced 100 percent that it's love after the first or second date? IGNORE THEM. Focus on the brain. On the logic. Turn back to your journal. Don't be afraid to ask questions, to seek out the possibility of red flags. Be suspicious (without *acting* overly suspicious). And don't be afraid to walk away if you unearth something you know in your head and your heart you probably cannot or should not live with if it doesn't agree with your <u>set of values</u>.

10. **Know Your Values**. Ah! Values again! Attraction, chemistry, passion, flirtiness—those things are fine and good and all, but they can't shake a stick at your values. Knowing your values is critical to dating. If you don't, how can you know if someone else's values are right for you? I do not suggest you try to find out what your date thinks about child rearing on date #1. But I do suggest that you know what YOUR values are so that you know what to look out for and how to assess the other person in time. Case in point, I went on a first date many years ago with a good-looking guy who asked if I wanted to get high. I said no thanks, and despite

the fact that his offer bothered me enormously, I kept dating him. I kept dating him because I didn't know my values. I knew I was *for* legalizing marijuana, but I didn't yet know that I was *against* dating someone who smoked it. I didn't know it was so important to me that the relationship would not work if drugs were involved. And it didn't. I eventually couldn't take his smoking. Had I known my values, I would have saved myself a lot of time and emotional angst.

To summarize, you need to hold people up to the light and really look at them and not be afraid of what you might see. Your happiness, security and peace of mind depend upon you being honest with yourself. And while I do not suggest scrutinizing people too early in the dating process, I do suggest being open to communicating, and being patient about cultivating a relationship. You will not get to know someone overnight. You cannot rush things. People who fall in love fast are red flags. YOU falling in love fast is a red flag. Healthy people are cautious, curious, protective with their emotions, with their heart. They don't call every two seconds, they don't profess love right away. They don't drink like a fish or do drugs or try to sweet-talk you into bed after a two and a half hour date. This is a different kind of date. Not that there's anything wrong with it. But you need to have lower expectations for a date like that. It's generally not the kind that might lead to a lifetime of shared values.

CHAPTER 34

How to Have a Healthy Break Up

"The saddest thing about love, Joe, is that not only the love cannot last forever, but even the heartbreak is soon forgotten."

–William Faulkner

"To want and not to have, sent all up her body a hardness, a hollowness, a strain. And then to want and not to have — to want and want — how that wrung the heart, and wrung it again and again!"

–Virginia Woolf, *To the Lighthouse*

You're back in the dating world. *Woohoo!* And all your hopes and fears are right there with you. And while every wonderful rendezvous brings you one step closer to your ultimate dating goals, that doesn't mean there won't be a few not-so-wonderful experiences out there. In other words, dating is not one and done. You still may have to go through a few flops and break-ups before finding the right fit.

A good friend of mine who had an ugly break-up with her long-term boyfriend recently said to me, exasperated, "Is there any such thing as a clean break-up?" I smiled and gave her a resounding, yes! And then I reminded her of the job she'd just left. She was working in the city as a graphic designer. She disliked her boss and hated the fact that there was no room to move up or out as it was a relatively small company. So she found another position with a larger firm and, without burning her proverbial bridge, gave two weeks notice to her current employer. Her transition went as smoothly as possible and everyone wished her well. In fact, she came back to her old company once a year to continue to help them with their annual Customer Appreciation Day. I reminded her of this "break up," and she quickly said to me that she wasn't in love with her company, nor did she have much emotionally invested. Leaving was an easy decision to make and to execute. But, she could have just as easily walked out yelling and screaming. Why didn't she? My guess is that in this situation, she used her logical brain verses her emotional brain. She knew that she still had some benefit to gain from keeping that work relationship as positive as possible. Maybe she needed a reference from one of her managers. Maybe she wanted to be able to visit her workmates. Maybe, because she's still working in the same industry, knew her reputation was important to uphold. Healthy break-ups, despite the hope, fear, pain and sadness that might accompany them, can still happen as long as we choose to use our logical brains versus our emotional brain.

One of the best things we can do to have a healthier break-up is to set goals for ourselves. Too often we live without goals and direction. Our life was on one track and it came to a screeching halt or it veered off-route into a ditch. Either way, a break-up marks the end of one direction and the beginning of another, and we need to reassess where we want to go from here. Below are a set of goals I created for myself to help me through a very painful break-up. Perhaps they could also help you:

1. **I need to (or would like to) redefine or simply re-examine my type of man**. I think this is crucial. Sure, I want the bad boy with tattoos and the cool heart of a serious lover. I want that "look" of sexiness and individuality or as I used to describe my ex, that "urban intellectual." And yet, I also want a family man. A man capable of loving and accepting the realm of family love. A man who is not afraid of the mini-van and the children and the fact that I have a life in the suburbs. A man who can handle reality. I am a very real woman. He would have to accept flaws, not perfection.

2. **I need to start to view myself in a more realistic light**. I am NOT a grunge girl, or a hippy chick. I cannot relate to people who do drugs (whether addicted or not). I just don't GET IT. I need to really ACKNOWLEDGE my success as a woman and stop settling for men way below my socio-economic level who have little or no ambition. I need to really see my positives and my achievements and recognize that they play a HUGE role in who I am as a person. When you think you are nothing, you accept people who also think they are nothing. My ex was a beautiful person in many ways. Physically beautiful, spiritually beautiful. But he could not take care of himself. He couldn't get his act together. I have to realize traits like that play a huge role in how a couple love and respect each other. The better I know myself, the better able I am to pick and choose someone more suited to my level of experience and growth.

3. **I need to refrain from contacting him.** He does not want to make that mutual connection any more so I must let him go. If he sends me an email, fine. I can respond as a friend. But the emotional-lover connection is gone. If he does reach out, I must place boundaries and not go back. I want this break up as much as he, and I must continuously remember that.

4. **I need to refrain from getting closer to my previous ex(es).** Even though, in the wake of *this* ex's rejection of me, it feels good to be with someone two exes back, someone who still loves me, it is not in my best interest. When we are alone, we tend to want to find someone quickly to fill the empty space. I cannot do that. I cannot pull from a pool of past lovers. I need to move forward and remember my goals. I need to remember that every day I choose not to get involved with these inappropriate men it is an act of self-love.

5. **I need to find a life--or better yet-- I need to acknowledge that I have a life.** Sure, from an outsider's perspective I look like I have everything. Beautiful kids, beautiful home, a career, an education, I have hobbies and work out, etc. And yet...inside of me I am not fulfilled. It's as if there is something more out there that I have not yet found. I either find *something*, or I make peace with what I've already got.

6. **I need to not focus on him or WHY he does not love me.** It's over. This kind of questioning doesn't resolve anything. If I ask myself why I like Reeses peanut butter cups but not Three Muskateers bars the ONLY answer is *preference*. Period. I have no right analyzing HIM. Pointless. How is knowing that he is a narcissist going to help me beyond simply knowing that I dated him? I need to know too that not everyone will think I am the

greatest thing that walked the earth. Oh well! Too bad. Get real, girl. **Do not take it personally**.

7. **I need to start to really live in the present.** Do not wish for the future or wallow in the past. NOW is all I've got. Sadly, that means kissing the comfort of fantasy goodbye. Fantasy thinking ("I wonder if he likes me?") is an In-the-Now killer.

8. **I need to be patient.** There is no rush when you live in the now. There is no hurry. Patience is a gift you give your heart. It helps you to realize that nothing can be rushed. Not the grass to grow or the flowers to bloom. The cycle of life brings all things forth in its own time. Patience also helps to abate "needing" and wanting.

9. **I need to get in touch with what I love.** Now is the time to embrace all those things that I can finally embrace FREELY...I can dance, let my hair grow, sing, wear ugly pajamas, not shave my legs...heck I can talk to myself if I want. I can be weird! And I am not going to be ashamed of what I gravitate towards. I don't answer to anyone right now. How lucky. I am going to see that I am lucky. If I want to watch Oprah's YouTube channel all weekend, who cares! I am going to be ME. And finally...

10. **I need to not be afraid of the path I am now on.** I am here for a reason. I have a choice. I can look at this as a disaster and try to run back, or I can look at it as a gift and move forward. I am going to try to choose to look at things positively. I am learning something, becoming something. And I am doing it alone. I am going to use this time to really define my worth. I will recognize my strength. Know that I am a fighter. And I am going to know in my heart that even though it feels as though I have lost everything, I haven't. I have what counts most. I still have me.

i.   **Dealing with Rejection**

Let's start here: rejection scares the hell out of most of us. Agreed? It's what keeps us from going up to strangers and asking them out on a date. Fear we'll be booed is what keeps us from going on stage and speaking publicly. And it keeps some of us from doing the things we love, for fear that we will be rejected by others who might be doing them better. But the worst kind of rejection is when we are rejected by those we consider to be the most important person in our lives—our spouse, our partner, our love interest, our crush. Rejection from this person is the absolute worst, because let's be honest, he or she is the one who defines and validates us and gives us our worth. When that person reject us, we feel worthless. And this is our first mistake. **No one defines us. And no one validates our worth, except us.**

But, back to rejection. It happens. And there's virtually no way on earth to avoid it. So…how do we handle it?

For starters, we need to change our perception of what rejection logically, actually is, not what we "feel" it is. So, step away from the gut-wrenching, terrible, awful, dreadful, unbearable feelings you feel about rejection and switch over to using your brain. Are you in brain mode now? OK, read on…

1.   **Rejection is neither good nor bad.** It's neutral. And yet we typically assign it as something negative. But, just for argument's sake, let's start to look at it as a positive force in your life. First off, it won't kill you. It's not a disease which can make you ill. It doesn't take any money, clothing, shelter or food away from you. It doesn't physically beat you up. And it doesn't change you in any way shape or form other than **help redirect you towards a new life**. It's often disguised as a loss, only to later down the road, be a gain, as most people will tell you. So, no matter how you "feel" about rejection's evil powers, try to keep things a bit more clear. Rejection, is neutral. At best, it's a positive force that pushes us to redefine our

lives and move on. The more we stay focused on the neutrality or positivity of rejection, the better.

2. **Rejection isn't personal.** This concept is tricky, and one that people have the hardest time understanding. Let me say it again: rejection is NOT PERSONAL. I'm sure you believe that if you were personally rejected on the grounds that your boyfriend doesn't like you anymore and even left you for someone else, then this is personal. But it's not! He's not rejecting **you** as much as he is opting to choose another life for himself. She's not rejecting you as much as she is selecting a different path to walk down. And while that may *seem* like rejection of who you are, there's actually a much deeper issue at hand. People come together, and ultimately move apart based on their set of Values. A value is a thing (a principle, a belief, a standard of behavior) that we regard as essential to our being, so essential, in fact, that without it, we feel lacking or wrong or worthless. It's a MUST HAVE, not a want or a wish. And when you reject someone, or they reject you, it's typically based on values, and not much else. When people's values are not aligned, the healthy response is rejection of the relationship. This of course, doesn't happen in unhealthy relationship. Why? Because love addicts or avoidants, for example, tend not to know their values, and because the idea of holding onto the relationship is far greater than any personal values, they remain. So even if someone is completely wrong, a love addict will still stay; out of fear, desperation, loneliness, and definitely not knowing their values. So start to see rejection as a healthy thing, a gift the other person is giving you by setting you free to make another choice for yourself. Remember, no one validates you or defines who you are. Only you do. So the more you figure out who you are, the more you will attract people who share your values. And while the risk of rejection can happen

any time with anyone, you will lessen your risk if you date people with whom you share similar values.

3. **Rejection is a huge part of nature.** Animals select one mate over another based on instinct to help perpetuate their species. Some animal mothers will reject their offspring. If you're a hamster, your mother may eat you if she determines she can't feed you. If you're a cat or a dog, your mom may stomp on you or simply refuse to feed you. Don't take it personally! It's called nature. In terms of our own bodies, think of all the things it rejects on its own. If you drink too much alcohol, say, or eat contaminated food, the body rejects these things by vomiting or getting sick. If we catch a virus or a bacterial infection, the body rejects these "bugs" by getting a fever. If we have a foreign object inside our bodies (like a cancerous tumor), the body uses all its resources to either get rid of it or protect against it by building a calcium encasement around it. The point is, rejection is part of life. And while we humans may have outwitted natural selection, we haven't been able to escape natural rejection.

When we think of rejection in these ways, and remove the emotional, negative feelings we associate with it, understanding that rejection is not personal can be very helpful. It is simply nature's way of redirecting you and letting you know that something isn't right–not because you are bad, no good, worthless, ugly or unlovable. It simply means you fit somewhere else. And that's a good thing. Rejection is a gift that allows you to consider new options– a more natural, organic path that you are currently denying yourself, if you hang on.

ii. **Not Seeing the Results You Want**

After I had my second baby, I felt it was time to work my ass off and get back into shape. I had 50 pounds to lose, zero willpower and chasing a baby and a toddler around the house didn't leave much motivation or time for my plan to become a Sports Illustrated model. I had my son about the same time Madonna had her daughter, and in three months, she was back to her pre-baby weight and on stage prancing around in her cone bustier and g-string. Meanwhile, I was doing everything in my power to get to a kickboxing class three times a week that showed no signs of helping me lose a single pound. I had to remind myself that Madonna had five personal trainers, two nannies and millions of dollars.

Many years later, long after babies, long after I was divorced, and long after I had spent years working my butt off to overcome love addiction, I met S and together, we fell madly in love. I thought I had finally found a truly healthy partner and that all my hard work paid off. *Wheph*. The climb up the mountain brought me to the summit! A mere eight months later, he dumped me.

Wtf?!

I cannot begin to tell you how blind-sided and betrayed by the entire universe I felt. How let down in myself and the whole world. How can you work so damn hard, for so damn long and not reach your goals? Isn't that the promise of recovery? Isn't that the guarantee of hard work? The universe answered back—"No." I didn't like the response. But, news to me, there is no promise. And there are no guarantees in life. I had heard it a million times before. I didn't want to believe it. So then? What's the point?

The universe didn't have an answer to that. But, I did. It came many months later. It came after S dumped me and I just completely threw my hands in the air and said, "I give up." After I sat on my bedroom floor, sobbing for days straight, curled up in a ball, something shocking occurred to me: what if I never find true love? What then? These questions were overwhelming. The fear of dying without ever finding love again seized me with terror and panic. I cried some more. I was, after all, 40 years old and the dating pool had all but dried up (at least, in my mind). If I never found love again, what would I do? The answer to this question for many is an easy one. But to a love addict, it's fraught with intense dread and difficulty because we can see our life no other way, because our whole life has been focused on obsession over this one thing. Letting go of that thing is akin to jumping off a cliff. It's instant destruction. How can we possibly let go of our dream? And yet, in my logical mind I had come far enough to know that letting go would not kill me. It wasn't fair, and it wasn't what I wanted. I felt like a complete failure. But I knew this experience would force me to reevaluate and reconfigure my whole life in ways I never expected. And, when I finally accepted that I wasn't going to find the healthy romantic, permanent love that I had craved my whole life, I finally stopped looking, and a funny thing happened. I looked around my room. I looked at the ceiling. I looked at the four walls. I looked at my kids tumbling their toy cars and trucks all over my bedroom floor. I thought of their boundless love. I thought of my boundless love for them. I thought of my family. My close friends. My car. My dishwasher. The trees in my backyard. My writing. My health. My breath. My brain. My spirituality. And a hundred other things I had in my life that I could be grateful for. They were good. At least, I'd better start thinking so because they were all I had. It's not that I gave up. I want to make that perfectly clear. It's that I decided, then and there, that I would choose another path to happiness, and additionally, I would choose to be grateful for what I had instead of bemoaning what I didn't. It was this moment that would define the next 10 years of my life. It was this moment that I recognized true joy is not what you obsess over or think you should have. True joy is what is in front of you right now, at this moment. Whether you like it or not. And, it is the gift of having a creative mind that offers you the possibility to find joy in other places, in places other than the one place you thought, you hoped, you'd find it.

A reader of my blog named Rachel recently reached out, as she does from time to time, to tell me that she's been working like crazy over the past year to become healthier. She's also been sober for three weeks, and hasn't engaged in any relationships for the same amount of time and was feeling really strong in herself and positive. And then, *bam!* An old friend of hers who was, according to Rachel, an alcoholic and love addict, recently posted a picture of herself on social media with her new boyfriend captioned, "Love of my life!" Rachel was furious and hurt and disappointed. How can I work so hard and see zero results and then she comes along, worse off than me, does no work, and she finds the love of her life?! I congratulated Rachel on her sobriety, and implored her to hide the friend, at least for now. But, after that, I didn't know what to say. The truth is, I can't figure this out for her. I can offer help, guidance and advice, but, she—we all—have to figure this out for ourselves. No one can convince anyone that little Miss *Love of My Life* won't get dumped in a matter of weeks, or that Facebook can be a brutal trigger-zone that makes so many of us think everyone is better off than us. No one can reconfigure the thoughts in your head to say, "Hey, I'm doing OK. If this is my best, I am going to accept it and try to find joy in everything I do." And no one can sit you down and persuade you with all the force in the universe to understand that romantic love is not guaranteed, but you can live an amazingly full, loving, powerful life without it. Only you can convince and persuade yourself of these things. And when you do, it's a game changer.

As a former love addict, I now know addiction and obsession are paradoxes. When we have an all-consuming lust for something that really doesn't exist or can't love us back in return, what do we actually have? Nothing. And yet, it's so hard and so painful to give up nothing. For some, love itself is that same paradox. Russel Brand, comedian, recovered addict and author of *Recovery, Freedom from our Addictions* has a great line in one of his YouTube videos regarding addiction and pain: "There's an essential you that's trying to realize itself and you're not realizing it because you're being distracted by the external coordinates of a world that wants you to be a consumer, a civilized being, instead of a connected, spiritual force." I will add to his list a "consumer of love." We live in a world that wants us to be consumers of love, to believe that our biggest life's achievement should be a whirlwind Hollywood romance. It's not.

He goes on to say that everything and everyone has an intended purpose. He uses a tree as an example, saying a tree not impeded in its growth becomes the great redwood it was meant to be. In his book he asks, "When are you going to recover the person you were born to be?" And this is the deepest message I can share with you here. That whether you find love or not outside of yourself, you will always have a gargantuan amount of work, joy, lust, love, spirit, beauty, mystery and energy within you that desperately needs exploring. For most of us, our inner selves are unchartered territory. When the end result of all the work you've done on yourself seemingly doesn't pan out, it's time to pull out your bag of tricks—your mysterious inner world. It's time to discover your spiritual side, to uncover lost details of your past, lose yourself in the wonder of why you do what you do. The meaning here is simple if you accept it: there are other routes to happiness and they are within you.

The driving force of Girl Rebuilt is my unshaken belief that the more you know about yourself, the more open and available you will be to healthy love. And, the better able you are to recognize what's right for you, as opposed to creating a fantasy version of what you think is best, the closer you will be to the source of connecting with people who also know themselves and want healthy love. Don't lose hope in your own power. Don't lose hope in your search for love within you.

PART V:
RELAPSES, RESOURCES
AND RULES, OH MY!

Sigh! We're at the end of what has hopefully been a challenging but enlightening journey that will most likely continue for you long after you close this book. At least that's the goal. And so the following section is filled with a few reminders, loads of resources, and further reading. Remember, you can also find a gazillion resources on GirlRebuilt.com, read the blog, post comments, and participate in our community!

CHAPTER 35

Fell Back Into Your Old Ways? Here's a Quick Fix

"Never confuse a single defeat with a final defeat."

–F. Scott Fitzgerald

Success versus failure is not always black and white. There's no distinct "finish line" to success that once crossed, leads to bliss, perfection, and the absence of failure. But there *are* bad choices you can continue to make which will hold you back from progressing towards feeling emotionally and mentally healthier. Here are some mistakes you could still be making:

1. **Continue to talk about/analyze the person you can't seem to stop thinking about:** While we all must give ourselves a much-needed grieving period to get over a relationship, we need to somehow recognize a point in time when our grieving has gone beyond

what might be healthy. The jury is out on how long an actual grieving period should last. It's different for everyone. But talking about, analyzing, fantasizing or stalking the ex long after the relationship ended may be behaviors that are doing more harm than good. This is not constructive grieving, this is trying to hold on. And while grieving in itself is a process of anger, sadness, disbelief, and a myriad of other emotions, acceptance and letting go must be the end result.

2. **Vent (about how miserable your life currently is)**: I'm convinced that venting is an art. The longer you do it, the better at it you become. And the irony of venting is that as you become better at it, you feel worse. Yay! Why is that? Because venting, although helpful for blowing off temporary steam, accomplishes absolutely nothing. It's just another way to obsess over someone or something that is completely unhealthy for you. It's just another way to stay anchored to your addiction. So, don't be fooled by all those blogs that glamorize collective venting. Venting is only worth its weight when it leads to a positive outcome. Like, maybe, you moving on?

3. **Blame "him" (and everyone else) for your problems**: We all know that none of your problems have anything to do with you but rather all the jerks who messed up your life, took advantage of you, held you back, never loved you, lied, cheated and broke your heart. You didn't ask for any of this, right? Heck no. So…when it comes to really assessing the situation at hand, and your ultimate happiness, don't take any responsibility. Blame others! And likewise, depend on them for your happiness. Happiness, after all, is something that comes from outside sources, not within. And you have no control over your own attitude, your own behavior, or the fact that you have to deal with this situation in the first place. Right??? Oh, and one more bit of advice: blaming others is

so much easier and will never challenge you to think that maybe, just maybe, you do, after all, have responsibility for your actions. So, if you really want to just take it easy and continue depending on others for happiness, blame them for not being what you need and want them to be.

4. **Trust your fantasies**: When you were a kid, you created big dreams of love and happiness and castles and unicorns. None of it was real, but it was a necessary process that either helped you begin to identify dreams that would eventually shape your reality, or it was a defense mechanism that protected you from a reality you could not manage, or scared you. Chances are, if you're a love addict, those "fantasies" you still carry with you are defense mechanisms that served (past tense) to protect you, but now, wreak havoc on your ability to deal with what's really in front of you, as opposed to what you wish were in front of you. The more you spend in la la land, the less time, knowledge and experience you will gain in the real world, learning real world skills to help you actually achieve your goals. So, if you plan to get a big fat F in recovery class, trust those fantasies in your brain and keep telling yourself that they speak the truth. Of course, they've never steered you wrong before, right?

5. **Remove all boundaries, let everyone in and say or do anything you please**: Yay! Freedom! Who needs or wants boundaries?! They have such an unappealing reputation, especially if you're a child of the 60s or 70s. And while good, healthy boundaries serve to protect you and those around you (they keep bad, unhealthy people out of your life and likewise, keep YOU from saying or doing things you really shouldn't), let's face it, they hold you back, make you responsible, and deny you that childhood fantasy that everyone will love you and be good to you if you just give them a chance.

6. **Cause lots of drama**: When you were a teenager in high school… oh, the drama!_Remember? Well, don't give it up. Continue to gossip, manipulate, and act totally histrionic at the smallest sign of strife. Because who needs to grow up and act rational? Not you. Acting like a teen, making mountains out of molehills and getting involved in other people's problems is exciting! Or dangerous! Or riveting! Heck, it's your own little slice of Hollywood. It gives you the perfect excuse not to face your actual problems, or work on them, let alone interact with grace and dignity.

7. **Don't change anything**: Don't change your behavior (notice I used the word "behavior," I didn't say change YOU). Keep doing exactly what you've been doing_(notice I used the word "doing" not "being"). Continue to hang around toxic people, and of course, keep pursuing the person you're obsessing over (how's that working for ya?). Keep frequenting places that compromise your desire to be healthy and safe (bars, online dating sites, the street your Person I am addicted to lives on). Really, why bother changing? Change is hard. It's actual work! It requires the meaningful attempt to alter or modify one type of behavior for another, for the sake of improving one's situation. And you have no interest in improving your situation. You like things as they are (that's an educated guess, or you wouldn't be reading this book), so…simply ignore my words and keep doing what you've been doing. The definition of insanity, after all, is doing the same thing over and over and expecting a different result. But then again, you don't want different results, do you? You want exactly what you've got, er, except you want HIM to change. But not you.

8. **Don't reach out for any help or take any advice**: There absolutely IS a light at the end of the tunnel, but you need to know how to navigate that tunnel. It's not a straight line. It's more like a

maze. And whether you turn to reading books, chatting on a Love Addiction forum with others, or attend LAA meetings, one or all of those things will help guide you. Why? Well, for starters, you never learned how to love in a healthy way (love can be learned!), you most likely have low self-esteem (self-esteem can be improved with more knowledge), and what you've been doing up to this point obviously isn't working (people with more experience, with years of recovery make great guides!). But, you're an adult and probably know it all. You probably resent advice, and hate to be told what to do. Well, take my advice, doing it on your own, without the coursework or without help from teachers will most likely get you a D or F. Try doing brain surgery without any prior learning. Coming out of love addiction is equally as challenging!

9. **Replace your current toxic, unavailable bf with another one**: This one always works so well. When you can't have a successful relationship with Guy A (for whatever reason), at least you can go out and replace him or her with Guy B or C, equally bad choices. And you can continue to do this until hell freezes over because there's an infinite amount of bad choices out there to be made. If you want an "F" for figuring this all out, this is the way to do it. Repeat the same mistakes of the past without ever changing and without ever recognizing that real change doesn't mean just changing the players around and expecting different results, it means redefining what you find attractive, acceptable and meaningful. We so often tend to thing that we will get different results from different people, and we're always so flabbergasted when different people treat us exactly the same as those who have come before. Does that tell you something about human nature? That while there are subtle differences between us, we still react to people one way: the way we teach them to treat us. When you teach people

to treat you differently (healthier) than you did in the past, you tend to attract a different (healthier) caliber person (those who can step up to the plate and provide the kind of relationship that you expect), AND those, like your Person I am addicted to, who start to notice that you expect more of them usually cannot step up to the plate. Change must come from within YOU, not the player. Unless you want an F.

10. **Never find out what your values are/Continue to believe you're worthless**: Why are you in this situation to begin with? Well, 99.9 percent of it is because you have low self-esteem. How do I know? Because the very second (well, maybe a little longer) a healthy person with healthy self-esteem recognizes they are not being treated decently, kindly and lovingly in a relationship, they don't stick around. Period. Love addicts do. Why? Because love addicts don't have the same level of intolerance for things like neglect, avoidance, physical, mental or emotional abuse, manipulation, and so on. And whether it be because they were never taught self-esteem from their parents, or simply don't have a healthy perspective on their own lives doesn't matter. What matters is that there are certain components to self-esteem that you need to possess in order to change and be healthier. Here is the most important component of self-esteem again: it is to have VALUES. A value is a thing we regard as super-important and believe we deserve in our lives for no other reason but that it is something that will make us feel alive, comfortable, and happy. Being treated with kindness is a value. Believing that you should never be physically beaten is a value. The trouble is, either we don't know what our values are, OR, more importantly, we have a vague idea of our values, but don't stick to them. We walk around and puff out our chests and say "No man will ever hurt me again!" and then hop into bed with the first hot

guy we pick up at a bar and only later find out he's a player. Having self-esteem means having values, and sticking to them! We don't just talk the talk, we walk the walk. If you know in your heart that every time you date someone who drinks heavily or does drugs it makes you feel uncomfortable, then that means you have a value that says: I do not want drugs or alcohol in my life. It also means you don't listen to that value. Success in recovery means you put your values ABOVE your need for a man. Self-esteem means you put your health and safety ABOVE your desire to get laid, above your desire to connect to someone as quick as possible, and above your desire to feed your hunger for anything that makes the pain go away. Don't write down your values or stick to them if you want to fail at recovery. Believing you are worthless, or going through life without a "Values" road map is a surefire way to guarantee a unhealthy, unhappy life.

CHAPTER 36

Essential Laws of Love

"Rivers know this: there is no hurry.
We shall get there some day."

–A.A. Milne, *Winnie-the-Pooh*

There is no law book or list of rules for personal responsibility when it comes to a quest for healthy love. So... I decided to create one. Here it is.

Law #1: Thou shalt strive to be a mature, responsible adult: Unhealthy love is all about stunted growth; rebuilding yourself is all about growing up. To successfully rebuild you really need to give up childhood survival mechanisms like addictive behavior, acting out, manipulating to get your way, chasing after unhealthy fantasies, and burying your head in the sand by focusing on your partner. In other words, learn healthier ways to manage your life.

Law #2. Thou shalt not avoid thy personal responsibilities: Unhealthy love is about using your partner or relationship as an emotional distraction so that you can avoid yourself, your responsibilities, and that which you fear the most. Find out what you fear, and face it.

Law #3: Thou shalt take care of thyself: You are your best investment, so treat yourself as such. Eat well, exercise, challenge your brain, be an integral part of your community and block harmful people from your life. Your body and mind are temples. They are sacred places. Do not pollute them with bad food, negative people and defeatist thinking. If you can care for and love others, you'd better care for yourself as well.

Law #4: Thou shalt exercise thy logical brain as much as if not more so than thy emotional heart: Well, at least until you get used to exercising your logical brain. But unhealthy love choices tend to be made by the heart and emotions when logic isn't involved. Don't allow your emotions to make decisions for you, without enlisting the help of your logical brain (which can detect red flags and recognize safety). Let the pendulum swing in the opposite direction for a time. Give up "thinking" with your heart and try to think with your brain. Or both!

Law #5: Thou shalt have a life of thy own: It's time to quit depending on others for your happiness. Why is it everyone else's responsibility to make you happy? What role do you play in your own happiness? Search for activities and emotionally and spiritually stimulating pursuits you can do on your own in times of solitude. This is how you begin to know, like and trust yourself.

Law #6: Thou shalt learn to accept and if necessary, forgive thyself: Look in the mirror. What do you see? Do you wish you saw someone far more perfect? Flawless? Wealthy? Famous? Get over it. You're not perfect nor will you ever be. No one is. But that does not mean you are not loveable. Even the most handicapped, disadvantaged, challenged people in the world are still worthy of love. And so are you. But if you think you can just waltz out into the world and expect to be validated and loved by others, you're in for a bit of disappointment. When you do that, it's hit or miss. You never know who will like you and who won't. But guess what, when the love and validation comes from within YOU, you always know what you're gonna get. Make peace with the mistakes you made in the past, and move on to being your best source of love and strength.

Law #7: Thou shalt not participate in harmful or hurtful behavior, to thyself and others: No affairs, no sleeping with or becoming emotionally bonded to a married or otherwise unavailable person, no cheating, no stalking, no physically, mentally or emotionally harming others for your own personal benefit, no acting out in ways that may harm or hurt yourself or others. And enough with the Facebook stalking. already. "I felt great after seeing my ex on Facebook, living out his new life without me," said no one ever.

Law #8: Thou shalt abandon obsessive fantasy in exchange for reality, and stay in the now: Obsessing over every Tyler, Zach and Justin you meet, falling in love hard and fast (in your imagination), and becoming hopelessly addicted to someone is all fantasy-based. About one percent of what's going on might be driven by reality. Let all that go and stay in the now. What does that mean? It means every time you catch yourself "wondering" or "day-dreaming" or fantasizing about someone new (or even your ex) STOP, and bring yourself back to what you are physically doing. If you're doing nothing, find something to do. But stay present in only that which is happening now. Love addicts create their addicts, and fantasy is how they do it.

Law #9: Thou shalt be true to thyself and thy values: Many of us do not know what a value is, let alone what our personal values might be. If there's one thing you learn in rebuilding yourself, learn your values. They are your map. They help define who you are, what you need, and who to look for and connect with in the world (when you're ready).

Law #10: Thou shalt no longer be a victim: Chances are many of your dysfunctional behaviors were learned from dysfunctional caretakers. They may have physically abused you, mentally abused you, or even neglected you. But, as an adult, you not only have the responsibility to care for yourself, you have the FREEDOM to care for yourself in much healthier ways than ever before. So, quit blaming your parents, and the world for what you *don't have* and be grateful for what you *do have*: you're alive, and you have the opportunity to learn healthier ways. You can start now. No need to forgive whoever messed you up (although it helps), but do recognize that you're the captain of the ship now, and you are in charge of your own destiny.

Law #11: Thou shalt live and let live: Stop trying to control everything and everyone. It's too much of a task to take on. It is said that people who have had traumatic or chaotic pasts tend to be very controlling in their adult life. As adults, even though we may have the power to control our own lives and our immediate environment, we cannot control everyone and everything. Every person we are in a relationship with is beyond our control. That's why it's essential to surround yourself with people who address your innermost needs. If you don't like chaos, don't fall for a guy who is impulsive and unpredictable. If you like excitement and spontaneity in your life, don't fall for a girl who prefers to be at home watching Netflix all weekend. Accept what you cannot change; but ONLY if you can handle it in your life. If you can't, don't accept it. Move on and reconfigure the players in your life.

Onward!

Here's where you pat yourself on the back, or maybe go out and buy yourself a new pair of shoes; maybe get a massage. Whatever makes you feel like you've won a prestigious award or ran a marathon, do it! You set a goal to understand yourself better, a goal to start rebuilding yourself and redefining your relationship with love, and you achieved that goal by getting to the end of this book. And so now that you are using your logical mind, no longer entrapped by fantasy-thinking and ready to face reality instead of avoiding it, here's a little fun fact I will leave you with about the history of "love."

Where did our contemporary notion of love come from? Have we always loved in the same way? Did cave couples look longingly into each other's eyes and grunt sweet nothings to each other? Probably not. Joseph Campbell, mythologist, storyteller and author of *The Power of Myth* believed that romantic love as we know it today came from the Troubadours, those Robin Hood-like wandering minstrels who wrote and sang love poems at court for noble ladies of the twelfth century. Before the middle ages, love was sex. It was based on lust, or what was known as Eros, "the erotic, biological urge," which drove humanity to procreation. There was, of course, "love thy neighbor" kind of love from the bible, as well as spiritual love for God; and, love that oftentimes existed between couples in arranged marriages. But by the twelfth and thirteenth centuries, Campbell writes, there "was one of the most important mutations of human feeling and spiritual consciousness, that a new way of experiencing love came to expression." That love was romantic love. It was, as Campbell describes, "the seizure that comes in recognizing... your soul's counterpart in the other person." Love suddenly became personal, focused and obsessive. But, (and here's the important part), it began as enter-tainment for the nobility. And much like jesters or jousts, courtly love, as it was known, was dramatic, spectacle-like, and hugely amusing. In fact, chiv-alrous rules were created by knights who had to go through all the phases of dating before winning the heart of their object of affection. And while this style of love essentially began as harmless courtly entertainment, it eventually became something we all had to have. Intense, "pure" love—that began as fantasy and fiction over 900 years ago—is, today, a profoundly ingrained (and unrealistic) expectation of how love should be. We're not troubadours or ladies in waiting! We've had 900 years to hone our skills and become better and smarter at loving, and by the time this book goes to print, I'd like to think that we're on our way to a new "mutation of human feeling—" that which leads to conscious, beautiful, wonderful, fulfilling, grounded, realistic love.

I think the love of the troubadours was love addict love. It was unhealthy, often unrequited, and drama-driven. And that being said, I really hope this book has empowered you to take your 900-year-old belief system, crush it, and create a new belief, ie, the belief that love doesn't incur pain. At least not the toxic kind. And love isn't abusive or neglectful or cold or lonely. And that you're worth far more than the scraps you used to survive on.

Hotlines, Recovery Facilities & Treatment Centers,

Books & Online Resources

Hotlines

SAMHSA's

National Helpline

1-800-662-HELP (4357)

Substance Abuse & Mental Health Services Administration

samhsa.gov

The Recovery Village

(352) 771-2700

www.therecoveryvillage.com

Recovery Facilities & Treatment Centers

Five Sisters Ranch

https://www.fivesistersranch.com/

California

The Meadows

https://www.themeadows.com/

Arizona

The Ranch

https://www.recoveryranch.com/

Tennessee

The Refuge

https://www.therefuge-ahealingplace.com/

Florida

Books

A Fine Romance, Judith Sills

Addiction to Love, Susan Peabody

Awaken the Giant Within, Anthony Robbins

Better Single Than Sorry, Jen Schefft

Co-Dependent No More, Mellody Beattie

Don't Let Your Emotions Run Your Life: How Dialectical Behavior Therapy Can Put You in Control (New Harbinger Self-Help Workbook), Scott E. Spradlin

Fear of Intimacy, Robert W. Firestone and Joyce Catlett

Feeling Good, The New Mood Therapy, David D Burns, MD

he's just not that into you, Greg Behrendt & Liz Tuccillo

Living, Loving & Learning, Leo Buscaglia, Ph.D

Man's Search for Meaning, Viktor Frankl

The Self-Esteem Workbook, Glenn R. Schiraldi

The Tao of Pooh, Benjamin Hoff

Online Resources

Girl Rebuilt

https://girlrebuilt.com/

Love Addicts Anonymous Forums

https://loveaddictionforum.proboards.com/

Women who love too much- Support group

https://www.dailystrength.org/group/women-who-love-too-much

ACKNOWLEDGMENTS

I would like thank Susan Peabody, my mentor and my friend, for her support and inspiration since 2008, as well as the Love Addicts Anonymous community. Thank you to my editor, Susan Krawitz for all your hard work helping me bring this book to fruition. Deep thanks to my husband Douglas for believing in me and encouraging me to continue with this project. Thank you to my mother for all her wisdom and undying faith in me. Thank you Dennis McDonald, my step-father, for being a wonderful rolemodel, not only as a loving husband to my mother, but a loving father, and author. And, thank you to all the Girl Rebuilt followers and readers for the mountain of praise, encouragement and kind words you gave me throughout the years. You are my heros.